BURFORD PAPERS

By permission of Mr B.T. Batsford.

The Great House, Burford.

BURFORD PAPERS

Being Letters of Samuel Crisp to his
Sister at Burford; and other Studies
of a Century (1745–1845)

By
WILLIAM HOLDEN HUTTON, B.D.
Fellow and Tutor of S. John Baptist College, Oxford

LONDON
ARCHIBALD CONSTABLE & CO Ltd
16 JAMES STREET HAYMARKET
1905

BUTLER & TANNER,
THE SELWOOD PRINTING WORKS,
FROME, AND LONDON.

Preface

SUCH unity as these "Studies of a Century" possess is due to all of them, I believe, having been written either to or in a house at Burford, in Oxfordshire, and so I call them all *Burford Papers*. The letters which form the earlier part of this volume have been most kindly placed at my disposal by Mrs. Edward Egerton Leigh, of Broadwell Manor House, Moreton-in-Marsh, who has also helped me more than I can say by her stores of knowledge about all that belongs to the Leighs and their kindred and friends. The further illustrations which we gain from these letters of Samuel Crisp of the literary circle in which Fanny Burney moved at the time of her first great success will, I hope, be welcomed by all those to whom Dr. Johnson and the Thrales, as well as the author of *Evelina*, are old friends. I think that the other details, more domestic, of the letters —medical, pecuniary, and the like—are also worth preserving ; and certainly the picture which is given of the writer himself is a delightful one.

The other papers in the book were all (or nearly all) written in the house where Mrs. Gast lived when she received the letters of her brother, Samuel Crisp. I have described different parts of it in the course of the volume.

The letters of Samuel Crisp have never been printed before ; and, of my own sketches, those called " In the Other House," " Some Oxfordshire Jacobites," " A Spanish Court Painter," " A Bath Evening," " The Rev.

v

PREFACE

Richard Graves," and " Sydney Smith : A Contrast," are now published for the first time. The others have appeared, at intervals during the last ten years or more, in *The Cornhill Magazine, The Guardian, Literature, The Treasury,* and *The Pilot,* and I desire to express my grateful thanks for permission to reprint them, as also to the proprietors of *The Treasury* for the use of the three illustrations connected with Sterne. The papers have, for the most part, been considerably altered and added to since they first appeared. Besides the thanks that I owe to Mr. and Mrs. E. Egerton Leigh, I wish to say also how grateful I am to Mr. Coldicott, of Ullenhall, for the help of his wide knowledge of the literature of Barrells and Warwickshire generally ; to Mrs. Tollemache, of Batheaston, who showed me her interesting house and garden ; and to the friends whose company has enlivened the expeditions for which the writing of these essays has been an excuse, and among them especially to Canon H. C. Beeching, because he has also read my proofs and saved me from several errors.

The period covered by the book is about a hundred years, from " the '45 " to the death of Sydney Smith. None of it seems to me so very far away when I remember that my father's father was born in 1750.

W. H. HUTTON.

The Great House,
  Burford, Oxon.
    July, 1905.

LIST OF CONTENTS

LIST OF CONTENTS

LIST OF ILLUSTRATIONS

ix

Think, listener, that I had the luck to stand,
A while ago, within a flowery land,
Fair beyond words ; that thence I brought away
Some blossoms that before my footsteps lay,
Not plucked by me, not over-fresh or bright ;
Yet, since they minded me of that delight,
Within the pages of this book I laid
Their tender petals, there in peace to fade.
Dry are they now, and void of all their scent
And lovely colour, yet what once was meant
By these dull stains, some men may yet descry
As dead upon the quivering leaves they lie.

   Behold them here, and mock me if you will,
But yet believe no scorn of men can kill
My love of that fair land wherefrom they came,
Where midst the grass their petals once did flame.

WILLIAM MORRIS.

Burford   Papers

Burford Papers

I. THE TOWN.

A LAND of forest, and downs, and little streams, now sluggish and deep, now shallow and swift. That is the country between the royal lands of Wychwood, where first King Edward saw Elizabeth Wydville, and where Queen Elizabeth and King James hunted, and whence, till within living memory at the disafforesting, the Bishops of Winchester had bucks each year, which they would give to Oxford colleges of which they were visitors. It lies between these forest lands, whose past is still preserved in the local " assarts," where the very meaning of the name has been forgotten, and the valleys of Windrush, and Lech, and stripling Thames. That is the country, still unknown to railways, but through which the great coach road runs from London, which of all others in these far-away lands, seem to have lost all the fame it had a hundred years ago. Then there were great heroes and great families, and yeomen of gentle birth, and old ladies—as we shall see—in touch with the London life. Yearly there came down crowds of fashionable folk to the races ; still an old gentleman remembers being held up by his father to see George IV go by. Daily there passed the flying coach, and not rarely royal persons would hurry by in their carriages to drink the waters of Cheltenham— " which," as the old testator says in *Money*, "nearly gave me my death." When agriculture ceased to be a mine of wealth, and when the railways passed the district by ; when the forest had been thrown open for a large part of its area, and when trees had all along the high ground been cut down

3

recklessly to enlarge the arable fields; when at last the coaches ceased to run and the great families began to sell their properties or live away from them, when in " the Agrarian Revolution " the old small families, *armigeri* many of them and college-bred, died out or sank in the social scale, the old life passed away ; and the nineteenth century before it had covered thirty years saw a very different society from what the eighteenth had known. The past remained only in memory, sometimes memory of grim and cruel deeds. On a lonely patch of ground stands an old Jacobean house, typical of the beautiful Cotswold building, but now unroofed and forlorn, where men still tell that children were born and buried whose mothers fled secretly from London and returned again, never to tell of what the Cotswold lands kept safe. In one village hall a highwayman lived and kept great state till the London runners unearthed him. Such are among the memories ; and imagination runs riot among the rustics, who tell what their great-grandparents saw.

If the life has changed, the buildings remain, and the style of the whole district has a beauty and a character of its own. So we in the Cotswolds—and others outside, too—have at last begun to rediscover. And, indeed, there is no more cheering feature of the new-time interest in old things than the rediscovery of the beauty of old house-buildings. How well we remember, long after the care for old churches was revived among us, the days when an old house was thought uncomfortable, unfashionable, and fit only to be swept away. How many a worthy clergyman restored his old church and pulled down his old house. How very few there are now left of the fine old parsonages which were standing two centuries ago. And it was not till so many of the houses and buildings of the olden days were destroyed that we discovered how far more convenient, as well as stronger, they were than the new ; and we are only just beginning to awake to the fact that they were also far more beautiful.

Notably this Cotswold land is a land of small houses, such as poor folk may live in, but such as to-day rich folk cannot surpass for beauty and fitness. The characteristic work is everywhere, in all this district, of the grey stone which comes from the plentiful quarries, and which has no superior for strength and durability if it is used within the area from which it is hewn. Mainly this is true of the Cotswolds, but they may be made architecturally not unfairly, in spite of pure geography, to stretch into Northamptonshire and Worcestershire, where the general character of the building is varied by the introduction of rows or layers of red ironstone at regular intervals in the limestone walls, or by the addition of wood and plaster fronts here and there. The main work is always due to the nature of the stone found in the local quarries : sometimes it is found in large blocks, sometimes in thin layers, and the walls show this at once by the alteration of the method adopted. The general effect, however, is still much the same ; it is one of strong, solid greyness. The stone, says Mr. Dawber truly (in his *Old Cottages, Farmhouses, and other Stone Buildings in the Cotswold District*) "is usually quarried from about April to October, after which the quarries are closed for the winter months. It is generally obtained by clearing away the upper layers of inferior stone and loose brash, though sometimes it is mined for, as most of the Bath stones are. When first quarried it is rather yellow in tone, but [it] becomes bleached by exposure, and is quickly covered with lichens, for which it seems to have a peculiar attraction. It is an admirable weather stone, as much old work in the district testifies."

The country covered by the style includes few towns of any size to-day. The best known are Cirencester, Painswick, Northleach, Burford, Chipping Campden : and Broadway, Bibury, Lechlade, and other villages of more or less importance belong to the area. Practically—with some ridiculous modern examples of preference for the far less useful brick —the "whole district is essentially a stone one" in its buildings. The houses are in almost every case the work of two periods of prosperity—the first that of the wool industry, which was the great source of wealth to the towns I have mentioned, and, indeed, to the whole district of which they form part ; and, secondly, of the agriculture which to a considerable extent replaced the wool as a source of wealth in the seventeenth century.

The buildings are very different from those which the nineteenth century erected. In the first place, they are essentially harmonious, rather than contrasting, with the natural scenery : the soft mellow grey seems especially attuned to the long stretches of bare blue and brown which you see as you stand on a high point, and look over valleys and hills, in surprising variety, for miles of view towards the horizon. In the soft shadows of the narrow lanes and close-built villages of Warwickshire something more abrupt and striking in the style of building is seemly, but on the Cotswolds the sharp airs, the sense of freedom and breadth, contrast to break the dominant thought. All there is plain and very simple : the chief features are the exquisite proportion, the absence of ornament other than conventional and traditionary, the mark of dignity and quietness in strength. The beauty of the grey walls culminates in the steep-pitched roofs, always of stone slates, graduated from the eaves to the ridge, and having a plain stone crest at the top.

Such is the land into which we are to be brought. And the special district is one in which the Cotswold style culminates, and the house we come to is one in which an architectural style of larger scope and history adopts in a manner the local methods and shows how well it can harmonize with a style so diverse.

In the valley of the Windrush, seven miles above Witney and eighteen miles from Oxford, has stood for at least twelve hundred years the ancient town of Burford. It was there, in 752, that Cuthraed with his West Saxons defeated Æthelbald of Mercia, and brought the boundary of Wessex north of the Thames. Plot, in his delightful *Natural History of Oxfordshire*, and Kennett, in *The Parochial Antiquities of Ambrosden*, believe that the custom of carrying a mimic dragon up and down the town on Midsummer eve—a custom that is now dead, but may be revived—dates back to this time, and was a memory of the dragon of Wessex. Certainly, there is a ridge above the

BURFORD A HUNDRED YEARS AGO.

town still called Battle Edge, with a round clump of firs on it, doubtless a barrow, which looks long backward into history. In story, urban and territorial, there are great historic connexions for town and guild and church. Many notable names in English story have their links with the town : Gilbert de Clare, Earl of Gloucester ; Hugh le Despencer ; the Neviles—and notably the King-maker ; Edmund Harman, King Henry VIII's barber, a worthy member of the College of Surgeons ; Sir Lawrence Tanfield, Chief Baron of the Exchequer under Elizabeth and James I ; his eccentric daughter, the wife of Henry Carey, Viscount Falkland ; and then the great Lucius himself, who sold the property to William Lenthall, Speaker of the Long Parliament. The house in which these later personages dwelt was built by Sir Lawrence Tanfield, and there James I visited him ; Lenthall added a private chapel. He died in 1662, and his son, Sir John, succeeded, whom Anthony Wood calls " The grand Braggadochio and Lyar of the age he lived in " ; and so the family went on to the times of which we are to speak.

But if the " ruling family " had often changed, the church was the most enduring feature of Burford, and still is. A splendid edifice, incorporating work that is Norman, Early English, Decorated, Perpendicular, and the late Jacobean, it remains a history in little of the town's prosperous days. In the middle of the eighteenth century it had high pews and higher galleries, and was mapped out among the townsfolk with an extraordinary precision. The old chantry chapel, dedicated probably to S. Peter, was turned into a family pew for the lord of the manor ; but the pulpit from which Oliver Cromwell had addressed the Levellers in 1649, and the font on which one of his unfortunate captives had cut his name, still remained unharmed. Monuments were plentiful on the walls, but the finest, the quaint Italian painted marble, sculptured, memorial of the Tanfields, occupied a whole chapel to itself. Burford was, at the time of which we are to speak, no doubt not very active, or polemic, in its religion. It was in the time of Francis Potter (1734–1746) as vicar, that John

Wesley paid his first visit to the town, which he thus records in his Journal :—

Wed., Oct. 3, 1739.—" After leaving Oxford, about six in the evening I came to Burford ; and at seven preached to, it was judged, twelve or fifteen hundred people, on ' Christ made unto us wisdom, and righteousness, and sanctification, and redemption.' Finding many approved of what they had heard, that they might not rest in that approbation, I explained, an hour or two after, the holiness of a Christian ; and in the morning I showed the way to this holiness, by giving both the false and the true answer to that important question, ' What must I do to be saved ? ' "

He preached again at Burford, " about eleven," on his way from Oxford to Tiverton, November 15, 1739, and again on his way back on December 6. Again, on January 7, 1740 (1741), he preached, and early in the next year, after a visit to Mr. Gambold (of whom more anon), at Stanton Harcourt, on February 18, 1741 (1742), " walked on to Burford, on Thursday to Mamsbury, and the next day to Bristol," not too tired, it may be guessed, to preach at any of these places.

Early in the next century (1804) I find a reference in a local paper showing the growth of dissent. Mr. Francis Knollys was vicar, and Mrs. Gast (the chief lady of my tale) was dead. So long as she was alive, so far as I can judge, the Church which she so lovingly served was " in possession " at Burford.

" The same day a neat place of worship, for Dissenters of the Independent denomination, was opened at Burford, in Oxfordshire. In the morning, Mr. Coles, of Bourton, preached from Ps. cxxii. 7–9 ; and Mr. Hinton, of Oxford, in the afternoon, from Isa. lxii. 6 ; Mr. Cobbin, of Banbury ; Mr. Hughes, of Battersea ; and Mr. Williams, of Fairford, engaged in prayer.—The cause of religion formerly flourished at this place ; and it is sincerely hoped a revival will be experienced. Mr. Smith, the pastor, labours also in the adjacent villages. Seventeen neighbouring ministers, and several respectable members of their churches were present ; and a pleasing solemnity rested on the services of the day."

The lady who received the letters we are to print was preserved from this. She was a plain Churchwoman.

Hard by the church stood, and stands, the Grammar School. Perhaps it never flourished more than in the eighteenth century, when it taught a Prime Minister and a court painter ; but it flourishes still.

The good houses in the town were not few. There were several famous coaching inns, some of venerable antiquity, some of modern design, to meet the demand of the coaching world—*The Lamb*, *The Bear*, *The Ramping Cat* (a name which humourised the town badge of a leopard rampant), *The Bird in Hand*, and *The Bull*, the last famous for the company it held when the races were run—the great races which made Burford's fame in that century more than anything else. Among the private houses was one beautiful building in late classical style in the High street, which survives, transmogrified, the residence then of a small squire. It was not alone in dignity. And it is of another, in outward appearance perhaps more dignified still, that our tale is to be told, which comes from Burford a century and a half ago.

Connected with an old house in this old town a large packet of letters has lately come to light. They belong to a family famous in literature, the family of the Daddy Crisp who was so kind to Fanny Burney, and they deal, several of them, with a time when her fame was at its height.

II. THE PEOPLE.

The people, the house, the letters,—we may well take them one by one.

And first the family. Samuel Crisp was a man of letters and of fashion who in 1754 produced at Drury Lane his tragedy of *Virginia*, when Garrick himself played Virginius and Mrs. Cibber Virginia. That, for the world, was his title to fame, for the play, if it was not a first-rate success, was much talked of, and was published in the same year by Tonson. To his friends Crisp was known as a man of fortune and good temper, who had already spent some time travelling abroad, and had settled, or seemed to settle, recently in a " villa " by the Thames and become the friend of peeresses and blue-stockings, of actors and men of learning. He was never married, and he had no brothers. He had, however, five sisters, four of whom come more or less into the letters he has left us. The eldest, it seems, was Anne, who never married, and who bore in the family the nickname of " Scrip." The second was Mary, who married a Mr. Phesant. The third, Martha, died quite young, in 1727. The letters show her to have been a quaint, charming girl. The fourth, Sophia, married a Dutch merchant, Philip Gast of Rotterdam, on August 18, 1724. At that time her residence is given as Canterbury, and she had the distinction of being married by " Nicholas Brady, lecturer of Clapham." The youngest, Theodosia, was Mrs. Lloyd. It seems that probably after her parents' death, and when her brother was travelling abroad, Mrs. Anne Crisp—Mrs. she is always called, though, as Mrs. Delany says, " she has vowed to live and die a virgin "—settled at Burford, Oxfordshire. She thus was within eleven miles of her kinsman, Mr. Crisp, " the eminent lawyer of Chipping Norton," whose daughter was the first wife of Bishop Talbot, the father of the Lord Chancellor, who was the patron of Thomson and lived at Great Barrington, little more than three miles from Burford, on the Gloucestershire border. In earlier days Mrs. Delany, then Mary Granville, had lived near Chipping Campden—which again is but twenty miles from Burford—and she had formed, it seems, no very high opinion of Anne's wits, for when she compares the two sisters she reports, as we shall see, from a friend, that Mrs. Gast " is very ordinary in her appearance, but an excellent creature, and far superior to our old acquaintance in understanding."

Mrs. Delany in one of her letters tells a tale from which this description comes, and which shows us the two sisters very quaintly.

" I must tell you a story of our old friend Nanny Crisp, though it cost me half a sheet more of paper. She has a sister Gast,[1] younger by several years than herself, who has been abroad, and is a widow in very bad circumstances. Mrs. Bernard, who told me the story, says she is very ordinary in her appearance, but an excellent creature, and far superior to our old acquaintance in understanding. A sister of Mrs. Bernard's was asked by a gentleman of a very good estate who has only one daughter (a child), if she could recommend a wife to him who was qualified to make him a good companion, and to educate his daughter ; she immediately thought of Mrs. Gast, as he neither insisted on *youth, beauty,* nor *fortune.* She told him she could recommend just such a person, who would make him a happy man. (They were at this time at Oxford, Nanny Crisp and her sister at Burford) ; it was agreed that Mrs. Price should carry him there to breakfast ; she did accordingly, and what do you think happened ? *He falls in love with Crisp,* and will not hear of Mrs. Gast ! but Crisp had vowed to live and die a virgin and will not admit of any addresses."

For several years Mrs. Gast lived in Southern France, at

---

[1] The printed copy says *Gough*, obviously a mistake. *Life, etc., of Mrs. Delany,* vol. iii., p. 52, Series I.

Parcaut, and bitterly does she complain in her lengthy letters—in which, as their present owner truly says, there is " a great deal of twaddle "—of the difficulty of travel, of getting news from England, of coming home. At last, her husband being dead, she determined to return and live with her beloved " Scrip." In which county is Burford, she writes on April 13, 1748, and how far is it from Bristol, for that will be the way to come, doubtless, and from Bordeaux. So, through 1749 and 1750 the letters drag on. It is so difficult to get away. On September 22, 1749, she says " Three ships have arrived here from London, and all of them are freighted for Ireland. There is so little trade from hence to England, that it is quite a misery to get a conveyance thither by sea." At last she overcame her difficulties and found her way to London and thence to the wilds of Oxfordshire. There she settled with her beloved " Scrip," and it took wild horses—or, rather, the quietest possible, when their reluctance was at last overcome—to drag them from their home. Sophia Gast was at her brother's deathbed, it would seem. But the two sisters lived on at Burford. There they died, and were buried, the register shows, Mrs. Ann Crisp on February 28, 1776, and Mrs. Sophia Gast on April 21, 1791 ; and a marble tablet in the church simply records that " under this stone lie the remains of Mrs. Ann Crisp and Mrs. Sophia Gast, above forty years Residents in Burford ; blessings to the poor and the ornaments of Society." But of this more hereafter.

The " society " of Burford cannot have been very large at that time. There were the Lenthalls at the Priory ; Mr. William, the squire, unmarried, who " died suddenly of an apoplexy," and was buried November 12, 1781 ; his brother John, who died in 1785, having married Ann, daughter of the Rev. Christopher Shute, of Broadwell, Gloucestershire ; Jane and Mary, their sisters [1]; and John, the son of John and Ann, who was High Sheriff of Oxfordshire in 1785. " M.L." became a great friend of the Crisps, but was a constant invalid. At the Vicarage from 1771 was

[1] Jane died Dec. 21, 1780, Mary, Jan. 18, 1794, both unmarried.

Mr. Francis Knollys, son of Charles, who claimed to be Earl of Banbury, and was Vicar of Burford from 1747 till his death.[1] But distances were not far in those days, and there were many good houses in the neighbourhood. From time to time, too, people would stop on their way through to Cheltenham, and Oxford dons would write letters and send books. In her younger days, Samuel Crisp tells in one of his letters to Fanny Burney, Mrs. Gast " was a great favourite with an old lady who was a particular crony and intimate of old Sarah Marlborough, who, though much of the jade, had undoubtedly very strong parts, and was indeed remarkably clever. When Mrs. Hinde (the old lady) would sometimes talk to her about books, she'd cry out, ' Prithee don't talk to me about books ; I never read any books but men and cards.' " I do not know whether the people at Blenheim ever came to see Mrs. Gast at Burford, through their old and round-

---

[1] The claim goes back to 1632, when Sir William Knollys, Earl of Banbury, died. He was born in 1547, and had married in 1605 Lady Elizabeth Howard. Two sons were born, in 1627 and 1630 ; but on his death the inquisitions of his Oxfordshire estates, at Burford, April 11, 1633, declared that he died without male heirs. The claim of the elder son was kept up till 1813, when the House of Lords decided against it. A long epitaph in Burford church commemorates Charles, Earl of Banbury and Vicar of Burford. I think it is worth quoting : " Within the chancel of this church are consigned to earth the bodies of the Right Hon. and Rev. Charles Knollys, M.A., Earl of Banbury, Viscount Wallingford, and Baron Knollys of Grayes, 20 years Vicar of this parish, and Martha his wife. He died March 13th, 1771, aged 65. His Countess Sept. 9th following, aged 64. By whom his Lordship had issue six sons (five of whom had been in the service of their Majesties George II and III) and three daughters. William, who succeeded to his father's titles and estates, who died without issue August 29, 1776, aged 59, lies buried by the side of his parents. This tablet as a testimony of respect to the memory of their honoured and beloved relatives was erected by their youngest son Samuel, who served in the 31st Regt. 34 years. Five thereof a Lieutenant in Germany, where he was severely wounded at the battle of Minden August 21st, 1739, and Francis, M.A., Rector of East Leach Martin and Vicar of this Parish."

13

Lymm, in Cheshire, and of Middle, in Shropshire, in the same year, and died in 1758. There are two letters from him at Oxford in 1757 to "dear Scrip and Gast." On October 13 he says, "I do not remember to have heard you mention a sermon of Mr. Gambold's [1] which I think a very good one, and therefore I send you three of them, which I desire the Professors and Miss Lenthall will allow a place in their respective Libraries," and again a fortnight later, "By a gentleman who is going on the Glo'ster coach I have an opportunity of writing to you." Burford was not really out of the world, for it was on the highway from London to Gloucester, the way that all the world and his wife went to Cheltenham.

I have mentioned the Lenthalls as the chief friends of the ladies who dwelt in what the leases call "the Great House," but Burford was not without other notabilities. The Grammar School had its head master, who combined its duties with those of a country living, sometimes—as the registers show—Asthall, sometimes Yelford, neither of them many miles away. In 1753 Sir William Beechey, perhaps the favourite English Court painter of his age, was born in the town, and an art chronicler tells that he "was, at the proper age, placed under an eminent conveyancer at Stow, in Gloucestershire ; but a volatile flow of spirits, a bright

---

[1] I do not know what this sermon was. The only sermon of Mr. Gambold's that I know of is—

CHRISTIANITY. TIDINGS OF JOY.

A
SERMON
PREACH'D BEFORE THE
UNIVERSITY
OF
OXFORD
AT ST. MARY'S
On Sunday, Decemb. 27, 1741.
By JOHN GAMBOLD, M.A.,
Vicar of Stanton-Harcourt in Oxfordshire.
Publish'd at the request of Mr. Vice-Chancellor
OXFORD
Printed at the THEATER for Edward Broughton Bookseller : And are to be Sold by Messieurs Knapton at the Crown, in Ludgate Street, London.

and active imagination, and a mind eagerly bent upon inquiry, was not to be chained to the desk of a provincial conveyancer long enough to acquire any deep insight into that abstruse profession." So, no more Stow, and no more Burford. Charles Jenkinson, afterwards Lord Liverpool, and for so long prime minister, who was born near Charlbury in 1727, must have been a boy at Burford Grammar School when first Mrs. Crisp came to the town.

Another inhabitant of Burford whom Mrs. Gast must have known well was Mr. William Chavasse, surgeon. He died on February 6, 1794, aged 57, and his wife on the 24th of June in the same year, aged 53. " They lived united 33 years," says their epitaph in the church, " giving and receiving mutual happiness among 15 children." Of Mr. Chavasse the epitaph says that he was " to his neighbours, the friend of peace, and to the poor a kind and zealous benefactor. His skill was aided by candour and urbanity, whilst his family was guided by discretion."

In August, 1753, Horace Walpole came to Burford and saw the Lenthalls' House. Thus, some years later, a writer in the *Gentleman's Magazine* describes the Priory and its treasures :—

" Mr. Urban, [*July* 11, 1799.]

" Of the priory at Burford, in Oxfordshire, the only mention which I find in Dugdale is its valuation temp. Hen. VIII, *viz.* £13 6s. 6d. Mr. Lenthall's mansion-house there is called the Priory, and is probably made out of the old building. There is a small chapel, now disused, but the pews, pulpit, etc. remain. The ceiling is full of stucco-work. In one compartment is the Adoration of the Shepherds, with *Gloria in excelsis*, etc.; in another Abraham offering up Isaac. On each side of the door-way stands a small angel on a pedestal. Under one is written,

Exue calceos tuos
Servabimur.[1]

---

[1] Mr. Urban's correspondent has of course, bungled. The texts should be read across, as *Exue calceos tuos, nam terra est sancta,* and *Salvabimur quasi per ignem.* They can still be seen.

" Under the other :

Nam terra est sancta
Quasi per ignem.

" The texts are mentioned whence the words are taken·
Over the door seems to be a representation in bas-relief of
a bush in flames.   I say, *seems*, because, unless explained by
the above inscription, it would not be readily acknowledged
as such.

" In a handsome room upstairs are many pictures.   At the
end hangs one of the Speaker Lenthall in his robes, seated
in a chair, his lady sitting by him.   On his right-hand stand
two sons, the eldest a youth, the other in petticoats, a
feather in his cap.   Behind stand two daughters, one of which
is particularly handsome, and in front is another daughter.
On the right-hand side of the room hangs the famous
picture of the chancellor Sir Thomas More, and his family.
The first figure is Sir John More, his father, in a red gown,
seated.   On his left is Sir Thomas, in a black gown, his
collar on, also seated.   On his left stands his son, in black,
reading ; and behind the two first stands a lady, who was a
ward of the chancellor, and married to this son.   To the
left of the son, in front, are the three daughters of Sir
Thomas, Margaret, Cecilia, and Elizabeth ; the two former
are sitting, in conversation, the latter stands behind them.
On their left are some relations of the family ; an elderly
man and his wife, seated ; behind them stand two sons,
Christopher and Thomas More, the former a man about 30,
the latter a youth about 18 : all dressed in black, and each
figure has a book in hand.   Over the last group is represented
a picture of a lady, the wife of Sir John.   Over several of
the heads are coats of arms with the wife's arms empaled.

" *Qu.* Whether the last group are not the family seated at
Loxeley,[1] near Guildford, in Surrey ?

" Near this hangs a picture of the great Duke of Tuscany,
and of Machiavel, his secretary, writing, and taking instruc-

[1] Loseley is the place meant.   It belonged to another family
of Mores.

tions from the duke. There are several portraits : Oliver Cromwell (behind the door) ; Sir Kenelm Digby ; the Earl of Pembroke, with his staff as lord chamberlain ; the Earl of Holland ; two of King Charles the First ; Gondemar, the Spanish ambassador (over the door) ; and several other noblemen. "Y."

A more particular description of the house says that it had two wings "and a middle projection, in which is the door, somewhat in the form of an E, with scalloped gables of that kind which distinguished the beginning of the last (i.e. the xvii) century. It is of the stone of the country, grown dark with age. The inside consists of a large hall, on the sides of which are a dining-and drawing-room, and on the left a heavy staircase of the same style, hung with old portraits, most of them probably left by Lord Falkland, when he sold the house, for there were amongst them Lord Chief Baron Tanfield in his Judge's Robes, and his wife, whose name was Symonds. This staircase leads to the large drawing-room, hung round also with portraits, amongst which is the famous picture of the More family." [1]

The pictures—there were many more of them, as we see from the description already quoted, clearly obtained by Speaker Lenthall—must have been interesting, though they were only "the refuse of Charles I's collection, the best having been got from him by Lord Clarenden after the Restoration"; but Horace Walpole says "The inside of the mansion is bad and ill-furnished." The family were already beginning to be a little reckless and a little poor ; and so the next century brings the inevitable sale.

Riches, however, if the tale be true, came to their house, but not to the Lenthalls themselves. A newspaper of this time tells the following tale, which it entitles, "Getting a Prize" :—

"Mr. Lenthall, who was descended from the Speaker of that name, while he lived at Burford, had a very good butler, who one morning came to him with a letter in his hand, and

[1] This is now at Cokethrope Park, near Witney, and is described in my *Sir Thomas More*, pp. 89–91.

rubbing his forehead in that indescribable manner, which is an introduction to something which the person does not well know how to communicate, he told Mr. Lenthall that he was very sorry to be obliged to quit his service. " Why, what is the matter, John ? has anybody offended you ?—I thought you were as happy as any man could be in your situation."—' Yes, please your honour, that's not the thing, but I have just got a prize in the lottery of £3,000, and I have all my life had a wish to live for one twelvemonth like a man of two or three thousand a year ; and all I ask of your honour, is that when I have spent the money, you will take me back again into your service.'—' That is a promise,' said Mr. Lenthall, ' which I believe I may safely make, as there is very little probability of your wishing to return to be a butler after having lived as a gentleman.'

" Mr. Lenthall was, however, mistaken. John spent nearly the amount of his ticket in less than a year. He had previously bought himself a small annuity to provide for his old age ; when he had spent all the rest of his money, he actually returned to the service of Mr. Lenthall, with whom he lived many years."

Skelton figures the Priory at the beginning of the nineteenth century at its greatest extent. Then Ackermann shows it in 1827 with one wing already gone.

Near it is the beautiful seventeenth-century house, a typical one of the Cotswold style, still called the Old Rectory, though it is long indeed since Burford had a rector.

Up the hill, across the river, are some beautiful houses of still earlier date, and in the valley the property, bearing the ancient name of Lady Ham, which once belonged to the merchant family of Sylvester, whose monuments take a whole aisle to themselves and whose warehouses the plate of 1816 shows along the river bank. Of the Great House itself about 1750 there seems to be no picture ; but it must have looked very much as it looks now.

BURFORD PRIORY A HUNDRED YEARS AGO.

III. THE HOUSE

And now for the house. It stands in what has been from time immemorial called Witney Street, the road that leads to Witney, about half-way up the hill which rises from the Windrush to 430 feet above sea level. It has a fine late Renaissance front, a classical design which reminds one not a little of the earlier houses in Bath, and has nothing like it in the near neighbourhood. In the days of Mrs. Crisp and Mrs. Gast the kitchens, a long series, must have been, as in London houses, partly below ground. There are four steps up to the front door. You enter on a hall, which has a door opening at the back on the small paved court, from which two steps upward lead to the walled garden. The hall, and the passages above it, are panelled in deal, painted a dull red colour, on which there are designs in all the panels. In the hall are Faith, kneeling with a flaming heart in her hand, and at her side a desk initialed I.H.S., and books of devotion above her, *Holy Living and Dying,* Comber on the Common Prayer, *The Whole Duty of Man,* Stanley's *Lives of the Philosophers* ; Hope, a lady in the dress of the early eighteenth century, looking upon a harbour, with an anchor at her side ; Charity, suckling two poor children ; Venus, with a Cupid and a Satyr ; Justice, with her scales, and above her Fortune blindfold. The smaller panels hold here and there a cornucopia or a cherub. On the stairs are a grim skull, with *Resurgam* under it, various figures of saints and prophets, a Crucifixion, and a copy of Guido's S. Michael, now in the Louvre. On the landing above, which leads into a large room looking into the garden, are—much more roughly painted—the Ecce Homo, the Epiphany, the Agony in the Garden, and Jacob's ladder ; above the door is Atlas supporting the globe, with a view of the house itself in the background. On the ground floor, opening to right and left of the hall, are rooms panelled also, but with no mural decoration. Above are a series of small rooms, divided only by wooden partitions and opening out of each other, ending in one which has many sacred emblems painted on the walls. This last room has out of it a little room looking on the stairs. Was it a powder closet ? Or was it a vestry, for the room itself may very well have been an oratory, from its sacred paintings ? Perhaps the house belonged once to Non-jurors, and here they worshipped. I like to think that it was so, but I can find no certain clue.[1] I do not even know who lived in it before Mrs. Crisp—and the only suggestion is that a painting on the door of a cupboard on the ground floor, of a merchant in a furred gown, tempore Georgii I, is a former owner, perhaps the builder of the house, while a tradition says that it was a dower house of the family of Fettiplace, whose tombs dignify the church at Swinbrook, two miles off in the Windrush valley.

Was the first owner one " Thomas Castle, burgesse " ? Mr. W. J. Monk suggests it. His tomb in the churchyard bears at the head the sign of a castle, and has this inscription :—" Exuviae Thomae Castle, Probi, Prudentis, Pacifici, Pii, Sacramento Militis Re Christiani, Pro Christo scilicet semper Castellani, Qui terram reliquit Anhelans Coelum attigit, Climacterico sic vere maguo, Maij 14to, 1690." The register shows his burial two days later. The quaint conceit of the epitaph is like that of the mottoes in the house, and a castle (of a very different kind)—they are neither of them heraldic—appears on the wall of the oratory. All the pious books I have named above were published before 1690. Castle was one of the bailiffs of Burford in 1665, 1667, 1679, 1687. John Castle, who died in 1726, and was, I suppose, his son, left benefactions to the town. But to return to the house.

The top floor is one long room, which seems never to have been entirely furnished, from the old pieces of panel found

---

[1] But see below, p. 121.

here and there on the walls. It has a copper at one end, in fashion of the Dutch houses, where to-day all the house washing is still done. Additions have been made to the house,—kitchen, scullery and so on, with two good bedrooms above them, on the east of the court leading to the garden, and the large room already mentioned at the west.

In this house Mrs. Anne Crisp lived, perhaps from as early as 1735, when her brother was on his grand tour, and her sister lived on till her death. Had they rented it from the Fettiplaces? It is possible, for Sir George Fettiplace was living at Swinbrook as late as 1741, and an account, about 1790, of Swinbrook after saying that " from the road this seat appears to be a respectable old mansion, standing in the valley, at the edge of the village, backed by a fine park," adds that " it now belongs to Mr. Fettiplace (probably maternally descended from this family), who is at present abroad. His next brother is resident abroad." Did he take the house on Mrs. Gast's death? One association of it with the Fettiplace family is perhaps preserved in the name of a lane which touches it and divides the house from other property of the same owner, and bears the name of " Pytts Lane." Mrs. Pytts, daughter of Sir John Fettiplace, has a tomb in the church at Swinbrook ; and a Dr. Pytt (?Pytts) lived in the Great House from about 1810.

At the time of which we are to give the records Mrs. Anne Crisp was dead and Mrs. Gast lived at the Great House with her servants, some of whom are mentioned in the letters, and at times, it would seem, with the company of her sister Theodosia, if indeed it be Theodosia Lloyd whose burial is entered in the register July 2, 1779, as " Mrs. Theodosia Crispe."

IV.   THE LETTERS

And now for the letters themselves.   Each is carefully docketed with the name of the writer and the place whence it was written, the dates when it was written and received and answered, and sometimes a short note of the important facts related.   Pieces, or single words, are frequently cut out, no doubt because they are regarded as specially private, in the manner in which Fanny Burney prepared her own letters for literary use.

The first is from Samuel Crisp, Chesington, January 25, 1779.   It was received on the 27th, answered on the 30th, and Mrs. Gast adds that she " wrote also February 27." " Concerning Dechair's proposal " she docketed it.   It is indeed for the most part a letter of business.   It shows " Daddy " Crisp advising his sister on their little pecuniary affairs, and throws some light on a subject which is much read about nowadays, the monetary transactions— so very simple they seem to us—of the eighteenth century. In the last paragraph we come to the literary interest.   Of this a word later on.

LETTER No. 1.

CHESINGTON, *Monday, Jan.* 25, 1779.

DEAR SOP,—

I yesterday received yours and one from Mr. Mathias at the same time, in which he sent me a copy of Dechair's letter, the same as in yours.   I immediately returned him an answer, which he will have this afternoon ; in which I told him my opinion was absolutely and finally to finish the whole business at the stated time in March, according to agreement ; that if he did not then pay in the whole £1,200 the stock should be sold directly for what it would fetch, and that he must then pay down the remainder that should on balance be found due, or give such ample security for said remainder as we should be satisfied with ; that if one or other of these conditions were not complied with, that the Bond should immediately be put in Suit. If I may advise you from this absolute determination I would not depart the breadth of a hair. Consider the slippery chap you have to deal with—if he should dye or steal abroad, you'd probably never get a farthing more than the stock would then fetch, which, in my opinion, is much more likely to fall than rise. Nothing was ever so difficult or impracticable as his most courteous offer of allowing you the £9 7s. 2d. overplus of interest, which the stock produces. Ridiculous ! because, let him pay you the whole £1,200 he owes you, with the £30 for his half year's interest, and with that £1,230 —at the present price of 62—you may now buy (with the addition of only £10 more out of your own pocket) no less than £2,000 4 per cent., which, instead of his offer of £69 7s. 2d. as interest for your mony, would produce you £80. Ridiculous indeed ! and impracticable, because, if his plan were adopted, it would on your side be an *Usurious Contract* for taking more Interest than the Law allows ; and consequently subject to forfeiture with treble Damages. As to the hardship on him of selling out stock to loss, 'tis what everybody is subject to ; and in this Case he may thank himself ; for he would never let you rest till you parted with the Chapel, which was an unquestionable security, and to oblige him and prejudice yourself you consented to accept one that is quite insufficient ; and now, contrary to all reason and justice, he wants you still further to entangle yourself. You must be resolute, and at a word with him, and declare you will accept of no other conditions than what are mentioned. I have wrote to Mr. Mathias to the same purpose.

As to Fanny and her Journals ; both the first and second I have copied ; and if I knew how to convey them to you,

I would do it, on Conditions nobody should see them but M. L. I have had a long letter from her besides ; as she conceals nothing from me ; she is not afraid of the imputation of Vanity, by sending me a list of the first Rate people in the Kingdom, that have paid such high honours to her Book as are hardly to be equalled. Get yourself in order, and be sure to be here sometime in April at farthest. I have still, and suppose I always shall have, bad nights, and not very good days, but must be content. Adieu ! Ham and Kate send Love.

Yours sincerely,
S. C.

A note as to this. In the old rambling house at Chesington (now spelled Chessington), which is no longer standing, Samuel Crisp lived with his friend, the owner, Mr. Christopher Hamilton, from about 1764, and here Fanny Burney first visited him in 1766. " This," says Mrs. Ellis in her edition of *The Early Diary of Fanny Burney*, " may possibly indicate the time when the Hall became a boarding-house." Strictly speaking, it was not a boarding-house in the modern sense of the term ; strangers were not received, but friends came and sometimes paid for their board if they made a long visit.

I suppose the " Kate " was Miss Kitty Cooke, a " boarder," who is described, good though she was, as dull, uncouth, and absurd, and " Ham " was her aunt Miss Hamilton, who since her brother's death was the owner of the house. A delightful house it must have been, with quiet and the charm of companionship for the old, and frolic for the young. " Dear, ever dear Chesington," wrote Fanny Burney in 1786, " whereat passed the scenes of the greatest ease, gaiety, and native mirth that have fallen to my lot ; " and there is in the diary of Susan Burney, her sister, an amusing description which brings in the serious Mrs. Gast (or at least her clothes), too, joining in the fun. " Monday night after supper we were all made very merry by Mr. Crisp's suffering his wig to be turned the hindpart before, and my cap put over it—Hetty's[1] cloak—and Mrs. Gast's apron and ruffles —and in this ridiculous trim we danced a minuet, with Hetty personifying *Madame Duval*, while she acted *Mr. Smith* at the Long Room, Hampstead "—this, of course, a scene in *Evelina*, Fanny's famous novel.

From 1773 at least some of Fanny Burney's writing had forced its way in MS. to Burford. First went the Teignmouth journal and then a number of her own letters to " Daddy," and from 1778 Daddy copied Fanny's letters to Susan and sent them too. At first Fanny seems to have protested that they were shown by Mrs. Gast to her Oxfordshire friends, but she soon relented ; but she said to Daddy, " I expect you will enjoin her to read them quite alone, or, not to be cruel, to poor sick Mrs. Lenthall, under an oath of secresy and silence." " Mrs. Lenthall " was Mrs. Molly Lenthall, the M—— L—— of this letter. The date, it will be noticed, is just a year after Fanny became famous by the publication of *Evelina*, or, rather, after the book appeared, for its authorship was a secret for some time.

The second letter was written at Chesington March 28, 1779, received the 31st, and answered April 3. It describes the triumph of the young authoress.

LETTER No. 2.

DEAR SOP,—

Your letter, tho' not quite what I could wish, yet gave me some Comfort—when you come, by all means bring Betty with you—as to inconvenience at Burford, really I think it madness to sacrifice your own great Comfort and Convenience to that of other people's ; and as to additional Expenses, ask Yourself this plain Question, viz : whether at our time of Life, it is of Consequence whether we dye £30 or £40 richer or poorer ? but, above all, whether for the sake of that £30 or £40 left behind us, it is worth while during our short Lease, to deprive ourselves of that Assist-

---

[1] Esther Burney, the eldest sister. Fanny was the second girl (her brother James being two years older) and Susan the third.

ance, Consolation, Attendance and inward Satisfaction, which results from having our own people about one, who know our ways, whom we have long been used to, and can depend upon ; and all this, forsooth, to save £30 or £40 more for the next Tenant ? Away with such wretched Reasoning !—besides, by a letter from Mr. Mathias[1] this morning, I find by the Disposition of y^r money, which he has rec^d from Dr. Dechair, He has fairly increased your income £18 10s.—he has for £600 of the money bought you £50 a year in the Annuitys for 29 years ; and with the remaining £600 by this time has purchased in 3 p. cents. £950—this will bring in £28 10s.—Total £78 10s. instead of the former interest of £60. Now for an account of my-self. I stand in the first place totally self-Condemn'd, for my own notorious Indolence and Disuse of Exercise thro' the whole Winter, besides a most senseless Disregard to a proper Diet of Regimen for the sake of indulging Appetite for the present moment. I think I cannot put my Crimes in stronger Terms. I have accordingly suffered for them in proportion—an Encrease of all my former Complaints, with the addition of swelled Legs, and restlessness. Kate and Ham at last insisted on my sending for Dr. Lewis, who accordingly was here on Friday—he gave me a most severe Lecture and I think has effectually rous'd me out of my Lethargy—he will not as yet prescribe any medicines, but has prescribed me a Regimen as strict and severe as his Lecture, which, like other terrified sinners, I promise and intend faithfully to observe ; and I have this small en-couragement, that already I find some of their good effects —my two nights past have been better, and my legs not so much swelled as they were. This is something. He is to attend me again next Friday, and proceed then as he finds me. So much for self.

I am quite glad Nanny Graeme is at last made happy and contented, and by your Account and the newspapers, that

---

[1] I suppose this was the " King's resident " at Hamburg, of whom we hear in other places as connected in business with the Burneys.

he is Cap^{tn}. of the Roebuck Man-of-War, and a Knight.
I think he has all the symptoms of an Admiral about him.
Lady Hammond ! Well God bless 'em both ! I think you
may fairly claim a great share of the Merit of bringing this
Match about.

As to Fanny Burney, she now in a manner lives at
Streatham ; and when she was, not long ago, at home for
a week, Mrs. Thrale wrote to her to *come home*. As you
say, she is so taken up with these fine Folks, I imagine we
shall see but little of her now. She is become so much the
fashion, is so carried about, so fetéd from one fine house to
another, that if she wished it, it is now really almost out of
her power to see her old Friends, as she us'd to do. When
I foretold her in my last letter, that I expected this would
be the Case, she disavow'd the thought, and said if the gain
of new friends were to deprive her of the old ones, she
should regret the Exchanges. I know Dr. Johnson, Mrs.
Thrale, Mrs. Montagu and some more of the Wits are driving
hard at her to write a Comedy ;[1] and by a Hint from Hetty
(which must be a profound Secret to M. L. and all the
World) I have reason to think she is actually at Work.
Mrs. Montagu holds a grand house-warming and Festival
on Easter Sunday (or Monday rather, for she is a mighty
good Woman) at her magnificent new-built house, which is
then to be open'd for the first time for the Reception of
Company. All the Wits and Genius's in London are invited,
and Fanny among the rest, together with the Thrales and
Dr. Johnson. I imagine she reserves an intended letter to
me till that is over, when perhaps she may give me some
account of it, tho' possibly I may flatter myself in vain,
considering the Changes occasion'd by Change of Circumstances and Station ; but Hetty told me she intended
writing soon. However, I have not heard from her a long
while ; but Basta, things must be as they may, as ancient
Pistol says.

---

[1] See *Diary and Letters of Fanny Burney* (1904), i. 204, *sqq.*, where
Fanny describes in February, 1779, how Murphy and Thrale pressed
her to write a comedy.

Adieu, get well as soon as you can, contrive your matters so as to come soon, and be sure to bring Betty ; if she comes. Queere if there would be much difference in Chaising it all the way ? and what differences ? If you are not quite stout when you set out, the Journey and Change of Air, and Change of Scene, especially if you have Betty always at your Elbow, will certainly do you good.

Y^r affectionate LEM.

Yes. Sunday, March 28, 1779. Ham and Kate full of Love, etc.

I have no idea why Samuel Crisp now takes to signing his letters " Lem." Is it a nickname, and short for Lemuel ?

The husband of Nanny Graeme was Sir Andrew Hammond, R.N., commander of the *Roebuck*.

The next letter, written April 9, was received April 11 and answered on the 17th, and is full of news, which Mrs. Gast very carefully noted on the back.

LETTER No. 3.

DEAR SOP,—

In answer to y^r Queries about my old comp., I shall tell you that this day Sennight, according to Appointment the Dr. came and pronounced me to be much better. The swelling of my Legs and other Symptoms, owing to indulgence and want of Exercises, such as thirst, fidgets, Itchings, slow feverishness, sleeplessnes, &c., &c., &c., manifestly indicated a tendency to dropsical complaints ; and the Dr's. orders hitherto have only been a most strict and laborious Regimen of Exercise and great abstemiousness in Diet, particularly as to Liquids. My Observance of these Rules has been attended with some success ; my Legs are less swelled and other matters easier. I was this day morning by 10 o'clock by appointment to have gone

over to the Dr. to Kingston ; but a most profuse, and
I hope, a critical sweat, forbid any such attempt, besides
the gout in my Elbow, which increases in pain every hour ;
so I was obliged to send over to excuse me to the Dr.
When able I shall either go to him or send for him ; I want
to know what farther I am to do ? what medicines to take ?
whether Spa or any Steel Waters.

Who advises the Blister on y^r Arm ? Sure 'tis a strange
Remedy for Rheumatics ! You say y^r self you are in some
respects better than you were ; why can't you come here,
and bring your maid ? You say not a word in answer to
all I wrote you on that Subject. Dolly Price was here
last week, and said you proposed coming to Ches. in April.
Why don't you say something about it ? I have just now
rec^d. a letter from Hetty.[1] She has been dreadfully ill above
this month, and her Boy with a putrid Fever and sore
throat. I must transcribe one piece of news. " I have
just heard that Miss Ray (L^d. Sandwich's mistress) has lost
her life by a mad clergyman who pretended love for her.
The story runs thus—tho' we have not heard the particulars,
yet the *fact* is undoubted—that as she was walking thro'
the Piazza's of Covent Garden Theatre last night to her
Chair, or her Chariot—this hot-headed Parson (who it
seems she has refused to marry) discharg'd a Pistol at her,
which killed her on the spot, and another at himself, which
only wounded him. He was immediately secured." This
is a terrible story ; Miss Ray was a very great Friend of
Dr. and particularly of Jim Burney, the Lieutenant ; was
an exceeding Decent good sort of Woman, if you'll excuse
her Frailty, and the mother of several Children, who were
brought up in Ld. S^s House. Fanny, I find, lives in a
manner at Streatham. I have not yet heard from her,
and now begin not to expect it. Ham and Kate send
much Love. The new Mrs. Penny is far from well, has a
sore Breast, &c. Adieu. My Elbow is very painful.

Y^r affectionate LEM.

CHES., *Ap.* 9, 1779.

---

[1] Hetty Burney was the wife of her cousin, C. R. Burney.

The case of Miss Ray was, of course, one of the famous scandals of the century, and a curious light it throws on the manners and morals of the age. A word must be said about it.

Miss Ray, the daughter of a staymaker in London, was the mistress of John Montagu, fourth Earl of Sandwich, famous as " Jemmy Twitcher," and the mother of several of his children. She lived in his house, sang at his concerts, and was painted by Gainsborough. James Hackman, who was in turn a mercer's apprentice, a lieutenant in the 68th, and a priest of the English Church—his ordination as deacon February 24, priest, February 28, and institution as Rector of Wiveton March 1, 1779, is one of the ecclesiastical scandals of the century—fell in love with her at Hinchingbrooke, and repeatedly offered to marry her. On April 7, 1779, he shot her as she was leaving Covent Garden Theatre, and vainly endeavoured to kill himself. He was hanged on April 19, less than two months after his ordination. A famous book of the period is *Love and Madness*, a pretended issue of the letters that passed between Hackman and Martha Ray. It was published in 1780, and written by Sir Herbert Croft, the clever author of *The Abbey of Kilkhampton*.[1]

The next letter is dated May 7, 1779, was received on the 9th and answered on the 20th. Mrs. Gast notes " Latin names and account of the two sorts of nightshade from Dr. Lewis's book." They evidently frightened her.

It was in May that Fanny, at Streatham with the Thrales, notes that Mr. Murphy came to call and insisted on seeing the first act of the unfinished comedy and praised it warmly, though, as Fanny thinks—and events show she was right —" probably out of flummery"

---

[1] Cf. below, p. 164.

THE LETTERS

LETTER No. 4.

Dear Sop,—

Immediately on receipt of yr letter, I sent to Dr.
Lewis; entirely for yours and M. L.'s satisfaction, and
nothing Else : for I could have answered your Queries and
quieted your fears with certainty (at least my own fears)
upon my own Authority ; however, I have a better : even
his own words, of which I send you underneath a Copy
out of his own Book, which is deservedly so celebrated
and in so high Esteem. I do this now that you may lose
no more time ; because the violent rains that have fallen,
I dare say, frighten him from venturing on our Roads, and
I don't know when to expect him—when he *does* think
proper to come you shall know more,

"Solani vulgaris folia. Solani hortensis seu vulgaris.

"I.B. Common nightshade—the leaves.

"Solani lethalis seu Belladonnæ folia : solani melano-
cerasi.

"C.B. Deadly nightshade—the leaves.

"These plants grow wild ; the first in cultivated
"grounds, the second in shady waste ones. They
"have both been suppos'd cooling and discutient in
"external Applications and poisonous when taken
"internally. Late experience has shewn, that an
"infusion of half a grain or a grain of the dried leaves
"of either may be taken with safety, and that in many
"Cases the Dose may be increased by Degrees to five
"or six grains, that they generally occasion some con-
"siderable Evacuation and Sometimes, especially in
"the larger of the above Doses, alarming nervous
"Symptoms, which however cease with the operation
"of the Medicine." [1]

If the whole College of Physicians were to sit in Judg-

---

[1] The nightshade was much used in the eighteenth century, and it
was recommended by Linnæus for rheumatism. Cf. the *Medical
Botany* (with beautiful coloured plates), vol. i., pp. 61 sqq. (1819).

ment on this subject, you could not have a better authority for the outward application of nightshade in the way you mention. You see, his very words are such as they would be if he were to give a direct answer to your Question—*"cooling and discutient in external applications."* Nay, he even approves of taking it inwardly in small Quantities. You may take notice that the first Article, the "*Solani hortensis folia,*" is the plant you mention—that is, "leaves of garden nightshade," but to me they appear to be, and I believe are, the very same plant. You see, he makes no distinction as to their Qualities and Use. Remember, He only mentions *the leaves*—so I suppose they only are to be us'd ; but I should however imagine that as a thick Coat of boil'd nightshade is to be us'd, the stalks and berries all should go together, otherwise it might be difficult to get a sufficient Quantity.

I go on much as in my last ; my gout is so far remov'd that I stamp about as much as I can, but am too stiff in my Joints to use as much walking as I did before, Consequently can't get down my swell'd ancles so thoroughly as I did ; the weather too has been much against me. When I see the Dr. I shall question him about Mr. Slade's Medicine.

Make what haste here you can. Hetty Burney is now sitting by me, and sends many kind things to you. Fanny (but *Mum*) has actually finished a Comedy, which I suppose will come out next Winter. I understand *Mrs. Thrale* is much pleased with it. Dr. Johnson had not seen it when I heard. Ham and Kitty Finder send much love and wish to see you soon. If it were not for your foolish arm, you might come in the Stage to Hounslow and from thence to Ches. When you see Mrs. Chamberlayne, give my love to her. Adieu.

Y^{rs} sincerely,

S. C.

CHES., *May* 7, 1779.

In the next letter we are back among the doctors again,

with much strange advice for poor Mrs. Gast's rheumatism ;
but there is a charming ending on the unspoilt Fanny.

LETTER No. 5.

DEAR SOP,—

Your letter gave me much Concern, to find your
Rheumatics are so obstinate. I did not ask the D^r how
long the fomentations should be us'd ; but hardly think
you can expect much from 3 times trying it. Observe, I
did not send for him on purpose or fee him for his advice
about the Nightshade ; it was only occasionally I brought
it in, when he was here upon my own account ; for he has
of late had no less than 5 g^s of my money. But this I say,
in spite of all the Doctors in the world, great Cures that
are perform'd under one's own Eyes will always, and always
should (at least with me) have their full weight and carry
conviction, notwithstanding the Slight and indifference of
these Men of the Profession, who are too apt to hold Cheap
whatever is not according to Establish'd Rules and Practice.
Remember what I took out of his own Book about Nightshade. There you will find its Use in outward Applications.
All that he urged against it, and what was to be guarded
against, was the noxious Steams and Vapours of the plant ;
and if you could manage so, as by open doors and windows
to get rid of them, I should make no scruple to try the
Remedy ; at least if after a fair Tryal of his Fomentations
you find no benefit from it ; but yesterday there was here
a Family of the Torriano's, who have for many years ex-
perienc'd wonderful Cures performed by a Medicine of their
own in Rheumatics, which they call the Oil of Charity. It
is to be rubbed in, and I think warm or hot ; but they have
promis'd me the Receipt, and if it comes in time you shall
have it by this post. They are never without it ; and by
40 years' constant experience under their inspection and in
their own Family declare it to be inestimable, and to have
succeeded unaccountably, where everything else has fail'd.

I read to the D^r the whole account of Mr. Slade's Case
and the French receipt ; which very Receipt in the very

35

words, was sent him about 15 years ago. He pays little Regard to it, and says he has had so many Accounts of Wonders perform'd in particular Cases, by particular Remedies, which upon Trial have vanish'd into nothing, that till their Efficacy is better establish'd they are by no means to be relied on. He says my Case he does not think Dropsical; for you must know, since I wrote last and during my Gout, I have had several direct hot Fever Fits, which have gone off with profuse sweats, exactly like the hot Fit of an Ague. Now he says in Dropsies, as is an infallible Rule, that they never sweat—there is no such thing as sweats, then he adds, it is not ague neither, or intermitting Fever; but an Effort of Nature to throw off what is redundant. I have been extremely weak and languid, with great sinkings in my inside, and felt so hollow, as if indeed I had no inside. These Complaints, and also my great sleeplessness, are both much better, and I am now taking the Saline Draughts, which seem to agree with me. I am quite griev'd about poor Manchester. I wish you may succeed with Molly Lancaster. I am going to Kingston, and if I can meet with anybody that can give me a Draught upon somebody in London for the Money, I will contribute 3 guineas towards; and the Draught shall be upon the other Half Sheet of this whole sheet of paper. I have by my own illness, and now laying in a Stock of wine for the year, for I am forbid Cyder, and by a great many other Sundrys too numerous to mention, been of late so weeded of money, that I have not been so bare for a long while past; however, the 3 Guineas may serve a little towards travelling Charges up to Arlsey or Burford. If I should not meet with a Bill to Day, do you advance the money and I'll answer it by the first opportunity.

I can have no opportunity of sending Fanny's Journal that I know of, nor some other letters, since they are too bulky, so you must wait till you come. She is at the height of happiness and almost splendour; and is in a manner ador'd by the great Folks, and the bright folks. The Thrale family and Dr. Johnson cannot live without her. She is now with them at Brighthelmstone, comes back with them in a Week, stays with them till the latter end of August, and then goes with them and Dr. Johnson and Mrs. Murphy a Tour of pleasure through the Austrian Netherlands, and so on to Aix la Chapelle and the Spas.[1] They are to be out about two months, travel with the greatest Ease and Luxury and Leisure, and live at the rate of ten thousand a year !

With all this sudden Change, her head is not turn'd. She does by no means forget her Old Friends. Hearing of my Illness accidently at Streatham, she sent over a man and horse on purpose with a letter to Kitty at ten o'clock at night to enquire after me, and has since wrote me the most affectionate and affecting letters you can conceive. She always remembers you ; and in her Caution about Secrecy, she excepts you and says she is too proud of your Favor and Affection to desire you should be treated with reserve by her—there's a girl for you ! She says she will not leave England till she has been here to see me. Mr. Sheridan, the manager of all the playhouses and the operas, has been privately applied to about her play next winter, and says whatever comes from her he will receive with open arms, and as a great honour, let what will prior Engagements stand in his way. Adieu. Write, or get somebody for you to write soon. Kitty Finder and Ham send much Love.

Y^r affectionate LEM.

The next letter, dated July 27, was received on the 30th, answered on the 6th. Meanwhile, the play " The Witlings," had been sent for Mrs. Gast's perusal. But it was condemned by Daddy Crisp and by Fanny's father, and the poor authoress bore her disappointment very well and suppressed it altogether. " Well, ' there are plays that are to be saved, and plays that are not to be saved,' " she says, and warmly she thanks her kind mentor, and humbly she submits.[2] Perhaps she was consoled by meeting her

---

[1] See *Diary*, i. 254. The plan had to be given up on account of the war ; " the fears and dangers of being taken by the enemy," says Fanny.

[2] See *Diary*, i. 254, etc.

daddy's sister. On July 30 she wrote that to be with her at
Chesington would be doubling her own pleasure, and allowed
her to see the unhappy comedy. " I should be glad to know
what I would refuse to a sister of yours." Mrs. Gast was
actually prevailed upon to leave her beloved Burford and
come to Chesington. She went away, no doubt, for change
and relief after her sister Theodosia's death. A letter of
Susan Burney's, August 1, 1779, describes a visit to Chesington, where she found Mr. Crisp, Mrs. Gast, Mrs. Hamilton,
and Kitty Cooke assembled in the parlour, and tells how
they went to church, and saw Mr. Torriano, and so on.

In 1780 Fanny had had a long visit to Bath with the
Thrales. The next letter is divided between two interests
that bitterly distressed poor Mr. Crisp—the monetary, in
which he had been hard hit, and so was the more careful
for his sister, and the national, about which he was
always, says Fanny, " a croaking prophet," and now
was distressed and miserable indeed. It was in the
dark days of Whig dominance and British disaster, before
Pitt came to power to revive the nation's glory.

LETTER No. 6.

CHESINGTON, *July 27*, 1780.

DEAR SOP,—

You certainly did perfectly right in giving me an early
line of your arrival alive and with whole Limbs at your Nest ; [1]
for, to tell you the truth, We all here began to wonder, and
indeed somewhat to murmur, at your suppos'd delay, or
suppos'd Accident ; one or other—for as it was, Your letter
dat. 15th did not get here till the 20th. No matter for your
knocking up the house at 4 o'clock; no matter for the
people's being glad to see you, and cry for Joy—other
people are as glad to see you, though they do not cry for
Joy. We have been continually remarking ever since you
went, what a hollow place you have left in the house ; be

---

[1] I do not know if Mrs. Gast had stayed a year at Chesington, or
if this was her return from a second visit.

sure You make haste and finish all your trumpery odments and accounts, and come and fill up the vacant space before the End of October—what signifies —— ?

You say you were just stepping into Bed. I hope you got better sleep than I can do ; to say the truth, I can procure none, or next to none ; my inside is so relax'd and hollow, I can hardly feel that I have any, and an almost continual purging. I am just going to try a steel, a Medicine of which Dr. Lewis gives a most wonderfully favourable recommendation in his Book, viz. filings of Iron steep'd in Rhenish or old Hock ; now I think, as I have old Hock by me, I cannot put it to a better Use. I have this morning reced. a letter from Mr. Withers that the pipe of Wine is bottled, and I may send for it when I please ; he tells me such wine is not to be procur'd elsewhere in London. I shall send for it on about Tuesday next—it will be in prime order for you by October, therefore be sure to come by that time and give it the meeting.

Mr. Allen last Friday brought down young Mr. Hinde with him to Dinner here, and they were both very pressing to persuade me to advance the money on their houses ; tho' I had before given an absolute negative they urg'd me to consider the matter again. I required a few days, and on weighing and considering it in every light once more, I am clear, that in the present precarious situation of affairs, it is by no means advisable ; and so by this post I acquaint them. The news yesterday at Epsom, that came down by the Epsom Coachman, and by a Serjeant of the troops quarter'd there, just come from London *was*, that there had been another Riot on Tuesday with the Cry of *No Popery !* and that some of the Rioters were Shot and others apprehended. Whether this be true or not, certain it is that notwithstanding our triumph on our little Successes in Carolina, &c., yet we are in a very ugly hole in general. Certain it is, that a very formidable Spanish reinforcement, both of Ships of the line, and a vast body of troops, have effected their junction with the French Squadron in the West Indies, which gives them an undisputed and dreadful Superiority against anything we can bring to oppose them in that Quarter; so that our Islands are in immediate jeopardy there; and if Jamaica is lost, what will be the Consequence is dreadful to think of. The Dutch, too, 'tis expected, will declare against us, and not a single ally for us. What luck we have had at Charlestown, and since that in our Expedition to the Mexico Coast, will soon be all unravelled again unless Admiral Rodney can, against apparent Odds, stand his Ground till great Succours can be sent him; and how they are all to be procur'd the Lord knows.

I have by this very post desir'd Mr. Allen to demand Principal and Interest on the £1,400 lent by poor Scrip to Mr. Shaw. It is a shame at such a time he should have such a sum at 4½ P. Cent. Interest, and on houses too. At least I expect this consequence, that he will consent to advance it to £5 P. Cent., which will be an increase of £7 a year. Above all things, I charge you to lose not a moment in getting Your money from [*blank*] and I hope before now you have wrote to him. On Monday all the Penny's came and spent the day here. The young Bridegroom seems to have learn'd better manners since You saw him, tho' still he seems inclining to play off *the agreable*—the *nonchalant*— but I fancy he has been let to know by some means or other that he is not as great Consequence as he had suppos'd. He was much more Civil and attentive than I expected. Adieu, our Sop—mind what I say; prepare and plan your matters, so as to be here by October at farthest. Ham, Kate, and Payney [1] love you much, I am sure. I don't deal in professions and Speeches; however, you won't be much out of the Way if you are of opinion that nobody does more than Lem.

The next letter followed within three days of a letter that Mrs. Gast wrote on August 19. It is dated 22nd, was received 23rd, and answered on September 5.

[1] This was one of the two Misses Payne, " daughters of Mr. Payne the bookseller at the Meux Gate," one of whom, Sarah, married James Burney, Fanny's elder brother, on September 6, 1785.

THE LETTERS

LETTER No. 7.

DEAR GASTATION,—

In the first place, I think I am better and more comfortable than when you went. I *do* get some sleep o' nights, and don't so constantly feel that hollow inside in the daytime as I did. The Baker has just brought y^{rs} so I was resolv'd to scribble a word by him, tho' I had design'd to wait for an answer from Mr. Shaw, who, you know, pays you but 4½ P. C^t for £1,400. I bid Mr. Allen tell him he must for the future either pay £5 P. Cent., or else pay off his Principal. It seems he is gone his Manchester Journey, and won't be back till the 28th, and so I deferr'd writing till after then ; but as you require a line now You shall have it, and another when I can tell you Shaw's answer, which I make no doubt will be a compliance with my demand—that will be an additional £7 a year. I *do* desire, you'd write to Mr. [*cut out*] to pay you *off*—not content with raising his Interest, for You have no Security, and if shou'd dye You might be in a nasty hobble ; therefore write to him directly. I wonder you can be so indifferent about it. Fannikin and the D^r were to have come last night, and we expect them every moment till we see them. Fanny promises to show me her beginning of a new performance, which you have heard of. Don't you give any hint to Nanny Leigh or anybody else that she is engag'd in any other work, especially what work. Gabriel Mathias [1] three weeks ago brought his two daughters here to visit the Payney ; they are very agreable girls. The Eldest sings sweetly, and with infinite real true Taste ; her voice is not very powerful, but as clear as a Bell and as sweet as Milk. I told her she wanted nothing but a Shake, and Advis'd her to try for it, which she has promis'd to do. They were all vastly delighted with

---

[1] This was the uncle of Vincent Mathias, Queen Charlotte's subtreasurer, who was responsible for paying Fanny's official salary.

the place, and *us people*—no wonder ! They quite expected to have seen you, and were much disappointed, as they had heard much about you—and that not to your disadvantage. They long (the girls) (they write Payney word) to come and stay here sometime next Summer, they say We are charming Folks—and so We are to be sure. Do you be sure to make haste and finish all your domestic odments, and be here at furthest before the end of October. What should you do, in that Gulf, that Abyss of Dulness ? Hetty is gone for a Month with Dick to Ramsgate for Sea bathing ; little Fanny is come to Polly Hubbard's ; she had been very ill a great while, feverish, &c., &c., and Dr. Broomfield could make nothing of her ; at last she voided *one worm* almost as big as herself, and is now quite Jolly and well. I must finish, for Baker is impatient, and is to put this into the black Dog in the Wick for You to have on Wednesday night —that is to-morrow. Sally Payne has been here this fortnight with her Sister. She is a sweet girl, and is going in 2 days. She and Patty and Ham and Kate all run about me to know how you did, and when you come, and were mighty earnest to send their love. So Good bye. I don't hate you much.

LEM.

CHESINGTON, *Aug. 22*, 1780.

A month later he wrote another letter, still urging the good lady to come. Nanny Leigh was a " cousin " of the Crisps. She was the daughter of the Rev. Peter Leigh, Rector of Lymm,[1] and Mary his wife, daughter of Henry Doughty of Broadwell, Stow-on-the-Wold. Mrs. Leigh and her sisters Mrs. Green and Mrs. Chamberlayne were co-heiresses of their brother, who died without issue. Ann, who married Captain Frodsham, long survived him. They were both buried at Broadwell, and the inscription on their monument is worth copying.

[1] See page 15 above.

THE LETTERS

SACRED TO THE MEMORY OF
JOHN FRODSHAM, ESQ.,
POST-CAPTAIN IN THE ROYAL NAVY,
IN WHOM UNAFFECTED ELEGANCE OF MANNERS, POLITE LEARNING
UNIVERSAL BENEVOLENCE AND TRUE PIETY
WERE HAPPILY UNITED WITH BRAVERY
OFTEN TRIED IN THE SERVICE OF HIS COUNTRY.
HE DIED MAY 29, 1791, AGED 54.

ALSO TO THE MEMORY OF
ANNE HIS WIDOW,
WHO DIED OCT. 16, 1830, AGED 79.
SHE WAS THE DAUGHTER OF THE REV. PETER LEIGH OF LYMM IN
THE COUNTY OF CHESTER.
THE REMAINS OF BOTH REST IN A VAULT IN THIS CHURCH.
IN FULFILMENT OF THE INTENTION OF THEIR BELOVED MOTHER,
WHO WAS THE MOST KIND AND TENDER OF PARENTS,
THIS TABLET WAS ERECTED BY HER TWO DAUGHTERS,
THE YOUNGEST OF WHOM, EMMA, DIED AT BATH,
APRIL 5TH, 1834,
AND WAS BURIED AT BOX, IN THE COUNTY OF WILTS.

Letter No. 8, written September 24, when Fanny was still at Chesington, was received the 26th and answered on the 29th and 30th. It shows Fanny at the height of her fame and with her simple charm unspoilt by the adulation she received from wits and blue-stockings.

The words at the beginning of the letter make one rub one's eyes and fancy one is in the days of bicycles and motor cars.

LETTER No. 8.

CHESINGTON, *Sept.* 24, 1780.

DEAR SOP,—

The roads are now excellent.

The day after I rec^d. y^{rs}, I wrote to Nanny Leigh according to your direction, and in the best manner I was

43

able congratulated her on the approaching change of her Condition ; most readily accepted the Trust she wish'd, with an offer of any other Service in my power ; excus'd my not being able to attend her in person, from my ill-health and the necessity I was under of never sleeping from home. I then represented my wish (if possible) of receiving a visit from her and our friends at Hanwell together, when she was with them there, at the same time taking shame to myself for offering such a proposal when it was out of my power to offer any of them a Bed, our house being quite full ; but that if she could compass a visit, we would dine at her own time, and the days were yet long enough to perform such a Journey. As an inducement, I acquainted her Fanny Burney was here, sent her love to her, and long'd to see her, which she had no chance of doing unless she comply'd with my request, as her stay at Ches. would be longer than Nanny's in Town. At the same time, Compliments, &c., and very civil messages to Captn Frodsham. My letter went Sept. 8th, and consequently was at Mrs. Hughes's the 9th. Now this day being the 24th, and never having heard a word from her yet, I conclude she has finish'd her business in Town and gone back, as you say her whole Journey out and home was not to exceed 10 days. However, my conscience is clear. I have done my part ; and if she has thought better of it, and excuses me the Trust she offer'd, I shall not be sorry, as I am far from wishing to entangle myself in such businesses at my time of Life and state of health, from which nothing can be produc'd better than trouble and loss of time.

Now for other matters. Since I wrote last, I rece^d a letter from Captn Hinde in Hertfordshire, mentioning his great disappointment and claiming my promise to Mr. Allen to pay the expenses incurr'd by the writings and Council's Fees on account of the Mortgage. There was no occasion to answer him, but I confirm'd my promise to Mr. Allen by letter ; and I am now heartily glad, even at this great Expense (I don't know how much, but dare say not less than £15 or £16), that I have got rid of this business. I now find houses are become such a drug that they (comparatively) fetch nothing ; and more and more every day

44

are quitted, and remain untenanted at any rent almost. At this very time, houses in Grosvenor Square and Grosvenor Street and Brook Street (that us'd to be the Cream of London) and belonging to the new Mrs. Penny and her Mother Simmons and Mrs. Edward Penny, are empty, which 3 years ago were let for no less than £450 a year, and the Day before Yesterday Dr. Burney rece^d here a letter from his wife, acquainting him with a proposal made by the purchaser of a most magnificent house in Upper Brook Street that 6 years ago he bought at the price of £5,300 and which he now offers to sell for £2,500 ! Dr. Burney having money in Navy Bills and other Government matters, has for some time been hunting after some solid purchase or Security ; and rece^d this proposal in Consequence of his Enquiries. Besides this, the Court of Chancery for some time past, I find, has absolutely refus'd to Mortgagees that brought Bills to foreclose, the liberty of so doing ; on this Consideration, that money is now so very scarce, that the Mortgagers find it impossible to borrow money on the best securities to pay off the Mortgages they owe ; so all the relief the Mortgagees can get from Chancery is the appointing a Receiver to receive the rents, and pay them their Interest ; their principal, want it ever so much, they must content themselves to go without. Nash has promis'd Mr. Allen to procure a Bondsman to join with him in a Bond to pay the Interest [*MS. torn here*] but had not yet done so a week ago. Allen hunts him up [*MS. torn here*] very close, and will let him have no rest till he has perform'd his promise, and put into his hands the Policies of Insurance. Allen will soon send me his Bill of the unlucky Expenses of the Mortgage, which I shall acquaint you with ; and then you must send Mr. Mathias your letter to discharge it ; in such perilous times as these, you must not think of invading your Principal ; You must Tap a Bond ; it would be madness in You at your time of Life to distress yourself in the smallest degree to leave a little more, or a little less, behind You. Have you yet wrote to [*space cut out*] to pay off his Bond ? Upon my word, Sop, You ought not to let that matter Sleep. Personal Securities at such times at these ! Let me earnestly

45

intreat You to make a point of it, to get in that money directly. I don't know whether I told you before, that Mr. Shaw's answer about raising his Interest to £5 P. Cent. was, that before the ensuing half year's Interest (some time in October) is due, he will give Mr. Allen his final resolution whether to pay off the £1,400—or pay for the future £5 P. Cent.

Dr. Burney and Fanny, and first Charlotte, and then last Suzette in Exchange have been here these 5 weeks—went away yesterday. Fanny is to come and spend some time here in the Winter ; and (entre nous) is to work hard upon some plans she has, that I think will turn out highly to her fame and Advantage. She has absolutely made me promise not to give the least hint of what she is about ; but if you were present, she says, she would hide nothing from You. You would be astonish'd to know in what a manner she is courted, and almost adored by all the Wits—it would be enough to turn a shallow Brain. Mrs. Montagu, who holds herself up in the Clouds, has wrote her two letters since she has been here, soliciting her Correspondence ; and wherever she goes, she is follow'd and address'd as if she was Pope. These particulars [*MS. torn here*] Example must not be quoted, as if they should [*MS. torn here*] be reported, it might be attributed to her Vanity, and boasting of the favor she meets with, only in general that she is greatly admired. The whole Family of the Thrales last Wednesday, viz. Mr. Thrale, Mrs. Thrale, Miss, alias Queeny, and the Great Dr. Johnson, came over in form to make me a visit—their civilities and invitations were beyond Expression. Mr. Thrale wanted me to promise to come and spend a few weeks at Streatham ; and if I could be prevail'd on to come to them at Brighthelmstone, they would make ample room for me, a good Bed for the Season and all other good things ; they go there the middle of Oct[r.] A Noble Basket of Pine Apple, Melon, glorious Peaches and Grapes accompanied their visit. They torment Fanny to go with them, but she persists to come hither to me and work hard ; they will stay at Bright[e] till after Xmas. Mrs. Th. enquired much after You ; and Fanny says she said to her, *I like that Mrs. Gast, she*

seems a very agreable, elegant woman. There's for you ! Prithee
make haste and come up here as soon as You can, and leave
that stupid Burford. Jem Burney is come home from
rounding the world, and is to come here with Fanny ; the
Dr. had a letter from him (the first these 4 years), dated
from the Orkneys, about a week ago. Dispatch your Business and come directly. Special good wine—and plenty.
Fanny, Ham, and Kate are earnest in their desires to be
remembered to you.

Y^{rs} &c.,
LEM.

So Jem Burney the sailor was come home from seeing the
world to see Miss Sally Payne ; and Mrs. Thrale was eager
in her hospitalities, which Mrs. Gast was begged to share.
Do leave that stupid Burford !

What was the very secret bit of journal referred to in the
next letter ? Some family gossip, no doubt. The diary,
as we have it in print, it may be observed, breaks off when
Fanny Burney left Bath in June and is not resumed till
December 6. There are no letters from her between August
24 and that date. There is a gap, too, just at this time in the
letters of Dr. Johnson to Mrs. Thrale, which earlier in the
year had been so abundant, so we have, I think, no other
description of the " splendid " dinner on September 30.

The ninth letter, written September 28, 1780, from
Chesington, was received on October 1 and answered
October 7. Before this Mr. Crisp had written another letter
to his sister ; the tenth was written on October 2 and received
on October 4.

LETTER No. 9.

HOLLO GAST !—

Our William has begg'd and obtained of Mrs. Hamilton
a week's Holiday to go to see his Friends in Wiltshire ; and

when there, he has a great desire to make you a visit at Burford. He says you invited him, (when he told you his Friends liv'd at Swindon,[1] not far off) when he came into that neighbourhood, to come over and see you—so he has begg'd of me to give him a letter to You ; by way of a pretence and excuse for taking that Liberty. He is a very honest, faithful Fellow and deserves notice ; so I hope, and dare say, You will make him and his Uncle (who travels with him (a very honest Cock, an excellent Gardiner, and lives with Mr. Smith at Epsom) very welcome ; and if you can without much inconvenience offer them a Bed for one night, I believe it would be esteemed a most high Favour.

He talks of setting out next Thursday (Oct. 5) and of reaching Burford either on the Sunday or Monday following. Now, d'ye see, Fanny has just sent me a charming Packet of her Journal continued ; containing (under the Seal of strict secrecy) certain anecdotes, which must be inviolable, as You will be convinced, if I obtain leave to communicate them to you. Now, once more, d'ye see, if this Packet should be brought you by William on Sunday (which under pain of annihilation he must bring back carefully sealed up), are you such a Bible-Face as not to read them on that day ? You will receive this letter I am writing on Sunday night (which comes out from Burford[2] very early on Monday morning), I shall have it on Tuesday ; and then according to your answer I shall either send the Packet by Will, or not (I mean if I get leave). I am to go to-morrow to dinner to Streatham (for Mrs. Thrale and the whole Family will take no Denial) and then I shall ask Fanny's Consent ; without which I would not on any account betray my Trust. They insist on my lying there, and Mr. T. promises to send me back in his own Coach ; but I am determined at all events to return at night, tho' I suppose two hours in the dark ; for the thought of complying is death to me. I

---

[1] Swindon is twenty miles from Burford.
[2] This probably means that as the post leaves Burford early on Monday she must read and answer his letter on Sunday.

rece^d on Tuesday last a very pretty letter from Nanny Leigh, but she could not contrive to see me here and to be sure is by this time got home. If you see her give my love to her. I shall write again by Will, so good bye.

Your loving LEM.

Kate, Ham and Payney send much love.

CHES., *Friday, Mich^s Day.*

LETTER No. 10.

DEAR GAST,—

Tho' I wrote so lately, I now do it again to tell you that I believe our William will come over to Burford, from Swindon (where he is going) on Saturday in the forenoon, with his uncle ; for both of whom (I have told him) you will provide a Bed for Saturday night—therefore don't engage yourself for that day, because the packet of Journal I shall send by him will take You up a good deal of time to read, and they must be off the morning before it is light. I went to dinner, according to appointment, to Streatham on Saturday ; and obtained Fanny's leave. [*Here a large piece of the letter is cut out.*] Spy, or a Drawcansir. What she says is very true ; and therefore you must seal up your Lips. On the same Condition M. L. (whom I know to be true and trusty) may see what I send, if she likes it.

I met a vast deal of Company at Streatham, where everything was most splendid and magnificent—two courses of 21 Dishes each, besides Removes ; and after that a dessert of a piece with the Dinner—Pines and Fruits of all Sorts, Ices, Creams, &c., &c., &c., without end—everything in plate, of which such a profusion, and such a Side Board : I never saw such at any Nobleman's. A most Gracious Reception, and such pressing invitations to stay as I could hardly escape ; but I got away, and reach'd home by 9 o'clock, and glad I was to creep again into my own Nest.

Now to other matters. I yesterday rec^d a letter from

49
E

Mr. Allen, containing Mrs. Shaw's answer about raising his Interest on the £1,400 he owes You on Mortgage. He does consent that from the 17th of this month (October) he will pay £5 P. Cent. ; which you know is an addition of £7 a year [*letter torn here and below*] that day (the 17th) the half year's Interest   that time the increase of Interest.

an Express came   was call'd out, and when he returned look'd very   but did not say anything to disturb the Cheerfulness of the Company ; but William, who was in the Kitchen, tells me the Messenger said (what I find now all the News are full of) the Enemy had taken almost the whole of our Quebec Fleet, a most irreparable loss ; and added (but said it was not Confirm'd) that the news likewise was, that 8 homeward-bound Indiamen were taken.   O Dreadful ! the French are now so strong in North America, particularly Rhode Island, which they are in full possession of, that all our successes in Carolina and Charles Town will be vanished into Smoak; and 'tis said and believed, that the loyal Carolinians, forsooth, are all revolted again to the Congress ; in such a Crisis the worst is to be apprehended, and for my part I think nothing but hard ready money is to be depended on ; therefore as Iago says to Roderigo—*put money in thy purse ! fill thy purse with money !* Need I say any more to induce you, immediately, and positively to insist on your money from   ? Lose no time.   The next thing I have to say is, to wish you to come hither as soon as possible.   Why not here as well as that stupid Burford ? Upon my Word, in such times as these 'tis best to be upon the Spot ; immediate measures may be necessary to be taken ; and surely you may be as warm and comfortable here as there.   You know the Folks, and sick or well, You will be nurs'd and taken care of ; pray take this last piece of Advice in good earnest ; my advice I do say is generally right.   Fanny will be here a good while this Winter, and Jemm will be backwards and forwards from coming round the World; and I think you may in every respect pass your time as well here as filthy Burford.   Ham, Kate and Payney send you much love ; and Fanny at Streatham was particularly earnest to be in the most kind manner remembered to you ; neither are you violently hated by

LEM.

That needy Fellow Nash, I believe after all, must be severely dealt with according to Law—for he pays not the least regard to his word.

Mrs. Gast did not come, and, instead, gave a very poor account of her health. Things were sad, too, at Burford. Mr. Lenthall's sister was dead, and he himself not well. He " died suddenly of an apoplexy " a year later.

The following letter was written November 8, received 10th, answered 27th ; and the passage about Mackail interested Mrs. Gast for she dockets it as the important part of the letter.

LETTER No. 11.

DEAR SOP,—

I am quite glad to hear you say you are better, for your last gave a very chicken account of yourself—no appetite, no relish for anything, even port wine ; what I really believe, is your very best medicine ; pray get rid of all these pitifull feelings ; and if You come when you ought, there will be a tolerable Stock of port left, and exceeding good in its kind. You talk of sending Bank Bills ; if You can send Bank Bills, You can get somebody to give you a Draft on some other Body in Town for your Bank Bills ; which I had much rather have ; as a Draft is much safer than Bank Bills bandied backwards and forwards by the Post. As to [blank] and the [blank] this bitter cold wintry weather ; to say the truth, I do not wish for them now, neither shall I give any hint to encourage it ; on the contrary, I had rather they should suppose there is no room for them at present ; and indeed, tho' Jem is gone to Town

51

for a few days, I expect him hourly till I see him, for he is quite glad of a little rest and quiet and country Air and milk, &c., after being a Tennis Ball round the Globe for 4 Years and a half. He was my Guest for a few days, which with great Difficulty I could force upon him ; but now he *will* come upon his own Account, and make a good long stay, I believe, backwards and forwards the best part of the Winter ; Fanny too is to come soon, for she wrote me word a good while ago, that she believ'd she should be at Ches. *ere long and for long,* so that it would not be in my power to assure the other Folks of a lodging, unless by round-about appointments backwards and forwards to invite one set at a certain time, and forbid the other ; all which manœuvre I wish to avoid : besides this cold weather, I want to creep into the fire myself, in my own great chair, and not be obliged to do the honours, &c. ; whereas, I make Jem and Fanny make room for me, and never mind them, nor put myself the least out of my way for them. When you come, I will take care you shall see Jem's Journal, which is very entertaining ; and as well wrote, or better, in my belief, than any officer's of the whole Expedition ; it is judicious and solid likewise, and shows a depth of Knowledge in his profession, which will hardly be equall'd by any Officer in the Service, of his Standing ; but the Accounts of his Adventures, &c., from his own mouth are still more enlivening ; it would be endless to enter into particulars, so you must rest satisfied till you hear and see yourself.

If you see the Leighs or Frodshams, give my kind love to them, and tell Mrs. Frodsham when the deed of Trust comes to me I will Execute it and perform my Duty in it as well as I can for her Service, and with great Pleasure. What does Mr. Frodsham's ship do at Liverpool ? is it to be a Cruiser in St. George's Channel ? It may possibly be an advantageous Station in point of Captures, but it is a Devil of a dangerous Sea, especially in Winter. You say Sr Andrew is Commissioner as well as Govr—Commissioner of what ? Does he then give up his Ship, on being appointed Govr ? When do they set out ? Patty Payne is gone, and I know nothing about the binding your Books ; when I do, I will pay for them. I am really sorry for Jane Lenthal ; what will the Squire do then for a housekeeper, if she drops ? will he invite M. L. ? or his Brother and his Wife ?

As for self, I am much as usual ; not worse, I think. I am glad you and M. L. were pleased with Fanny's Journal ; when she comes she is to bring the remainder ; she desires me to acquaint Mrs. Frodsham, then whenever she knows she is in Town, she will find her out, if above ground.

When your letter was brought me in, I was reading Hume's *History of England*. 'Twas in Charles the 2nd's reign, in the Year 1668, when a bitter and bloody Law was made against the frequenters of Conventicles in Scotland, and as bloodily executed. The passage I met with struck me so that I will transcribe it and send you. Charles himself, touch'd with Compassion for the poor Sufferers, sent a letter to the Council to put a stop to such Cruelties ; but not being deliver'd in time to Sharpe the President, one Maccail in the interval was put to the Torture, under which he expir'd ; he seem'd to dye in a Triumph of Joy—

> " Farewell Sun, Moon, and Stars ; Farewell World
> " And Time ; Farewell weak and Frail Body.
> " Welcome Eternity ; Welcome Angels and Saints ;
> " Welcome Saviour of the World ; and Welcome
> " God, the Judge of All ! "   " Which were his
> " last words ; and these animated Speeches he
> " Utter'd with a Voice and manner, which struck
> " All the by-standers with Astonishment."

There is nothing in Homer or Milton more Sublime. Well, Good-bye ! come soon, and be well. Ham and Kate truly wish for You, and send you their Love.

Adieu, I don't hate you,

LEM.

A brief letter, received November 29, answered December 14.

LETTER No. 12.

DEAR SOP,—

I now write to scold You. Captain Graeme was here yesterday, and told me Mrs. Chamberlayne had rece^d a letter from you that you was far from well. Why did you not let me know it ?—d'ye think I don't care for you as much as Mrs. Chamberlayne ? Your last letter gave a different account of Yourself, and a hope that you were mending apace. I desire you'd without delay set me at Ease in this particular ; which I shall not be till I see your own hand ; and perhaps not that neither ; however, that will be some satisfaction, by letting me know the truth ; for suspense is worse than all. Thank you for the Gold Buttons he brought, but what signify Gold Buttons, if you are to be ill ? Be sure to get strong enough to come hither early in the Spring, and we'll nurse you to the full as well as your Folks at Burford can do. I am still a poor wretch—sleepless nights, Bad digestion, swell'd Legs, &c., &c., &c. Ham and Kate were much concern'd at Capt. Graeme's intelligence about you, for I am sure they have a sincere hearty kindness for you. I am sure so has

LEM.

I rece^d from Mr. Leigh of Westminster Nanny Leigh's marriage settlements, both of which I executed and return'd ; and Mr. Leigh was likewise to execute both and return me one, which however he has not yet done.

CHES., *Nov.* 27, 1780.

LETTER No. 13.

Written Dec. 15, received Dec. 19, answered Jan. 9, 1781.

DEAR SOP,—

Since Dr. Parsons's prescriptions do so little for you, according to your own Account, I think you have nothing to do but to make yourself up as well as you can and get into a proper plight to come to Ches. early in the Spring ; for I am sure when you were here, You were better than either Captain Graeme or yourself now Describe You to be, and as to nursing and attendance, You will be as well look'd after here, I'll answer for it, as at home ; and you'll find Kate as handy, as zealous, and assiduous about You, as your own Betty can be for the Life of her ; and Sally (now my maid) much more attentive, alert, and exact than honest Bet was. What secret Charms that center of everything that is stupid, Burford by name, can have for you, is, I own, quite past my Comprehension.

I am glad to hear so good an Account of Captn Frodsham, and heartily hope He and his piece will have good luck together. Mr. Leigh of Westminster sent me both parts of the Marriage Articles to Execute, which I did ; and return'd them to him to do the same, which I understand he has done and transmitted (by my directions) one of the parts to Mrs. Simmons at Millbank, which she will get convey'd to me as opportunity offers ; these Articles, by the way, seem to me to be drawn up in a queer odd way ; and if I had seen the Draught, before it had been engross'd, and executed by the parties, I believe I should have made some objections, and propos'd several Alterations. Did Mr. Jarvis see them, or was he at all consulted ? What degree of Reputation for skill in his profession has this Lawyer of Stow, who I find was employ'd ?

Now I am talking of Law matters, it puts me in mind to tell You I have some thoughts of new making my Will ; and of joining that honestest of beings, Jack Edison, of Basinghall Street (and whom I have had experience of, between 30 and 40 years) with You as a Joint Executor ; being fully convinc'd of his perfect integrity of disinterestedness, and likewise of his experience and conduct of business ; so that he would prove a very usefull Assistant to You, in Case of need ; and exclusive of that as You and I are neither of Us young, I think one would wish the due execution of a Trust, should not hang upon one single Life. This will of mine, that now exists, was made before either poor Scrip, or Doce, or Molly Lancaster died ; so that even the very wording of it anew seems in some measure requisite. I have not yet propos'd it to Jack Edison, but intend it, either by this post, if I have time, or else by the next. Mr. Allen's Bill is paid—I own I grudge it heartily ; but upon the maturest Consideration, and most perfect Conviction, I would do it again. Mrs. Simmons, like a fool, to whom I sent the Bill, to pay Mr. Allen, took a Coach to Lombard Street (which she charged to me) to receive the money at the Bankers, in order to pay him ; Whereas Mr. Allen (as I wrote her word) would call on her, and then he would have taken the Bill, and given her the Change out of it. As to Mrs. Frodsham's Annuity, I fear it can never answer—her £600 is now at £5 P. Cent., and brings her in £30 a Year ; and I much question if at her time of Life, she will get, upon good Security, above £7 10s. P. Cent., or £45 a year ; so that at that rate, she must sink £600 for an increase of only £15 a year income—surely that can never be worth while. Represent this to her ; and if she still holds the same mind, I will make enquiries. I will add one thing, which is, that as things now stand, and every security is ticklish, except Land—good Farms I mean—if I were to advise I would accept of nothing else ; and in that case, I dare say, she would not meet with an increase equal to her purchase money—and as to Land, she would be as likely, or more so perhaps, to hear of such a thing among the Country Attornies, than in London. That slippery Fellow Nash, I wish we could get rid of him for good and all ; but how, is the Question ? He promised Mr. Allen faithfully to give him a letter of Attorney to receive Rent of one of the Tenants to pay himself the Interest of your Mortgage, and to make over to your name and put into your hands all the Policies of Insurance of the several houses ; but he has done neither yet. I have desir'd Mr. Allen to give him no rest, and he must pay all Charges—the 18th of Jan. there will be another half year due.

At the time Mr. Thrale's Death was put in the Newspapers, he was perfectly well, and some days after, but has had since a most hair-breadth scape indeed. Dr. Sr Rich^d

THE LETTERS

Jebb accidentally came to Streatham in the afternoon, found Mr. T. and the ladies and other Company in the drawing Room, seemingly all well—the Ladies at their Tea, Mr. T. in his Chair by the Fire. When he came up to Mr. T. and ask'd him how he was ; he made no answer ; he observ'd his Eyes rowling in his head—he felt his pulse and cried out, Hey day ! why, what are you all about ? Why this man's very ill ! Up they all started in a fright ; the Dr. then shook him and at last made him get out of his Chair ; he then cried out he was very cold, and had a shivering Fit. The Company all thought of nothing but a return of the same Fits he had had before, and if Dr. Jebb had not been there they would have instantly had him blooded, like an ox, as he was before. Providentially his presence prevented this discipline and certainly sav'd his Life—he ordered him instantly to bed, to be plied with hot white wine whey— stay'd with him 3 hours watching his Pulse ; declar'd some Crisis was coming on ; ordered the whey to be made quite strong, and ply him all night with it. Next morning early return'd ; ordered him to drink large quantities of Port, above a bottle a Day, and a large proportion of brandy mix'd with the Port—likewise to give him the highest things to eat, and as plentifully as he could take them—port with brandy without all Stint. The bystanders were frighted, but the Dr. persisted, and at last by this hot work produced a violent Boil in the Nape of his neck, which indeed proved a Carbuncle ; he still went on heating him and feeding him up in this manner, which he continues to this hour, and by his bold and judicious proceeding has obtain'd what he wanted. His Carbuncle has been open'd before ripe, by orders, vast quantities of crude undigested blood squeezed out by violence with most excruciating Pain, and now this envenom'd Carbuncle is become mild, cool, digests great Quantities of laudable matter ; the patient is easy, comfortable in Spirits, and Sharp, the famous Surgeon, and the Dr. both declare him a restor'd Man, and in all probability the secret, and dreadful cause of his several late dangerous attacks, is radically and effectually remov'd ; there's a Cure for you ! Fanny and Jem are both now with me, and

Fanny sends much love ; so do Ham and Kate ; and so does

LEM.

When I see Mr. Payne, I'll ask him about binding the books.

Fanny Burney was now hard at work on *Cecilia*, and she spent part of the early months of the year at Chesington. So did Jem, intent, no doubt, on Miss Payne.

Of the next letter, written on March 1, 1781, received on the 4th, there is no note of the answer—only a fragment is preserved. Poor Fanny terribly overworked herself at her novel, and told Daddy Crisp that she had " very narrowly escaped a return of the same vile and irksome fever which with such difficulty has been conquered." She pretended that it was " all from vexation " because the Thrales, who had planned to take her to Italy, were now going to take Dr. Johnson instead. " As their journey was without limit, either of time or place, as Mr. Thrale's ill state of health and strange state of mind would make it both melancholy and alarming, she [Mrs. Thrale] could not in conscience think of taking *me* from my own friends and country without knowing either whether or for what length of time." Poor Fanny, it was a bitter disappointment, but Mr. Thrale's health was worse than they knew, and the journey with Dr. Johnson to Italy was never taken. What we have lost !

LETTER No. 14 (*a fragment*).

And after settling that she should return home the Thursday went back to dinner—poor thing. I carried her back to her Father's, and there was Mrs. Thrale at 2 o'clock, and had brought Dr. Jebb to meet her, that not a moment might be lost. I return'd back the same evening ; I have had a short note from her since ; the Dr. attends her every Day ; he says something is wrong, but he has no doubt of setting her up again. Mrs. Thrale sees her every day ; often twice, and thrice. They have a ready furnished house for 3 months in Grosvenor Square. Fanny seems to have become a public Character ; the house is throng'd from morning till night with How dy'es and enquiries after her from half the great Folks in Town. Mrs. Thrale has taken me so much in favor for my kindness to Fanny, that she sent by her *her Love* to me—there's for you ! She is about a mighty pretty entertaining Work which not a soul has seen a word of but myself ; but not a Syllable of this must transpire ; her close application to it from morning till night I believe contributed not a little to her present Illness,[1] for she is, like her Father, indefatigable and ardent in all her pursuits. Hetty has been very ill. I saw her in Town for half an hour. She looks like the Edge of a wornout knife ; but still pretty. She has been in great danger of a Miscarriage. She has got her sweet little Girl up from Worcester. Jem has been a good deal here since he came home ; he is in hopes of a Ship in May or soon after. Their last Voyage is ready finished, but as there must be a good many plates, it can't come out yet. Poor Simmons has had her house broke open, and lost to the amount of above £100. Kit bids me tell you Bob is well ; and that the Yew Hedge is to begin cutting to-morrow. Mrs. Penny has got a Boy. So my poor Fellow Traveller is gone ! How has she left matters ?—how much to Dumpling ? How does the Squire go on ?—what is his Plan ? Send me a Burford Journal. Dr. Lewis has been upon the decline these 2 years, and kept at home, and gone to no patients ; and since then, A Dr. Anderson, who has been settled at Kingston these 7 years with a small Share of business, has started forward at a great Pace—is sent for far and near, and they say has perform'd extraordinary Cures—has set up his Carriage and drives the World before him. Poor Dr. Lewis died about a month or six weeks ago. 'Tis lucky for the neighbourhood that there is still a very able Physician within call. Nothing of Graemes or Hammond do I know. Mrs. Graeme borrowed Evelina. Is Mrs. Bund the

---

[1] See *Letters*, i. 460.

Miss Cox I once knew? Mrs. Thrale is become a mighty visitor of the Duchess of Cumberland and wants to carry Fanny there. Mr. Thrale is well, but I fear not quite regular enough—too much feasting. I have been very queer for some time, sleepless and indigestion; but believe the Gout has a mind to be about my house, and consequently the other complaints not quite so bad. Mrs. Dr. Burney has sent her poor little neglected Girl, Sally, over to Geneva, to her half sister, who ran away with an adventurer from Paris—did you ever hear of such a Scheme? Kate and Ham both well and send much Love; neither are you much hated by

LEM.

N.B.—a Burford Journal.

The next letter follows quickly, written March 13, received March 14, answered the next day.

LETTER No. 15.

TUESDAY, *March* 13, 1781.

DEAR GAST,—

Admiral Jem is my scribe; he is now here a second nurse, though to say the truth I have but little occasion for nursing, being wonderfully better than could have been expected: fever quite gone, sleep and appetite returned; in a very few days I hope to be about again and promise to be more regular for the future. I am greatly mortified to hear you give up all thoughts of coming to us. I hope the longer days and warmer weather will make you alter your resolution. The Fannikin is growing better apace, and Hetty, I hear, is mending. For my own part I must say Mr. Hemmings has attended me very carefully, judiciously and successfully, so that no Doctor Jebb or any other Doctor was wanting. I wish you was here and Admiral Jem could show you Journals, Maps, plans, Charts, &c., that would make you very happy; besides a thousand little anecdotes and particulars worth all the rest. You shall be sure to hear from time to time how we go on here. Ham and Kate send their best love and so does Jem.

All this I vouch to be true, witness my hand.

JEM.

Pray remember the Burford Journal.

Before the next letter Mr. Thrale was dead. A letter Fanny had from his widow is endorsed " Written a few hours after the death of Mr. Thrale, which happened by a sudden stroke of apoplexy on the morning of a day on which half the fashion of London had been invited to an assembly at his house." The account which Samuel Crisp must have written to his sister seems to have perished, for the next letter is two months after it occurred. Written June 4, received June 6, but not answered till September 29.

LETTER No. 16.

CHESINGTON, *June* 4, 1781.

DEAR SOP,—

I inclose You Mr. Allen's letter, which will inform You what You are to do, relative to your Mortgage from them for £1,400. Observe, Shaw says, if he can call in his money time enough, he will pay off the Mortgage in October next, tho' the notice is for April 1782 ; but at all events he will engage to pay it in April. You will see Mr. Allen's inclos'd letter was wrote on Friday the 1st of this month ; and both he and myself began to fear that Tyler (by his seemingly avoiding to meet, or answer Mr. Allen) intended to shuffle off both his first and second proposal, of gradually paying off that Rascal Nash's Debt, &c., particularly that comfortable circumstance of paying down immediately £100, part of the principal and all Interest to January last ; but yesterday (Sunday) Mr. Allen came here and show'd me a note from Tyler, wherein he confirms his intention of paying off, now, the £100 and Interest ; but will not bind himself to go on paying £100 a year, as he first propos'd, tho' he intends it ; and if he neglects to do so, We may then take our Remedy, just as we can now ; so that at all events, what he pays is so much gain'd, without trouble. This I have agreed to ; and Allen says that the ground Rents (£42 a year for 56 years to come, clear of all deductions and Taxes, your Title to which nobody disputes, and for which the houses built thereon, Rented at about £250 a year, are a most unexceptional Security) are valued to be worth the greatest part, if not the whole of the remaining £600. This Villain, Nash, has, it seems, since your Mortgage, Mortgaged them over again to a poor widow in Hatton Garden for £500, of which She will lose every Shilling. Allen says such a Scene of complicated Villainy, as he is now discovered to have continu'd, is not to be match'd in the opinion of all the practises in the Law he has mentioned it to ; so that upon the whole we shall be well off, and escape without being sing'd. Allen thinks, as I do, [*cut out*] has not behav'd handsomely ; but from the Account in your letter, I would wait longer.

I am now something better, and walk about, and up and downstairs without a stick, and if I can but keep up to the good Resolution I am continually making, of a very Temperate Regimen, I hope to gain Strength apace ; but the Old Adam is Stubborn, and hard to Conquer. Why, Gast, you seem to give up all Chance of coming hither this Summer, for which you are—I won't say everything at my Tongue's end—but a Scrub, at least. As for the Hammonds, I wish them all good things ; but readily excuse their visit. In your last letter, before that rece^d yesterday, you say, speaking of little Sam,

"*He mentions Cruttenden as having deceiv'd him, talks of having had various loses, has still enough to live in affluence, but acts like a fool and Madman and can't manage for himself.*"

This you have worded so that I cannot well understand whether Cruttenden, or Sam, is this fool and madman, that can't manage for himself ; tho' I think it would be strange if Sam gave such a picture of *himself*—but you go on and say of him,

THE LETTERS

" *There is sense and strange incoherence in his letters*, &c., &c., &c." So that I am puzzled more and more.

I gave Kate and Mrs. Fisher your letters yesterday, for which they both return thanks, and Kate will answer soon. Mr. Thrale's Brewhouse and Stock in Trade is sold by the Exc^{rs} for £120,000 ; upon a Valuation, on his Death, it was valued at £150,000, but no set of men could be found who could engage in such an undertaking, but [at] a price considerably below its real value, so that Mrs. Thrale's friends (and I think rightly) judg'd it better to dispose of it on these terms than for her to continue on the business, and lye at the mercy of Clerks and Agents. She and her Children are now at a Certainty. She is to have £1,500 a year Jointure, and her own Estate £700 a year, on which there are upwards of 20,000 fine oaks, that would now fetch 20 shillings a piece, the worst of them, but they are to be (by her own choice and Resolution) sacred from the Axe. Mr. Thrale's own Estate in Lond. about £1,000 a year (besides Streatham) is to be the Eldest Girl's (who is to be made an Eldest son of) and I understand her share of the personals (besides these two Estates) will be about £50,000 ; the Remainder to be divided among the 4 younger Girls—Mrs. Thrale to have Streatham for Life. Fanny is now there, and I believe is likely to become at Last a sort of Fixture to the house. Mrs. Thrale and Dr. Johnson can't breathe without her.

Dr. Burney and Madam din'd here yesterday, and have left the agreable Suzette behind them. Jem has been here some time ; the Dr. would have stay'd longer, but was oblig'd to return, in order to make his appearance at Court this day ; he is now at the Top of the *Ton*. He is continually invited to all the great Tables, and parties, to meet the Wits and Grandees, without the least reference to Music ; and among the People, that neither employ him, nor care a straw for his Skill in an Art, which they never think about, he has now half a guinea a Lesson from all his scholars, the old ones as well as the new, and 4 Guineas Entrance ; and has this year more Scholars and business than ever he had in his Life—there's for you ! Hetty's Charles, likewise, has a great deal to do, and comes more and more into Vogue ; this is very comfortable in such distress'd times as these. Hetty has been very ill, but is got much better ; she is to Kitten, I understand, the latter End of August, or beginning of September. Suzette desires her Compliments. Ham and Kate and Jem Ditto.

God bless You.

LEM.

The next letter, written July 13, is long and business-troubled.

LETTER No. 17.

CHESINGTON, *July* 13, 1781.

DEAR SOP,—

Your account of Yourself is not a very pretty one, and I don't like it. Cold in your head, neck, Earack, Jawack, &c., &c.—but little Strength at present !—talk of coming for a few weeks if better ! What a P—signifies a few Weeks ? Come for good and All, and we'll make one Partie ; or if you won't determine upon that at once, come this Summer time, and stay the time round till the next, and see a little. Poor Ham has since I wrote last had an Attack, that we all thought of the most alarming kind ; it was a fair trial of Skill between a naturally excellent Constitution and that horrid hollow-ey'd Goblin, Death ; it was a violent inflammation of head and Face ; in Short, a furious Erysypelas or St. Anthony's Fire, attended with dreadful bilious Complaints ; and to compleat the distress for near 3 Days nothing would stay in her Stomach, either food or Physic. We sent away directly for her Sister Simmons, then at Chelmsford in Essex (50 miles from Ches.). She rece^d our letter the next morning at 12 o'clock, set out immediately, and was here the same evening at 9 o'clock. Hemming was very doubtful about her ; however he has manag'd her with great Skill and Success—bleeding and Bark and

Fomentations—these applications to noble, sound Stamina have set her up again; indeed her illnesses have ever almost been of a kind to be soon determined one way or other; and now (tho' she was seiz'd not above 3 weeks and a few days ago) she trots up to the Brewhouse, and toddles after her Pigs and Poultry again as usual—not that she is yet quite in *statu quo*; her head is still sore and her strength not yet quite restor'd, but all Danger over; she mends every day, and sleeps like a Top every night. I assure you, I pass'd many very uneasy, restless nights and days on this occasion. I should have been obliged to seek other quarters and quote another Plan; for I should never have taken upon myself to have paid Rent for Chesington, and kept house there. I suppose I must have endeavour'd to have prevail'd on Kate to take some little petty dwelling in, or close to some market Town, and have been half ruin'd by buying furniture, and moving and breaking every thing I have here; then, thought I, if Gast would but come up, and Join purses, and keep house together, we could well afford to pay rent, and stay where we are; and by the help of the Meadow, Orchard, Stable and Coachhouse, could keep a one-horse Chaise to carry us backwards and forwards, where we should want to go; and then we should be in a situation not to give up wholly all society and agreeable Friends, by being in possession of a dwelling, where there would be rooms and Convenience now and then to receive and entertain them. In that Case, the Name of the house-keeping should be in Kate, because then the Burneys, the Paynes, &c., &c., &c., with other pleasant People, might contribute to our delight and amusement and at the same time pay for themselves, and we should still as we pleas'd treat our own Visitors as usual; but by the House being kept on, in Kate's Name, we should avoid the unpleasant Sound of keeping Boarders. Weigh this well with yourself; and may you have the Grace so to apply it as to bring forth the Fruit of good living and dying at Chesington along with honest Lem. Amen, Amen. Bring your maid with You; take up a good hearty resolution and the business would be half over. If we can but continue to make the short remnant of our Lives comfortable and easy, is the leaving behind one a little more or a little less a Consideration worth attending to ? If once you can bring yourself upon the whole to relish this plan, what should hinder you from having all the little Conveniences and Indulgences you lay such a stress upon at Burford ? Your own Bed, your various Easy Chairs, all your Odments and Fancies, that to we Old Folks are very Essential and serious matters ? Once more, I say, think of this and with a good will too.

I yesterday rece^d the inclosed, by which you will see the little dirty Act of that Scrub Fellow Tyler, who I am strongly inclin'd to think has all along been privy to the Coqueries of his most villanous client Nash. You see he wants to shift off if possible the payment of even the one hundred pounds he has so often offer'd backwards and forwards ; and hopes that the bait of our gaining an additional £15 a year for clear ground rent of part of our mortgage ground, will induce us to forego our claim of his promise. To be sure, a clear additional £15 a year for above 50 years, is a very great and indeed unexpected stroke in our Favour, and increases the Value of our Security to a large amount ; it is worth above £200, and will be wholly our own ; but then observe, it will be a very great Advantage to Tyler himself as well as to Us, to have the ground (which when we are paid will be all his own) cover'd at other people's expense with very profitable buildings. You will see what Mr. Allen (very judiciously) has done by his answer. I have wrote to him approving all his measures, and desiring him to manage the affairs entirely by his own opinion ; promising to ratify and confirm his proceedings in consequence thereof—when you have rece^d and considered his letter, return it me. You need not return the other thing—his writings into Your hands may be a sort of check upon himself ; but will by no means enable you to recover your money from that quarter ; nothing but his assigning by proper Deeds his Mortgage to you, and making it liable to pay you off your Debt, by putting it out of his own power to reassign his Mortgage to his Debtor without your Concurrence, can give you any claim upon it, or impowers You to recover Your Debt out of it ; so that you will still remain as You are, with no other Security but what You have already—his personal security only—a piece of paper forsooth !—his Bond !—because he chuses to have his own hands free, at your hazard ; and because he won't be at any expense to make You easy and secure—if this Estate is not agreed for and soon sold, all I know of the matter is, that he should not serve me so. When I had wrote thus far, Mr. Allen's second letter dated the 11th came in, which was a most welcome one ; as now besides the additional clear £15 a year secur'd to us, we shall get out of that Rascal Tyler, and that other Rascal Nash's hands ; and besides receiving down upon the Nail £100 principal and the whole year's Interest which will be due the 18th of this month, £35. I say, besides this, Parkinson binds himself to the payment of the whole Principal by instalments of £100 a year, together with the Interest as it becomes due ; this is a real acquisition of a solid Security, which that shuffling Scoundrel Tyler never meant to do. By the return of the Post I answered this last letter of Mr. Allen's, highly approving of the Proposal of Parkinson and of his own Conduct in the affairs, so that I hope we shall now have everything settled satisfactorily, and that soon.

As to myself, I am now upon my Legs again, and stump about pretty bold—but indigestion and want of sleep still are my Companions—in great measure I must own, I believe, thro' my own fault—want of resolution to abstain, in point of Diets. Oh, Gast ! that Old Adam is a powerful Obstinate Antagonist ! I must cry out Ill fare our Ancestor impure ! as Milton says. However I don't quite give it up ; I go on making good resolutions ; if you were to come, perhaps you might fortify them—make the Trial. Since I wrote last Captn Graeme and his wife came and staid one night. Jem has got a Ship, with which (and with great reason) he is highly dissatisfied ; he is now cruising under Admiral Darby's Orders, off the Lizard, in quest of a 74 Gunship of the Line, that parted from the Fleet.

I have acquainted Mr. Edison with my request, which in the most obliging manner he consents to ; and I shall set about that matter soon. Oh that I could obtain what you complain of !—your *usual bad custom* (as you call it) *of sleeping too long in a morning !* Ham and Kate send much love, &c. ; that of Lem is not wanting. Adieu.

When I hear next I will write again.

Return Allen's 2 inclos'd letters.

PS.—Since I had finished and folded up this letter the Baker brought in a 3rd from Mr. Allen—read all 3 in their orders. What a set of Scoundrels.

LETTER No. 18.

Written Oct. 16, 1781, received 19, answered Nov. 10.

DEAR SOP,—

I write now, as You desire a Speedy answer, concerning little Sam. He cannot be in abler, or honester hands than Mr. Allen's ; and I would have you recommend him as strongly as you please, for I am confident he will come up to the best Character you can give him ; You may tell him You and I both have employ'd him in many transactions, which he has perform'd with much skill and Integrity, and with fair and reasonable Expenses ; but take care, I beg you, not to involve me in any Correspondence with the tiresome selfish Animals. I would not be pester'd as you are for more money than I will Name ; and I don't want to affront him, which I certainly should do by resolutely not answering his letters ; and I shall warn Mr. Allen in my turn, to avoid in his intercourse with him bringing me into question, or referring anything to me. You may hint the same thing to Allen, when you write to him. I ask'd him for his Bill on your Account relating to Nash's affair, which he has managed with a Degree of Dexterity, as well as indefatigable Care and trouble, that you could have no Notion of, unless all the particulars at full length were explain'd to You ; I shall therefore only tell You in General, that there was a Flaw in our original mortgage, occasion'd by that Rascally Felon's concealment, that if Mr. Tyler (Nash's Attorney and second mortgage of our houses) had been aware of, he might have been in as bad a pickle as the poor widow in Hatton Garden, who (I told you) will lose every Farthing of £500 she lent on the same Houses. But now everything is made firm and Solid, and nothing can hurt Us. Allen would not even tell me myself of the Danger We were in, till he had got all over, and now our Security is undoubted.

He has made out your Bill, which I was surprised to find so little as £14 odd shillings, and part of this out of his own pocket. I would therefore have you write to Mr. Mathias as soon as you know he has any money of yours in his hands to pay Mr. Allen, and think yourself happily off. Inclos'd I return Your Note. Do you design to let [*cut out*] go quietly on in your Debt for £500, on no other Security than his Bond ? Do you never hear from him now ? Can you not fix him to Name a certain time, when he will pay you, out of his great [*cut out*] and other Property ?—or is it to be left to his humour and his pleasure when he will deign to honour You with what is Your own ? I declare, I can't think of his proceedings, and answers to your demand, and his refusal (to give You what security he can give, because of the Expense) without Indignation ! Well, You must do as you please ; But if I was his Creditor, I would soon show him the Difference.

I don't at all like your Account of Yourself. Stomach and Bowels—want of appetite—grow big—breath oppress'd —Cough a good deal !—and do You design to go on, on your own head, and Burford Doctoring any longer ? I am convinc'd, in my own Mind, You want Jumbling about. What infinite Benefit did You receive by travelling round the World from Burford, to Manchester, Cheshire, London and Chesington ? How are Your Limbs after the desperate Fall, as it might have been, You had downstairs, with your Legs doubled under You ? Seriously, I do firmly believe, if you will come up hither early in the Spring (and surely You must be disabled with a Vengeance, if you cannot bear being Carried into, and in, a Post Chaise) the Journey, Change of Air, &c., will be of infinite Service to You ; for Physic, to old, crazy Frames, like ours, *is all my eye and Betty Martin*—

(a sea Phrase that Admiral Jemm frequently makes use of)—
I had yesterday half a Pipe of excellent Old Port (25 Dozen
and 2 Bottles) laid in, which our excellent worthy Friend,
Mr. Mathias procur'd for me, which will be in prime order
for Drinking when You come up (For I shall not touch it
myself till then, as I am constantly drinking Cyder of my
own making, which I really like better, and agrees with me
better ; and I have besides left of my old Stock above 5
Dozen of Port, which likewise I believe I shall hardly touch
myself, and am now Preparing to make 4 or 5 Hogsheads of
this Year's Cyder, so that I probably for the future shall be
no great dealer in Wine). Now, all these Premisses being
put together who the D——l, d'ye think must drink this
Wine, if You don't—lay these things to heart, and then
honestly draw the Fair Inference.

All our Jolly, Gay, Young Set (Alas !) are now broke up—
and went some weeks the Sooner on Account of Patty
Payne's illness, who was oblig'd to go to Town for help and
Advice. She had one tooth lugg'd out, while here, and has had
two more since ; and now is quite tight again. I find Jemm
has made some Progress in his Attempt of laying close Siege
to Sally Payne ; for in a letter from Suzette she says—
" James has din'd in Castle Street, *only four times* since he
came to Town (N.B. he has been in Town but 5 days).
The *other* day he spent at the Denoyer's ; Mais Je ne
crois pas, qui'l ait intention de se Noyer. He will be more
likely to *Sally* forth, and gain possession of the Castle.
His affairs are, I think, *en bon train*, but don't tell him I
say so."

Poor Mrs. Thrale and Fanny have both been pretty Ill
together—Dr. Richard Jebb constantly attending them ; he
won't take a Fee on Fanny's acc^t. tho' ever so earnestly
press'd ; he so greatly admires her, as he declares. I had
a Letter from her the 2nd of this month ; she intends to spend
some time here, when both she and her affectionate Hostess
are both better—at present she, by Dr. Jebb's orders (besides being 2^{ce} blooded) refrains even from Asses Milk and
Potatoes, as too nourishing ; and at that time, actually
liv'd wholly on *Turnips*, with a very little dry bread, and

what Fruit she lik'd ; but *nothing else* of any sort. Drink, Barley Water ; and Rennet Whey. As to myself, I am in the old way, neither better ; nor worse. Lovely weather ; Roads better than in the Midst of Summer ; but we are dreadfully off for Water—our Ponds and Pumps Dry, and but for Polly Hubbard's Well, we must go without Tea, Coffee and Water for Dinner. Mr. Woodhatch's Cart, with an empty Wine Pipe fetches Water from Ruxley River (a mile and a half off) for his own Family and ours for Washing, Brewing and even for our horse and Cow. Good bye. Love to M. L. Ham and Kate send much of D° and are quite impatient for You to come. Kate says she owes You a letter, and will write soon. I don't at all hate you.

LEM.

CHES., *Oct*. 16, 1781.

Poor Mrs. Gast continued to ail, and poor Mr. Crisp made light of his own ailments in comparison. Would that she would leave " that center of everything that is stupid."

Meanwhile two letters it seems had come, for Sam wrote again on December 29, finishing his letter on January 1, 1782. The letter reached Burford on January 5 and was answered on February 2.

LETTER No. 19.

CHESINGTON, *Dec*. 29, 1781.

DEAR SOP,—

I put off my answer to your two letters, till I could give you some intelligence about Electrification, which I here inclose. I think the account sent, gives You ample encouragement to come to Town ; if you can possibly bear the Journey—bring your Maid with You, and when you have been sufficiently *shockified* (tho' you see, they pretend to produce the Effect without Shock) come and stay the

Summer round at poor deserted Ches. I have near 30 Doz. of Port, old and sound, as yet not began upon and has now been in bottle about three months ; it is about 5 years old, and will be in high order when You come ; as a further inducement, you will see by this letter, that Susan and that gallant and agreeable Young Fellow (who very, very soon will be united to her) are likely to become your housemates here ; and I think you will be highly pleas'd with him—an open, unaffected, manly, intelligent Creature, as ever I know ; let all these Accounts put together have due weight with you. I don't know what to say about placing out your Money—there will be time enough before You receive it, to consider, and weigh the matter duly ; We shall then see more what aspect things wear—at present the prospect is dreadful ; and I am convinc'd Many People will do, as my Friend Mr. Wright did in the time of the last Rebellion, when I was with him at his Country house at Sunbury for several months till the news of the decisive Victory at Culloden, and the total defeat of the Rebels ; and in a Week after he pull'd out a small Box he had hid, and opening it, show'd me six Bags with 500 Guineas in each, which an hour afterwards, he and I in the Chaise with him, carried to Childs, the Bankers ; in times of such horrible Danger hardly anything but hard Gold seems secure, and the growing Interest seems scarcely an Equivalent for the Risk of the Principal ; besides, at such times, it is frequently impracticable to get one's Interest on the best Mortgages, and to redeem them impossible ; at present therefore let matters rest, and make no application to Mr. Stephens. Mr. Allen tells me he has wrote to You about little Sam. Thank you for Venison, which was dress'd for Dinner on the Sunday. Cooke's Voyage publish'd is not the Authentic one but put out by some of the Ships Company of an inferior Rank, merely to get a penny by starting before the true one can appear. At last, the Affair of that worthless Wretch C.———— is decided —the B^p of London absolutely refus'd to ordain him ; and advising him, at the same time, with Mildness, to think of some other plan of Life through Regard for ———— whose ———— He plainly told him that not only he could not

Ordain him, but that he was under a necessity of certifying to the Archbishop his refusal, and requesting him to enter a Caveat, in the Prerogative Court, against his being ordain'd at all. I am really glad of it, tho' they are all greatly afflicted at this Disgrace. I understand —— will try to send him abroad somewhere. Lord North's Brother, the Bishop of Winchester, and his Lady are grown most violently fond of the Burney Family—there is a whole heap of them now with them at Farnham for the Xmas Holidays ; and several more are going there. I hope it will turn out advantageously for them ; particularly for Charles and Hetty. I am glad to hear young Jack goes on so well, now he is come to his Estate, and consequently that [*letter torn, and below*] will exhibit a comfortable neighbour, in the room of

(I was going to say   )—but I will say   . Pray remember me kindly to Molly Leigh, and Mrs. Frodsham, when you see them. I am very glad the latter is got up so well again. I heartily wish her Captain, and my Captain Jemm may speedily bring home good fat Prizes and a Peace ; and then let the Sea rumble and tumble its Bellyfull ; while they, instead of swinging in a Hammock luxuriously sink in a down Bed with each of them their Girl by their Side.

I think, I wish neither the Gentlemen, nor the ladies any harm ; as to my own crazy self, I am not well—indigestion and sleepless nights seem to be settled on me, as an Annuity for my Life. Ham and Kate pretty comfortable ; they both send you much kindness and many good wishes ; and are in great hopes of seeing You in Consequence of Electrification. I have no Franks to my self ; but that don't signify ; wish away for dear Nation.

Yours sincerely,
LEM.

I began this letter two days ago, but this is New Year's Day.

The letter waited some while for an answer, and it was not till No. 20 arrived at Burford on January 27 and had had time to be digested that an answer was written, to both, on February 2.

LETTER No. 20.

Dear Sop,—

Burn You, Why don't you answer my last letter? Are your Rheumatics so bad you can't? I enclose a letter from Fanny, where at the bottom you will find Mrs. Byron, (who has had so much Experience of electrification) thinks you and your Maid may manage the affair to great advantage—in truth, I suspected Dr. Graham's[1] declaration, was selfish; and that he wished to draw People to Town, for his own Advantage; so that if You have a mind to try at home, I think 'tis well worth while to be at the Expense of Six Guineas for a Machine; therefore let me know your resolution, and I will try to procure one for You, if you approve it—send me ample directions what Days Your Burford Carrier sets out, what is his Name, and where he lives; that no time may be lost, if you will have one. My hand Shakes, as You may may see, and I am otherwise not well; Sleepless, fluttering inside and Indigestion. Don't communicate to any one a single word about Fanny's Book, which in a few months I suppose will come out. You see how triumphantly she goes on. If she can coin gold at such a Rate, as to sit by a warm Fire, and in 3 or 4 months (for the real time she has stuck to it closely, putting it all together, will not amount to more, tho' there have been long Intervals, between) gain £250 by scribbling the Inventions of her own Brain—only putting down in black and white whatever comes into her own head, without labour drawing singly from her own Fountain, she need not want money. She has been from hence above a month, on occasion of Suzette's wedding (who with her Lord is now here) and

---

[1] This is the notorious Dr. Graham, of " celestial bed " fame.

since She has been in Town, I find She is Courted, Caress'd, and sought after by the Wits of the Great Folk, it would be enough to turn her brain if it were not a pretty strong one. Suzette's Husband,[1] Captain Phillips, is a noble, Brave, open, agreable Fellow but 26 ; and I really believe, now he is married and settled (apparently in a high degree to his own liking) he will prove Œconomical, for which he naturally has a Turn—when not led away by high Spirits of Company. They both make us very comfortable here ; but I fear their stay will not be long, as he is under Recruiting orders, to go to Ipswich; however he has applied to his Colonel to change that place for Kingston, Epsom and their Environs, and if he succeeds they will probably be here a good while—wherever he goes, or stays, she is to be with him.

Good bye ! Kate tells me she has a letter to go in this only Frank. She, Ham and Suzette desire Love, &c. I don't hate You.

LEM.

CHES., *Jan.* 25, 1782.

After three weeks Sam wrote again on February 26. The letter arrived on March 1 and was answered on March 11. Poor folk, they were very busy with illness now, and looking ahead of their age into " electrical machines."

LETTER No. 21.

DEAR SOP,—

I should have wrote sooner, but waited for intelligence about the proper method of applying the Electrical machine for the Rheumatics. I believe there is no mystery in the matter, and the plain, simple, and only way is to electrify the parts affected ; but to do any good, it must be follow'd up constantly, assiduously and for a good while together

---

[1] Susannah Elizabeth Burney married Molesworth Phillips, afterwards Lt.-Col. in the Marines. He was a companion of James Burney in Captain Cook's last expedition.

every day ; however, begin gently, and try how You can bear it—'tis a new discovery, and you must feel your way in the Dark ; if you have any encouragement from your Trials with Hunt's Machine, make no hesitation about procuring one of y^r own directly, to have it always at Command. As to Suzette and her Man, they have left us almost three weeks, to the great Sorrow of Us all ; but there was no Remedy ; he was order'd off by his General, on a recruiting party to Ipswich ; and there they are together ; for Susan and he have agreed the matter, that wherever he is sent, She is to pack up her bundles, and trudge along with him, except he should be commanded abroad ; and in that case (which is by no means, I find, unlikely) she acquaints Kit, she should like to be with Us. He seems perfectly to adore her, which She returns very properly. He is a most ingenious Creature ; and such a Gentleman mechanic I believe is not in the Kingdom ; he has presented the Museum with Models of a vast Variety of Vessels, Utensils, Arms, &c., &c., &c., executed with his own hand alone with a degree of neatness and accuracy that cannot be surpass'd ; for which he has rece^d a letter of thanks and acknowledgement in form from the Governors of the Museum ; and a Ticket of Admission for ever for himself, and Company with him to visit every part of it whenever he pleases. These Models are of the many uncommon things he met with in going round the World. He is now but Six and twenty—a fine made, tall, stout, active, manly-looking young fellow as you shall see. I think Susan has great luck. I have rece^d a letter from her from Ipswich, full of Content, which I have not yet answered. As to my own Carcass, I find little alteration ; otherways than that, since I have totally left off Tea, and constantly breakfast on Coffee, my Stomach and inside don't feel so relax'd, and washy as before. Cyder (of which I have now got a pretty good Stock, and in tolerable drinking order) I find, agrees with me better than Wine or any other Liquor. My knuckles feel very Rheumatic or Gouty—I don't know which—weak however to a great degree. According to your Success in Electricks perhaps I may be tempted to try. As to Politicks, and money matters, I think things look but gloomy—those few that have any money are and must be anxious what to do with it. Surrounded with danger and difficulty on every side the new loan, 'tis true, fills as fast as they please to call for more and more—why ?—because Government pays a most monstrous Interest for the present—on calculation not so little as 7 P. Cent. The money Jobbers, English, Dutch, French even French—(in a word every where) that supply this loan, do it evidently to make a market of it ; not to keep it for themselves, but to sell it out again to advantage, as fast as they can to the Dupes that think of nothing but high present Interest, inattentive to the principal ; and as to that the Devil take the hindmost, the funds fall and must fall every day—the Consols this time two years were at 61 and 61½—Now they fluctuate between 54 and 55—7 P. Cent. fall in 2 years—but to go on paying the *Interest only* for any length of time (without thinking of Principal) of the Public Debt, is as impossible, as for me to lift up St. Paul's. One thing I like well enough just now. Mr. Shaw, who owes you on his mortgage £1,400, and who, you know, had Notice to pay it off, as in April next, has writ me a letter, asking me if I would consent that he should pay off £700 only at that time, and let the other half remain on the mortgage security another Year or perhaps less—to which I have for you consented—for the mortgage is a most ample Security for the £700, and himself a wealthy man. I wish all yʳ money was out as well ; if he had a mind to continue it on, longer when the time comes, I should not object myself. Of the [*word erased*] I have heard nothing of late. I am not sure they may not be a little up, at my declining to go there on account of ill-health, &c., but really [*word erased*] is too much—but then, I might indeed have [*word erased*] but the same [*word erased*] I am very glad the Hammonds are so Comfortable in their Banishment. As to [*word erased*] I think you are well off to be rid of his most tiresome Correspondence. I fancy Mr. Allen will hear no more of him. He is a worthless Character, I think—selfish and unfeeling. My Will, (which I told you, I meant to alter and join Mr. Edison with you in the Executorship) has been done a long while, and to him I have a good while ago transmitted a duplicate ; and I have several times intended, but forgot, just at the time I was writing to acquaint you of it. Acquaint me what opportunity I can have of sending it to you, and I will do it. Having just got a few franks I inclose 2 of Fanny's last letters, which with the others you may return when you have a good opportunity. You see it has got wind that she is soon bringing out a new Work ; so you will judge what you may communicate. My Franks are so small, I don't know whether I can inclose one to myself.

Good bye.
I don't hate you.
LEM.

My love to Molly Leigh and Mrs. Frodsham when you see them. Do. to M. L.

Send me a Burford Journal and how You all go on there.

Ham and Kate well and send much love to You.

CHES, *Feb.* 26, 1782.

————

Of letter 22 only a fragment is left. It was written May 7, received May 10.

LETTER No. 22.

(Part of letter which has been cut.)

As to Electrical Machines, and their price ; I think Dr. Graham spoke but slightly of a 6 Guinea one ; but that I don't quite depend upon. You say Hunt's had but little Effect—did he apply the full power it was capable of ? If you would have one I will write to Fanny (or to save time, and delight her, write yourself to her at Dr. B^s, St Martins Street, Leicester Fields) to enquire of Mrs. Byron what siz'd, and price'd Machine she thinks might be effectual ; for it you are encourag'd to make the Tryal, don't starve the cause, by an ill-judged Parsimony.

THE LETTERS

Of late I have been far from Well, all my Old Complaints, my swell'd neck is troublesome ; and the late very bitter pinching weather has not made me better—however this morning there seems to be a change and it has rain'd, and not so very sharp.

Fanny saw the paragraph about *Variety*—she knows nothing of the Author—they say 'tis poor stuff. She is so deep in her present Work that I quite let her alone at present, so Charlotte is her Deputy. I believe the 1st is printed off, and Mr. Payne is about the 2^{d}. She is now hard upon correcting the 3^{d} which he will have soon ; the whole 5 Vols. are to come out together. Dumplin seems a pretty agreable Creature—more of her when I write next—but I must finish or shall lose the post. Love to M. L. Kate and Ham send theirs. Horrid times ! Peace seems farther off than ever ! Coals have been very lately £5 a Chaldron in London ; now £4, and we have but very few left. Dreadful. Good bye. HONEST LEM.

In the next letter, after some lugubrious but not uninteresting business, we have a reference to the publication of *Cecilia* and the money paid for it. I have no idea who is the person, mysterious and miserable, whose name is erased and about whom so much is cut out. Nor will I guess who is the terrible lady at the end. The letter written May 23 was received next day and answered on the 30th.

LETTER No. 23.

DEAR SOP,—

I find our letters crossed each other—however somebody must acknow : So, here goes—first as to Stock ; I did on receipt of yours, write immediately to Mr. Mathias, recommending (if he approv'd) the Consols ; which by his answer, I find he did in part, but said he took time to look about him a little ; what he has done since, I don't know ; tho' by this time I suppose you do ; probably in D° 3 P. C^t Consols, as I don't see how he could do better. My opinion of Stock is the same it has been of a long time, viz. that they never can be a Solid and permanent Security ; as I think it impossible in our irretrievable Condition that this ruin'd Nation can hold on paying the National Interest on the Debt already incurr'd ; how then must it be, when that Debt is, and must be increasing every hour in so frightful a Degree ? Notwithstanding all this, we can do no better. We shall sink together ; the Stocks at present pay 5 P. C^t and perhaps may hold on, or at least pay something, while You and I live ; and when we are gone, those after us must look to themselves. Indeed, nothing but Land, good Farms, are to be depended on ; and even then, when the great Crash comes, will be miserably low—but let me turn away from this horrible prospect. [*Piece cut out*]

Since I wrote last Mr. Allen has been here, and according to his word brought down a Cargo of [*erased*] letters to him ; and a long verbal Account of him he gave me into the Bargain—such a one I hardly ever heard of anybody ; he thinks him (and so do I) at least half, if not whole mad. In one letter, he showed me, he says, *he has an ample Subsistance, good health, in no bad repute, and yet is miserable !* He gave Mr. Allen a particular of his Income, which is a clear £316 a year ; of which he does not spend quite half ; he torments him by letters, and visits ten times a Week, giving for ever fresh instructions for his Will ; and every time new Alterations, after Allen has drawn it up according to his last Orders—many of these directions are such ; so wild, and even contradictory, that Allen says, if he were to follow them, he himself would be deem'd a Madman ; and his reputation suffer in the World. He seems to proceed upon this Hypothesis. First, that all the World are Rogues and Villains ; next, that they are all in a Combination to cheat *him*—he is continually turning away his maids, and taking new Ones, on that Supposition—he is, it seems, at present in great distress on that account. He tells Allen he is convinced the present one Robs him, and yet does not know how to turn her away, as she was recommended to him by a family he is mightily connected with, and who had and have [*piece cut out.*]

I would sooner be a Toad, and live upon the Vapour of a Dungeon (as Othello says) than continue to exist in such a State of mind. So much for him. By your own account of yourself your Electrifying Scheme seems to be at an End ; and not without reason. You had better Success a pretty deal by the Jumble of travelling ; have you forgot the surprizing effect of your Rapid Journies, the first Season you came hither ? You seem'd new-made. Change the scene therefore as soon as possible—dispatch your beastly papers ; get out of your abominable Hermitage next y^r dreary, dismal Garden ; and bring hither yourself, your Maid, and those few papers you reserve for my sight. As to my own Carcass, it is a Scoundrel one, much out of repair, can hardly be propp'd up, and hardly worth that. Sleepless night and indigestion, &c., &c.

The new Ministry have just given honest Jemm a fine 50 Gun Man of War ; so now he must be a Post-Captain. I had a letter from him yesterday from Plymouth, where he is now extremely busy in fitting her out ; tho' she won't be ready to Sail in less than Six weeks, he is in the highest Spirits and Jollity on the occasion. Hetty and her Eldest Girl, I expect here for 4 Days next Saturday.

Fanny's Book can't be got out before the Birth-Day— great Expectations are rais'd about it.[1] Mr. Payne told me (I forget whether I did not tell You this before) that he and his Partner (Mrs. Cadell) in this Publication, did not intend to limit their generosity to the bare price stipulated (£250) if the work answer'd, as they imagin'd ; but that they intended (privately) to present her with a handsome pair of Gloves over and above—this he whisper'd to me in Confidence as a secret—this I guess will be t'other £50—a pretty Spill (£300) for a young girl in a few months to get by sitting still in her Chamber by a good Fire ![2]

[1] *Cecilia,* which appeared on Friday, July 12, 1782.
[2] Mr. Austin Dobson (*Fanny Burney,* p. 118), who had not seen these letters, rightly assumes that Fanny's adviser approved, but does not know of this " extra."

She is to come here after she is perfectly deliver'd of this new and promising Babe, and her month is up, and set about brooding and hatching another ; and I believe her Stay will not be a very short one, so that if you are not shocked at the Idea of being under the same Roof with her (She, I can tell you has the highest opinion and regard for you), I think the Intelligence might be an additional motive to induce and to hasten You to come this way.

Old [*erasure*] it seems has been pretty ill, of late ; and the rest were all [*erasure*] for it seems, She is grown more sour [*erasure*] than ever ; but, *Hauld a Bit !* She has made good her own Words—that nothing but a Cannon Ball will do for her. She should cry out, with the Devil in Milton, when he first view'd the happy pair in Paradise, *Evil, be thou my Good !* [3 *lines scored out here*]
and I have treasonable Correspondence about her. I must transcribe a short Paragraph in her last, to make you smile. " As to Precious (her nick-name) I really think she is just " now more intolerable than ever ; [*blank*] good Success galls " her most bitterly ; or else it is, that instead of being tam'd, " (as other wild beasts are) by going without meat, for her " health, it has made her more fierce and savage. Nothing " is said that she does not fly in a Passion at and Contradict ! " *Whatever is, is Wrong !* that's her Maxim. I think she " ought to be indicted for *Living* : for she is a Nuisance to Society : She is ' an unworthy mimber of Society ' " !

Pretty well this, for [*scored out*] but she deserves it all, and more poor [*scored out*] the best natur'd, inoffensive of beings, is the object of her extremest hatred.

Good bye. Ham and Kate send all kinds of good wishes, and long to have You come—so Come and be hang'd *directly*. I don't hate You.

Witness my hand,

CHES., *May* 23, 1782. LEM.

The next letter is the last, a letter full of sorrows, preluding the end of the writer, which was not far off. It was written on July 29, 1782, and reached Burford on the 31st.

THE LETTERS

DEAR SOP,—

I am out of all Patience at these cross Accidents happening just at such a time as this. I was in full expectation of seeing you at this place before now; and only waited thus long in hopes of telling you the Coast was clear and summoning you to come away. I had wrote likewise to Mrs. Graeme to the same purpose and acquainting her with your intention to come hither, was contriving that you should both meet here. I believe, nay, I am sure, I sometime ago mention'd the Burneys being here—the Dr., his wife, and Mrs. Young (her old Friend) came on Saturday 3 weeks, with design to return on the Tuesday. Madam in the meantime was taken so ill, she could not go back; and since that time she has grown so much worse, that it was thought to be a desperate Case, insomuch that the famous Dr. Warren, the King's favorite Physician, was sent for hither from London, who when he came gave but little hopes. She has ever since lain struggling between Life and Death, and has been thought actually dying more than once : particularly a week ago Mr. Hemming saw her, and said she would not live till morning; for that the Death Sweats were upon her. How it will end, God knows. She still lives, but without sleep, and almost without food. There is a little Tent Bed made up in her chamber, in which Kate and her Friend, Mrs. Young, by turns lye in every night alternately to attend her, as she is decid'd too bad to be left to a Nurse. I suppose Kate will be knock'd up, and the other, too, as they are oblig'd to be up every now and then, thro' the night. Her son was sent for up out of Norfolk and is gone again this morning. It is absolutely impossible for her to be mov'd, it seems; as Hemming says she would dye upon the Road; so that we are in for it to some purpose. The Dr. lyes up in Kate's Cabbin in the Garret. She has an ass here, and her milk seems to be her chief nourishment, for she is allow'd nothing of animal food, not even the weakest Broth, and is indeed become a mere Shadow. They say for the two last days she has not been quite so bad ; tho' this last night it seems was a bad one, almost wholly without sleep (it was Kate's night), of which she procures none without opiates, and hardly any with them. One would think this could not hold long ; but Hemming says now he does not foresee any immediate change, but thinks it will prove a lingering affair. How provoking ! The moment the business is decided, either by her recovery and removal home, or (which I think more likely) by her removal out of this World, You shall hear ; and then don't delay a moment, but come directly.

Now for business. What has been done with Gabriel Mathias ? Have you had your Account ? is your balance of Cash, Bonds, &c., &c., remaining in the late worthy good man's hands, yet laid out in Consols ? Have you rece^d from Allen a form of an Order to Mr. Mathias to deliver y^r Mortgage Deeds into Mr. Allen's hands ? The 18th of this month there was another £100 of Nash's Mortgage to be paid off by Mr. Tyler to You. What has been done in that affair ? Pray send me a particular detail of all these matters as soon as you can. Mr. Allen has been so busy and perplex'd that he has hardly had time to write, so that I have heard little from him of late.

I have seen in the papers an Account of the Capture of Capt. Frodsham's ship, and his own Imprisonment, for which I am much concern'd on his Wife's Account. If You have any intelligence concerning him and his Situation since his arrival at Brest, put it in your letter. Send me word how You hold out Yourself, and be sure to keep stout enough to make your Journey hither as soon as I can give you the Notice I wish for.

As to myself, my Digestion and Sleep are wretched. At times, I feel as if I had no inside ; but as I am in my 75th year, I cannot expect great matters in my favor. Therefore Patience ! Ham and Kate continue, in spite of trouble and watching, comfortably well and send much love. Adieu. Sick or Well, I don't hate you.

LEM.

CHESINGTON, *July* 29, 1782.

THE LETTERS

From this time the well-known letters of the Burneys, father and daughter, speak of the increasing illness of the dear " Daddy." His last weeks seem to have been full of pain, and it seems probable that all his nearest kin and friends were summoned to him. Fanny certainly was at Chesington, and so was Mrs. Gast, who read to him daily the prayer for the dying. On April 24, 1783, he died ; and he was buried on May 2 at Chesington. It was the end of the old happy, literary, and frolicsome life in the Hall.

Since that sad day Chesington has changed almost beyond knowledge. The old house is gone and replaced, and, though the hamlet is still quite countrified, London has stretched nearer and nearer to it, and the time has gone by when there was only one " safe route across the wild common," to which the clue was given as a secret by Mr. Crisp to his friends. But in the little church there still remains the epitaph written by Dr. Burney for his friend, Samuel Crisp :—

> Reader, this cold and humble spot contains
> The much lamented, much revered remains
> Of one whose wisdom, learning, taste and sense
> Good humour'd art and wide benevolence
> Cheer'd and enlighten'd all this hamlet round
> Wherever genius, worth, or want was found.
> To few it is that bounteous Heav'n imparts
> Such depth of knowledge, and such taste in arts,
> Such penetration and enchanting powers
> Of brightening social and convivial hours.
> Had he through life been blest by Nature kind
> With health robust of body as of mind,
> With skill to serve and charm mankind so great
> In Arts, in Science, Letters, Church or State,
> His name the Nation's annals had enroll'd,
> And virtues to remotest ages told.

Mrs. Gast was Mr. Crisp's executrix, and thus Fanny Burney's letters to him came into her possession. After her death her executrix, Mrs. Frodsham, restored them to the writer, and thus the publication of the letters, years after, became possible. It was then that the careful Fanny made so many erasures and " cuts." The later relation between the two ladies can be briefly told. It is concerned chiefly with the " literary remains " of the author of *Virginia*.

Part of a letter from Mrs. Gast to Miss Burney is printed by Mrs. Ellis in her *Early Diary of Frances Burney* (vol. ii. pp. 326–27). Thus it runs :—

" MY DEAR AND AMIABLE FANNIKIN,—

" Your much valued friend, and my beloved brother, in his last illness, said something, which on reflection appears to me as a hint, that he wish'd the scatter'd fragments of his *Virginia* might ultimately fall into your hands. The only compleat and perfect copy of his play, as he himself approved, was got into some hands, from whom he never could recover it. The then manager (it was thought from —— [1]) would not suffer the too much approved and greatly admired performance to be acted as in its pristine state, but insisted on many alterations, greatly against the author's judgment and inclination, which, however, he was necessitated to comply with, if he would ever have it brought on the stage. I have neither time nor capacity to select all the beautiful passages that deserve to be kept from the blotted papers, that had better be destroy'd. But as I would not omit even in the most trifling instance, doing whatever I thought he wish'd, I send you the whole, which you will please to dispose of as you think proper, selecting what you think worth preserving, and destroying the rest.

*　　*　　*　　*　　*　　*

" Your ever affectionate,

" SOPHIA GAST."

April 27, 1784.

The MS. which is preserved with the letters shows very considerable alterations, in whole speeches, insertions, altera-

---

[1] Fanny has concealed this word by scores of her pen. It appears to have been " jealousy." [Mrs. Ellis's note.]

tions of characters to whom speeches are given, and so on, chiefly from the beginning to page 10, line 190, of the published edition, and again from page 13, line 241. It is on the whole much shortened. The original edition was printed without the author's name in 1754. Bell's edition (1778) which has a picture of Mrs. Yates, in a hoop, with a large hat and feather perched on the top of her hair, is unaltered.

Then Fanny, it would seem, wrote to her friend's sister, for, writing from Burford on June 22, 1784, Mrs. Gast said to Fanny : [1]—

"The sight of that dear hand, which has so often given pleasure to my best beloved on earth, could not fail of awakening keen sensations in a heart so much his and yours. I don't apprehend he wish'd the relics I sent you should live in any memory but your own. Your approbation I believe was his aim, and might cause him regret about recovering the compleat copy. Very long absences, even from our childhood, makes it more than probable I knew less of his mind than his ' favourite ' adopted child, with whom he so frequently with great delight conversed. I cannot suppose that he thought of any future renown."

Fanny replied from Norbury Park, November 14, 1785, with an apology for delay, that she agreed that what he wished was no doubt that everything belonging to *Virginia* should rest in silence and quiet till at last it sank into oblivion. She added :—

"You will forgive me, I hope—I know indeed you will forgive me—for entering so largely upon this subject ; for though you have looked too far and too clearly to suffer your affection to overpower you, I am sure your best beloved on earth will ever be uppermost in your thoughts, and the grateful justice done his honoured memory by her whom you so truly call his favourite adopted child, cannot be offensive to you." [2]

After this, they only met once again. Fanny was busy with her court duties. On July 6, 1786, the *Public Adver-*

[1] *Early Diary*, etc., ii. 329–30.
[2] Letter in *Diary*, etc., ed. 1876, vol. ii., pp. 11, 12.

tiser announced her appointment as Dresser to Queen Charlotte. Through her friendship with Mrs. Delany, which had helped to fill the gap caused by Daddy's death, she had come to know the Royal Family ; and her new post kept her fully occupied. At last, however, on July 12, 1788, on the visit of the King and Queen to Cheltenham, her diary records : " When we came to Burford, where we stopped for horses, how I wished to have seen Mrs. Gast, my dear Mrs. Crisp's sister ! I knew she resided there, but had no power to visit her. I inquired after her of the inn-keeper and sent her my most affectionate remembrances."

And then again on August 16, the return journey : " When we stopped to change horses at Burford I alighted and went into the inn, to meet Mrs. Gast, to whom I had sent by Mrs. Frodsham a request to be there as we passed through the town. I rejoiced indeed to see again the sister of our first and wisest friend. My Susanna, who knows her too enthusiastic character, will easily suppose my reception. I was folded in her arms and bathed in her tears all my little stay ; and my own, from reflected tenderness for her ever-honoured, loved, and lamented brother, would not be kept quite back ; 'twas a species of sorrowful joy—painful, yet pleasing—that seemed like a fresh tribute to his memory and my affection, and made the meeting excite an emotion that occupied my mind and reflection almost all the rest of my journey. She inquired most kindly after my dear father and my Susanna, and separately and with interest of all the rest of the family ; but her surprise to see me now, by this most unexpected journey, when she had concluded me inevitably shut up from her sight for the remainder of her life, joined to the natural warmth of her disposition, seemed almost to suffocate her. I was very sorry to leave her, but my time was unavoidably short and hurried."

Poor, kind, sentimental Mrs. Gast lived on till 1791, a lonely life, I think, full of sickness, but devoted to the poor. I have already quoted the only memorial of her which remains in Burford Church. I will now give one which occurs in a local newspaper. I do not think it was ever erected.

THE LETTERS

EPITAPH ON A MONUMENT IN BURFORD CHURCH, OXFORDSHIRE.
UNDERNEATH LIE THE REMAINS OF

SOPHIA CRISP GAST,

A LADY OF THE MOST POLISHED MANNERS,
EASY AND WINNING ADDRESS, EXTENSIVE READING,
AND OF THE MOST SINCERE AND UNAFFECTED PIETY.
POSSESSED OF A SOUND JUDGEMENT, SOLID UNDERSTANDING,
AND A MOST RETENTIVE MEMORY, SHE HAD ACQUIRED
(BY UNWEARIED DILIGENCE, AND UNREMITTING APPLICATION),
BESIDES A CRITICAL SKILL IN THE ENGLISH AND FRENCH,
A COMPETENT KNOWLEDGE OF THE LATIN, GREEK,
AND HEBREW LANGUAGES.
HER FAVOURITE STUDY WAS THAT OF
READING THE DIVINE ORACLES IN THE ORIGINAL.
HER SOCIETY, WHICH WAS AT ONCE
ENTERTAINING AND INSTRUCTIVE,
WAS COURTED BOTH BY YOUNG AND OLD.
SHE WAS AN ORNAMENT TO HUMAN-NATURE,
AND AN HONOUR AND EXAMPLE TO HER SEX ;
FOR SHE EXPENDED HALF HER INCOME
(£300 PER ANNUM)
IN FEEDING, CLOTHING, AND INSTRUCTING THE POOR,
AND IN DONATIONS TO WORTHY, BUT DISTRESSED, FAMILIES.
FREE FROM THE PETISHNESS AND FRETFULNESS ALMOST
PECULIAR TO PERSONS ADVANCED IN YEARS,
SHE ENJOYED HER FACULTIES UNIMPAIRED TO THE VERY LAST.
IN MERCY TO THE INHABITANTS OF THIS PLACE,
HER LIFE WAS PROLONGED TO THE GREAT AGE OF 85.
HER MEMORY WILL EVER BE REMEMBERED
WITH ADMIRATION AND RESPECT
BY THOSE WHO HAD THE HAPPINESS OF HER ACQUAINTANCE
HER SOUL QUITTED ITS EARTHLY TENEMENT,
AND FLEW TO MANSIONS OF BLISS,
APRIL 13TH, 1791.

Her death was recorded thus in the press. I find the cutting, as I find the epitaph, in an old collection, but cannot tell whence it came :—

" At Burford, co. Oxford, after a short but severe illness, which she supported with becoming patience and resignation, in her 85th year, and universally regretted, Mrs. Sophia Crisp Gast. In her shone, with distinguished lustre, every virtue that adorns the Christian. Her sincere and fervent piety, great reading, universal benevolence, and numerous acts of charity, are perhaps, in the present age, seldom, if ever, equalled. Even at her advanced state of life, she was so cheerful and entertaining, that her company was courted both by young and old. By her death the poor will sustain an irreparable loss ; and her memory will be long revered by all those who had the happiness of her acquaintance. She was descended, in the male line, from Ellis Crisp, esq., who died sheriff of London, 1625, and from the celebrated Sir Nicholas Crisp, who spent £100,000 in the cause of Charles the First ; and whose father, Harry, was forcibly carried from the Isle of Thanet to Bruges, and with great difficulty and cost ransomed. (Bib. Top. Brit. XVIII. 175.) ”

The portrait of Mrs. Gast was painted by Fanny's cousin, Edward Francis Burney, an artist of considerable fame in his time, who survived till 1848. What has become of it I do not know.

And so the memory of these good ladies passed away. Old people would still talk of them, and their charities, years after the younger was laid to rest in the church. The name which Daddy Crisp seems to have given, in playful jest, to the old " Great House " in which they lived— " The Hermitage "—was still recalled, only the other day, by one whose memory, and that of his father before him, in Burford goes back very far indeed. But of what came to the house when Mrs. Gast was carried to her grave I know not. Her kindred at Broadwell, the Leighs and the Frodshams, would keep up the remembrance ; and, by a happy fortune, it is to the kindness of that family, still living in the handsome eighteenth-century house which Mrs. Gast no doubt visited, that I owe the power to publish these letters and connect through them the house in which I am living to-day with its past of more than a century ago.

Has Burford changed much in that century ? I often ask myself. Not much, I think, would be the answer of most of those who know it to-day. In the long High Street little indeed is changed. What was once the fine house of an old squire has become, since 1847—with its inside, floor, staircase and all, taken out—a Wesleyan chapel. Here and there a new window has been put in, or a new (and hideous) front been added to a shop ; but, for a new house, there is not one of them. Indeed, I believe there are only two houses in the whole town that Mrs. Gast may not have looked on, and one is a bank, which—one gathers from the correspondence—she might have been glad to have had in her time. As to the architecture of these two houses, it is kindest to be silent.

All that the devoutest lover of old days can wish for is that the beautiful town should undergo no further ill treatment. Local " restoration " does indeed mean cruelty to the past. Alas, that one should say so—and particularly since this is from no personal memory of the past which existed before the present Vicar, or I, or those who of recent years have best loved the town, ever saw Burford—the Church has yet, fine though it is to-day, and bright and sweet for its use, the glory of God, been gravely wounded. " The parish Church of Burford, on the Windrush, a sumptuously decorated building, is an epitome of the whole civic life and art of the later Middle Ages," says Mr. Mackail, almost too generously, in his Life of William Morris. In the middle of the nineteenth century pews and galleries were swept away ; but not all was wisely done. It was Burford Church, the same writer tells, that caused the movement, now happily successful in many parts of England, against the reckless " restoration " of thirty years ago. In 1876 Morris saw Burford as he passed through to Broadway : " The alterations going on in the beautiful parish church aroused his horror ; and at Broadway Tower he drafted a letter urging the foundation of a Society which might deal with such cases, and, if the destruction done by the restorers could not be stopped, might at all events make it clear that it was destruction and not preservation." Morris, his biographer tells me, would " never tire of talking about " the town. He has brought it again, one may say, into history ; and he has helped to preserve to us much that we value more and more to-day. Much, but not all ; for still the " restorer," no longer eccliastic but parochial or conciliar, is about his work. Within the last year the beautiful old " tolsey " where the tolls were paid in old days, has undergone the painful process ; and to-day you cannot tell which was old and which is new. The old glass has gone, the old barge-boards, the picturesque roughness of the old front ; instead and anew we have smartness and chimneys, with even that wildly unnecessary horror, a chimney pot—chimneys wholly out of keeping with the famous Cotswold type of chimney, one of the really decorative features of the old buildings. So the old changes, not wisely but too much.[1]

" Greetings to dear Burford. I hope no more restoration is going on." That is my last message from Kelmscott. May the pious wish ere long be fulfilled, and the memories of all the old beauty and kindness, the records of the past in its love for things fair and of good report, rest undisturbed. And with it, in these pages, one more memory of the literature of bygone days goes to rest.

[1] Cf. the book I have mentioned above, p. 5. A thorough study of it would do much to prevent the destruction even now going on in this lovely district. Mr. Dawber notes the destruction of an outside staircase at Burford, and the sad disfigurement of the ancient " tolsey " may be contrasted with his drawing of the building, which would supply modern builders with ideas, practical as well as artistic, of which they often seem sadly in want.

Among My Books

Among My Books

IN A DON'S LIBRARY

I HAVE often thought that it would be interesting to trace some of the changes in academic interests as they may be observed in the hereditary libraries, of which there must be not a few in Oxford and Cambridge. Not unnaturally, in spite of the abolition of all local restrictions, the same names tend to recur in the lists of University officials generation by generation, and it is a curious study to see how the men of to-day take after, or depart from, the ways of their forefathers. Where there is individuality so marked as to amount to genius the peculiar interest of the investigation ceases. What is interesting to discover is how the ordinary commonplace men who live in the Universities, generation by generation, show their literary interests, keep in touch with current fashion of thought, and slowly or with precipitate violence adopt the philosophical, political, or religious opinion that prevails for the time in the world outside.

I have often studied in a library which has been growing during the last century and a half in the hands of three Oxford dons, I am not to mention their names, which are, indeed, of no interest; but I may premise that the first held a Fellowship from 1737 to 1743, and then enjoyed two benefices till his death, still a bachelor, at the age of eighty-eight, in 1804. The second, a nephew of the first, was thrice married, but left no issue. He was born in 1764, and died in 1817, having been Fellow of his College (not the same as his uncle's) from 1785 to 1797. The library formed by these men, part of which had, no doubt, been twice located in Oxford rooms, then passed to a nephew of the second, who was a country parson, one loved by good men, a traveller, but not a particularly bookish man. He made a few additions to the books, and left them to his son, who brought back the books to Oxford, obtained a Fellowship at a third college, and still resides there. The first was six years a Fellow of Lincoln, the second twelve years a Fellow of Magdalen, the third has been for twenty-one years a Fellow of S. John's.

The library thus formed may fairly claim to be a typical one. All three dons were clergymen. The first became a Fellow of Wesley's College just after he left Oxford, and it is very likely that the two may have known each other in Lincolnshire. The second lived in the days of Pitt and the French Revolution. The third belongs to the era of " Lux Mundi " and the *Revue Anglo-Romaine ;* but a study of their books shows that there is a noteworthy continuity in the opinions which have been handed down.

The library, like all eighteenth-century collections, is rich in theology and sermons. For some of these, and especially a handsomely bound edition of the works of Jones of Nayland in twelve octavos, the present owner tells me with indignation that he has been offered a penny a volume. But there are very many books which appeal to others besides divines. Among those of the first collection are the 1622 edition of Hooker's works, and the first edition of the " Anatomy of Melancholy." By their side is Sir Walter Raleigh's " Historie of the World," and the great folio, with all its extraordinary illustrations, of the " Works " of Charles I. Fuller and Heylin and Hammond and Mede are hard by, and the works of Mr. Abraham Cowley, which, with Stowe's Chronicle and Meredith Hanmer's quaint translation of the ecclesiastical historians, formed no doubt, agreeable recreation for the country rectory in which the first of our three dons passed the last sixty years of his life. From these he could turn to Law's " Serious Call," or Hoadly's Sermons, or Sparrow's " Rationale," whose first editions are on the shelves. There is a grim portrait of him, by the way, on the wall not far from his books—a very serious old gentleman in a white wig.

His nephew, the second of the trio, was, from his portrait, quite a different type of don—a very neat, well-dressed young man, wearing his hair in powder, and of a pink and white complexion. He was not content to read only. He addressed Mr. Fox in an indignant letter " occasioned by his speech delivered on the anniversary of his election for Westminster, October 10, 1798," and he published an " Appeal to the Nation on the subject of Mr. Gilbert Wakefield's letter to William Wilberforce, Esq., M.P." In these the most excellent Tory sentiments are expounded with much vigour of expression and with some pleasing Shakespearian quotations. The doctor evidently took a great pride in his library. He noted when and where he obtained a book, and what he gave for it, and in nearly every one he wrote the motto from S. Paul, fitting indeed to a divine, $\phi\iota\lambda o\tau\iota\mu\epsilon\hat{\iota}\sigma\theta\alpha\iota$ $\dot{\eta}\sigma\upsilon\chi\dot{\alpha}\zeta\epsilon\iota\nu$—" that ye study to be quiet." He had a very fair collection of the classics, here and there a Delphin and an Elzevir among them. He had the sermons of Bishop Horne, his old president, of Porteous, and Bull, and Potter, and all the works of the saintly Wilson. But though he was well furnished with theology and the classics, it is clear that he had at least as deep an interest in history and the *belles lettres*. Besides Clarendon, given him by his College, he had all Robertson's histories, Watson's " Philip the Second " and " Philip the Third," Coxe's " Memoirs of the two Walpoles," Burnet, of course, and Bingham. He bought the first edition of "The Wealth of Nations," as well as of such donnish works as Warton's " History of English Poetry " and Dallaway's " Heraldry," which latter a friend of his vigorously corrected. But the characteristic feature of the good doctor's collection is the series of the Essayists. They are all in their first editions, lovingly bound in a sober brown calf ; the *Guardian, Spectator, Englishman, Craftsman, Tatler, Adventurer, World, Lounger, Looker-On, Connoisseur, Observer, Mirror*, down to the *Rambler*, the *Idler*, the *Country Spectator*, and the *Microcosm*. He was evidently a keen Johnsonian, for he has the octavo Boswell, the Dictionary, the Poets, " Rasselas," as well as the " Tour in Corsica," Reynolds's " Discourses," and Goldsmith. He had also all the *British Critic* and the *Critical Review*, and the *Anti-Jacobin*, to which he himself contributed. Fielding, Sterne, Pope, and Dryden, with Miss Burney's " Camilla," seem to represent his own tastes in literature. I suppose the noteworthy thing about these collections is that the reading of these eighteenth-century dons seems to have been confined to the Classics and English. There are a few French books, it is true, La Fontaine, M. de Voiture, La Bruyère, and Madame de Genlis, and, in Italian, Tasso's " Aminta," but nothing to show a real acquaintance with foreign literature. That reproach at any rate is removed from the dons of the present day.

Here the chief attraction of this Library of dons may be said to cease ; but I have been interested, too, in seeing what sort of a collection the possessor of this library, the descendant, indirect though he be, of these literary dons, has made for himself. One may go round his shelves and pick out books that he has evidently bought, and see if there is any clue to his own tastes and how far they are inherited.

There are of course books that mark his trade, the books he reads and scores, the books undergraduates will borrow and not return. There are the Thackerays and Scotts, the Dickens (in first editions I notice), and Tennyson, a volume or two of the first printed Indian books of Rudyard Kipling, some Ruskin and Church and Newman. Then there is all Pater, among them that rare little volume of reviews for the *Guardian* which contains his delicate appreciation of " Robert Elsmere " and rejection of its too limited view of life, and on the wall a photograph that once hung in the rooms at Brasenose, of a stalwart young warrior from the great Mantegna series at Hampton Court. If one could judge of the owner's taste in letters it must be from seeing that there does not seem to be a book missing of Robert Louis Stevenson, or George Meredith, or Thomas Love Peacock.

When I ask for personal associations, he shows me a book

with some pretty Spanish verses in it, or the " Pages from
a Private Diary " with the inscription *ex dono authoris*, or
"Weeping Ferry," or a life of Laud with a letter from Mr.
Gladstone about it, or learned volumes of Freeman and
Stubbs with their autographs showing how they came to
his shelves. But the books he has set round him are not all
of to-day. There is a Second Folio Shakespeare, not quite
complete, it is true, but clearly a much-prized possession.
There is the private issue of the great Marquess of Wellesley's
Primitiae et Reliquiae with an inscription in it to the editor
of his speeches, in his clear thin hand, as steady at eighty
as at eighteen. There is, in its old black leather cover, the
" Relation of the Conference between William Lawd, then
Lord Bishop of St. David's, now Lord Archbishop of Canterbury, and Mr. Fisher the Jesuite," printed in 1639. More
rare and precious still is a very delicate little volume in red
morocco, printed in the italic letter at Florence in 1556, " Il
Moro d'Heliseo Heivodo, Inglese : All' illustrissimo Cardin-
al Reginaldo Polo." There is also the 1520 " Epigrammata
clarissimi disertissimique uiri Thomæ Mori," with Holbein's
title-page. By it are some rare seventeenth - century
pamphlets, a medal or two which one does not often see
and Heber's Trinity Hymn, in his own MS. More modern,
but of equal rarity, are a curious little print of Dr. Pusey,
inscribed ·' From Christ Church College, Oxford," " published for the proprietor, 202, Sloane Street, Chelsea, Oxford
Theologians No. 7," and that leaflet referred to by Dean
Church in his history of the Oxford Movement, but never
seen, it would appear, till quite lately by any one of this
generation, which tells " friends " how they may procure
" Tracts for the Times on the Privileges of the Church and
against Popery," and how they may promote their sale.
The memorandum is partly printed, partly filled in in Dr.
Pusey's writing, and it is interesting not only in relation
to the movement and the methods by which its principles
were spread, but also in regard to the position of the
bookselling trade at the time.

It would seem as if even the modern don, so emancipate
and cosmopolitan, still survived among those who can

trace an ancestry of scholars. My subject to-day has a
clever drawing of Aubrey Beardsley's and a print of Holman
Hunt's with an elaborate pencilled explanation by the
artist, but he would seem to set as much store by a forest
tree sketched on blotting-paper by Dean Liddell and a
letter in the hand of Laud's secretary to the city of Edinburgh with the bold autograph signature " *W. Cant.*"

Two other " modern instances " strike my eye as I leave
the room. Here is the first edition of Mrs. Gaskell's " Life
of Charlotte Brontë," which for its plain speaking was immediately withdrawn by the publisher, and is now hardly ever
to be met with. Beside it is the little octavo of " Idyls and
Songs " by Francis Turner Palgrave, 1848-1854. On the
flyleaf is inscribed " B. Jowett, with F. T. Palgrave's love,
October 1854." Below this is a pencil note, " p. 48."
Now on page 48 is " The Birth of Art : Introduction. To
B. J." Up to that point the volume has at least been
opened. After that not a page is cut.

As I turn to leave the room my thoughts go back nearly
two centuries. It is most probable that none of these
three dons was a " man of the world," but their books show
that they did not care to fall out of it. The generations
seem to have given them much the same part to play, a
very ordinary one, that can be played, happily, without
noise and without effect. The first read and perhaps
thought, the second read and wrote, the third wrote and
taught. They were commonplace men, but they were
types that the Universities cannot yet afford to lose. Much
more in touch with books than with life, all of them, I
mused : and then the door opened and an undergraduate
came to tell me all about a football match, and I did not
envy them any more.

IN THE OTHER HOUSE

WHAT is there here ? I suppose you would call it the travelling library, the working tools of the man who spends his playtime in reading and writing. To-day the tables may be covered with volumes of Fanny Burney; next month there will be lives of the Saints or medieval chronicles. Generally you will see as many of the works of Richard Graves as the Cotswold hermit of to-day has been able to pick up, with Shenstone and Somervile and Jago to bear him company. Always there will be Morris —this is the very place in which to read *The Earthly Paradise*—his Life, as well as his poetry, and hangings and wall-paper, too, of his design ; Rossetti, and the Life of Burne-Jones ; and some things that may illustrate the most brilliant period of English Nineteenth-century Art. All Scott is here, and never very far from the hermit's hands.

But it is difficult to disentangle the two libraries. The owner always says that it is only when he is among the smaller one that he has ever time to read a book : among the thousands that line the walls of his college room he is only able to look now and then at the covers. But each is continually increasing—sometimes from a new fancy in literature, sometimes from a new subject of study imperatively demanding attention. Prints and pictures, too, will come to illustrate the interest, those caricatures, for example, of Pitt, at the time of the Declaratory Act, riding upon a " dun'd ass " ; of Charles James Fox riding on an elephant, with Lord North's face and having Burke to blow the trumpet before him ; of Warren Hastings being received with a bag of gold into S. James's, while Nuncomar swings in the background; of that most corrupt and unblushing of Nabobs, Mr. Paul Benfield, riding in Hyde Park and dubbed " Count Roupee."

So down into the rooms where the portraits are, the family ones—most notable the old great-grandmother, born in 1745, died in 1849, drawn when she was 103, and might have been twenty years younger—and the mezzotints of soldiers and statesmen. Here is Cornwallis, with the ribbon and badge of the Garter and a background of soldiers and elephants, from the picture by Copley. Here is Lord Milton, of the famous Yorkshire election, a present to the incorruptible freeholders of the county; Lord Moira, from the Hoppner now at Hampton Court, looking for all the world like a dried monkey; Mrs. Siddons, as the muse of tragedy, a beautiful mezzotint indeed; and the Prince Regent himself, by John Raphael Smith, in the very uniform he must have worn at Waterloo, with the Life Guards behind him.

Wellesley, delicate and sentimental, and Wellington, before any of the marked features had developed, are there. Turn the back of the latter towards you, and you will see written in bold printing-letters :—

WELLINGTON

THE

Enemy of his King

AND THE

Betrayer of his Country.

So the old Tory to whom the print belonged doubtless wrote at the time of Roman Catholic Emancipation or of the Reform Bill, and turned the face of the traitor to the wall. Fox is here, from the since-destroyed portrait by Reynolds, with his hand on the India Bill; and beside the mezzotint he hangs again, in his latest and coarsest time, a monster of obesity—" the triumph," says the owner, " of Radical principles." There are three of Pitt—the young buoyant face that Gainsborough drew; the older profile, where the nose is almost a caricature ; and then the beautiful face that Gainsborough Dupont gave him, more kind than nature. Last of all is that strange Charles III of Spain by Rafael Mengs, of which there is more to say. And so we leave the eighteenth century, and in the nineteenth see only the dignified presentment of the honoured Head of an Oxford College, who still lives but was born when George III was king.

So books and pictures work together ; and here and there an autograph, Wellesley or Castlereagh or Stubbs, illustrates what the owner has been writing about. And as the prints grow, so do the books. There are new ones, it seems, every day ; and whatever are they to be done with ? It is one of the day's pleasant moments when the string of the new parcel is untied : surely a man is not really avaricious who is greedy of books.

But there are accessions to the library which can never be looked at without a heartache. Thus came a great number of French and Spanish books, the memorials of a friend who can never pass out of remembrance. Once he wrote in the book that recorded his visits :—

> Al marcharme de su pueblo
> Voloi la cara llorando
> Ay, pueblecito de mi alma !
> Qué lejos te vas quedando !

Once again—it was the last time—he wrote those lines from the wonderful Poema de Roncesvalles :—

> Porta patet omnibus, sacris et profanis
> Non solum Catholicis verum et paganis,
> Judæis, hæreticis, otiosis, vanis.

and then the book, in which he could write no more, was closed.

So as life widens out its interests narrow. The vacant places mean so much more than those which are filled. I turn the pages of his books, and then I look out on the bright sunshine of the countryside which he sees no more. From one of his books the lines meet me :—

BURFORD PAPERS

Le ciel est par-dessus le toit
  Si bleu, si calme !
Un arbre, par-dessus le toit
  Berce sa palme.

La cloche, dans le ciel qu'on voit
  Doucement tinte
Un oiseau sur l'arbre qu'on voit
  Chante sa plainte.

Mon Dieu, mon Dieu, la vie est là
  Simple et tranquille ;
Cette paisible rumeur-là
  Vient de la ville.

So let these memories of him rest, in the house where, I know, he spent, as he gave, happy hours—rest till the hour when the day breaks and the shadows flee away

A GLIMPSE OF THE EXILED STEWARTS

I DO not know how to begin this paper, except by the commonplace that there never was a royal family so attractive as the Stewarts. If the interest which belongs to Mary, Queen of Scots, and to Charles I, skips a generation in James I and VI—and I am scarcely sure that it does when I remember " The Fortunes of Nigel " and the Gowrie mystery—if the interest of Charles II and of James II and VII is peculiar rather than general, the attractiveness of the last three princes shows no sign of diminution. And certainly it will not diminish so long as Mr. Andrew Lang keeps us among the companions of Pickle and Prince Charlie. It is most of all an interest of romance ; and when I say that I still remember the ringing tones in which Mr. Ruskin at Oxford, more than twenty years ago, told us, " I would have you remember that when I use the word ' romantic,' I use it always in a good sense." With all the errors and failures of the unhappy line, the romantic interest of the Stewarts is still that which belongs to devotion and self-sacrifice and chivalry and gallant courage.

> A wonderful Star broke forth,
> New-born, in the skies of the North,
>   To shine on an Old Year's Night,
> And a bud on the dear White Rose
> Flowered, in the season of snows,
>   To bloom for an hour's delight.
> Lost is the Star from the night,
> And the Rose of an hour's delight
>   Went—where the roses go ;
> But the fragrance and light from afar,
> Born of the Rose and the Star,
>   Live through the years and the snow.

When he has printed these romantic lines, Mr. Lang must add, " The eighteenth century, in its moments of self-consciousness, wrote itself down unromantic."

The glimpse which I can now give, from an old letter, belongs to the least romantic part, perhaps, of the life of the exiled Stewarts. It belongs to the time when James, the Old Chevalier, was living in Rome, when Charles Edward had finished his tour through the Italian cities, and was idling, in weariness of " the moth-eaten hangings and outworn furniture of the Palace of the Apostles, in Rome," and in dislike of " a city of priests and of curious English tourists." In February, 1741, Lady Mary Wortley Montagu saw Charles Edward and Henry Benedict at a public ball " in masque." It is from the letter of another English tourist that I am allowed, by the kindness of the possessor, to quote a description of the young Stewart princes at a ball in the house of one of the Roman nobility. The writer was Samuel Crisp, the " Daddy Crisp " of Fanny Burney and her sisters. Mr. Crisp wrote his letter to " The Reverend Mr. Shute,[1] at Broadwell, near Chipping Norton, Oxfordshire," from Rome on February 15 (New Style), 1739. He was then thirty-two, and it was fifteen years before the production of his tragedy at Drury Lane. He was on a tour in Italy, and an earlier letter had given an interesting description of Pompeii. At Rome he had been at many entertainments and balls, of which the most notable was at Prince Colonna's, given for the reception of the King of Poland's eldest son. His meeting the Stewart " pretenders " was an incident which he knew would interest his English correspondents greatly, even if they were not among those who looked for their return. It was a little later in the same year that Walpole himself sent a verbal message, by Carte the historian, professing his attachment to James III and VIII.

Thus Mr. Crisp's letter :—

" Last day of the Carnival was the Marchese Bolognetti's Ball, which I will give you a small History of, and so con-

---

[1] For whom see above, p. 12.

clude this voluminous letter. The Apartments were not so grand nor the Ball room so magnificent as at Prince Colonna's, but still very fine ; but 'tis on account of the Chevalier's sons, who were out of masque, that I give you this further trouble. In order to avoid all Dispute about Precedence, as I told you before, they were both in Masquerade Habits of two young Shepherds, very rich, white silk hats with Diamond Loops and Buttons. Bankes of White Ribbands at their knees, and shoes, their faces unmasked, notwithstanding which they were to be considered only as masques, not as Princes, and accordingly everybody called them Signor Maschera ; this was to avoid all Dispute with the Prince of Poland. I think I may say with truth they are two as fine youths as ever I saw ; particularly the youngest, who has more Beauty and Dignity in him than even one can form to one's self in Idea ; he danced miraculously, as they say he does all his exercises ; singing, as I am told, most sweetly, and accompanies himself, and is, in short, the admiration of Everybody ; these Accomplishments must come to him by the Mother, for I take the Father to be a Poor, Mean, Cowardly Bigot, and nothing more. Well, these two young Sparks sat on one side of the room, and the Prince of Poland on the other ; they had never yet spoke to one another, but the Marchioness Bolognetti (who is mighty fond of the Pretender and his family) was resolved to bring them Acquainted this time, and the sight of the particulars of all this, which I had very fully, pleas'd me very much. The eldest, whom they give here the title of Principe di Gallia, began the Ball with the prettiest Woman I ever saw, call'd the Bonaventura (I desire you'd toast her for my sake now and then, for she is quite beyond compare the Queen of all Beauty), and after him the younger. In about an hour, in came the Chevalier himself, in a purple and silver domino and masqued ; everybody made a great bustle to make room for him when he came in, and after he had gone up to the Marchioness, and some other Ladies to make his compliments, he came down to the end of the Room, where all the English Gentlemen were together, most of them unmasked, and stood among them. I believe he did it on purpose ; but nobody took any manner of notice of him, though he talked English for half an hour together to one of his attendants ; I was the very next to him, and he heard the English Gentlemen talking together all round him ; after some time the Master of the Ceremonies of the Ball came, and asked him by the name of Sire if his Majesty had a mind to see the young Princes dance ; to which he answered he should be very glad of it, and accordingly the eldest began, and while he was dancing I was got somehow or other within two or three yards of the Prince of Poland without knowing what was going to be done ; but when his minuet was ended the Marchioness Bolognetti, who sat next the Prince of Poland, called to Signor Maschera to come and sit by her ; which accordingly he did, and in sitting down made a bow to the Prince of Poland, who returned it and spoke to him ; so there was a conversation began between them, across the Marchioness Bolognetti, who, seeing her scheme take effect, got up and made them sit close together ; soon afterwards the second son, il Duca di York, as they stile him, had done his minuet, upon which immediately the Lady that sat next the Prince of Poland on the other side immediately got up and made room for him in her place, on which the whole room fell a clapping and cried Bravo ! Bravo ! I never saw anything so genteel as this young one's paying his court to the electorall Prince ; his looks, his gesture, all was the finest and most expressive that can be imagin'd, and I was near enough to hear now and then a Sentence ; they call'd cousins ; after some short space they both got up to begin English Country Dances, which they have taught all the Roman Ladies, who are much pleas'd with the fashion. I was not a little surprised to hear my old friends Butter'd Peas and Willy Wilkie struck up in a Roman Palace ; but here I must end for want of room, else I could tell you a good deal more, though I fancy you will think this is enough."

A few notes may be added to this interesting picture. The Prince of Poland was, of course, the son of Augustus II, whose succession had been assured by the long war and the complicated political intrigues which began in 1733. Dead enough that history would seem to be, and yet it is curious, and one of the things that book collectors and men of letters in time to come will note, that the Crown Prince of Siam actually wrote and published an essay about it recently, and that in English. Prince of Poland they called him politely, but he was never anything but Saxon. Friedrich Christian Leopold was born on August 23, 1722, so he was now not yet seventeen. Eight years later he married his cousin, Marie Antoinette, the second daughter of Charles VII, the Bavarian Emperor ; an " extremely clever, graceful, and lively " girl, Carlyle calls her, who was in later years the very practical correspondent of the great Frederick. Friedrich Christian turned out an insignificant creature enough, and passed more than forty years of aimless existence before he became Elector. October 5, 1763, saw him on the throne, and there he stayed but two months, dying without having accomplished anything, and leaving behind him a son who became the first King of Saxony. What a contrast were the tame insipidities of this Saxon prince, whose father held the Polish crown till his death, but who himself never succeeded in winning that perilous honour, to the exploits of the intrepid lad who was within six years to make Europe ring with his romantic quest !

As to the place, and the people who gave the entertainment, both have disappeared. I believe there is no Bolognetti among the Roman aristocracy to-day, but there is a Bolognetti Palace opposite the Gesu. The original and great Bolognetti Palace was in the Piazza di Venezia, at the top of the Corso. It was recently pulled down to give a view of the national monument to Victor Emmanuel. It had been bought early in the nineteenth century—some time in the twenties, I think—by the great Torlonia. It was not the great palace he possessed in the Borgo, built from designs by Bramante, of which Maziere Brady wrote such an interesting account. It was in the once Bolognetti palace that Torlonia gave his historical and famous balls, and, indeed, he seems to have bought this house simply for that purpose. It was said that every one who had a credit at his bank of over 500 scudi was asked ; it was thus, we shall remember, that Becky Sharp was invited, and went, leaning on the arm of Major Loder, to have her last sight of the Marquis of Steyne, in his collar and orders, his blue ribbon and garter, his red whiskers dyed purple, and the red scar on his forehead. The hackneyed stories of Polonia, as Thackeray calls him, will not bear telling again, but the description of his house is worth quoting by the side of Mr. Crisp's account of the ball which was given there a century before :—

" All the great company in Rome thronged to his saloons —princes, dukes, ambassadors, artists, fiddlers, monsignori, young bears with their leaders—every rank and condition of man. His halls blazed with light and magnificence ; were resplendent with gilt frames (containing pictures), and dubious antiques, and the enormous gilt crown and arms of the princely owner, a gold mushroom on a crimson field (the colour of the pocket-handkerchiefs which he sold), and the silver fountain of the Pompili family shone all over the roofs, doors, and panels of the house, and over the grand velvet baldaquins prepared to receive Popes and Emperors."

Mrs. Elliot, the " Idle Woman in Sicily," gives a not unpleasant picture of the house in her " Roman Gossip," and of its owners, and tells that it was there that Alessandro, son of the first millionaire, died as he came in from his drive.

SOME OXFORDSHIRE JACOBITES

In Oxford, as we all know, the Jacobite interest died hard. "That learned body wanted loyalty," in the opinion of the Georgian wits. There was, however, much cry and little wool, a great deal of toasting the King over the water, but no going out to fight for him in 1715 or 1745. The Jacobites, Hearne foremost among them, had often the laugh of the Hanoverians, but they had nothing else. The wit was with them, the victory with those loyal to "the Protestant succession." And all the revenge the vanquished could take was verbal. "James the Third and Eighth" proclaimed a preacher in the chapel of S. John's College ; but it was not treason ; he was only giving out his text, and it was this, "But the tongue can no man tame."

Oxford dons had only tongues, Oxfordshire gentlemen had swords. Would they use them for the Stewarts ?

The '15 and the '45 are matters of history. But what about those who never "came out" ? Then or afterwards there are many tales, some in books, some in men's memories that in the heart of the country are so retentive and yet so vague.

First there is the story that belongs to the once beautifu house of Adderbury, on the high ground at the north-west of the county. In 1743 it was the property of the Duke of Argyll. Once it had belonged to the famous Rochester, whom Charles II loved in his sins and Burnet in his repentance. When Skelton wrote in 1823, all he could say was, "In the eastern part of the village is a handsome seat in the occupation of J. Connor Field, Esq. ; a small remaining part of the former magnificent structure, which was the residence of the Earl of Rochester, is incorporated with this building. By tradition we learn that the old mansion once belonged to the great John, Duke of Argyll ; it subsequently came to the family of the Buccleughs." It did, for the daughter of John, Duke of Argyll, who died in 1743, brought it to her husband, Lord Dalkeith, who died there about seven years afterwards. The house was sold, and the Scottish lords passed away from the district.

John of Argyll was of course no Jacobite, though Horace Walpole insinuates that he was. But he was, if not suspect, at least tampered with. Lady Louisa Stewart, the daughter of George III's Lord Bute, and grand-niece of John of Argyll, who was born in 1757 and died in 1851, in her most entertaining Memoirs tells a story which she learnt from her aunt, who was brought up at Adderbury :—

" I once heard Lady Betty relate a circumstance that greatly contributed to depress her father's spirits in the last sad year of his life. Lord —— [1] (I have totally forgotten the name), a very old acquaintance, whom he had not seen since they were both young men, came unexpectedly to Adderbury. The Duke gave him the most cordial reception, showed him his grounds, insisted he should stay to dinner, and seemed so cheered by his company that the day passed over uncommonly well. But at parting, when he attended his guest to his carriage, ' *that creature*,' quoth Lady Betty, ' suddenly turned round on the step to whisper, " I had orders to give you this," slipped a paper into his hand, leaped in, and drove away.' It was a letter from the Pretender, full of high-flown compliments on his Grace's public spirit in opposing the Court : a conduct which, it might be hoped, was a sure sign of his having at last (though late) espoused the rightful cause, and resolved to reinstate his lawful sovereign. Support like his must ensure success ; and, were that once obtained, what reward could be denied him ? He instantly sent the letter to the King, together with another professing unalterable loyalty, and protesting his utter abhorrence of the treason suggested : protestations

---

[1] James Fourth Earl of Barrymore [editorial note]. This happened in 1742. See Horace Walpole, *Letters*, i. 182.

which were perfectly sincere ; for the Hanoverian succession had no steadier friend. Yet, that its enemies should have dared thus to tamper with him, and have interpreted his political conduct as forwarding their designs, wounded him to the very soul. He writhed under the insult ; could not forget it ; and Lady Betty affirmed that to his last hour it rankled in his mind."

The Duke was indeed unjustly suspected. But there were neighbours of his besides the reckless Barrymores of whom one would not be so sure. On the chief way from Oxford, a mile or two outside Chipping Norton, was the old inn at Chapel House, where four roads met. It was often, tradition tells, a rendezvous for plotters. Meetings were also held at the high lodge of Cornbury, at which were Lord Cornbury, Jenkinson, Cope, Basset, Lacy and others, and the lodge-keeper, who remembered them, would say that he believed a regular correspondence was kept up with the exiled princes till after the rising. In the villages round there were many families waiting to rise in 1745, if things had gone well with Prince Charlie. But the cat jumped the other way. There is a tale in Charlbury that a man lived till 1822 who had carried food to men resting in Cornbury Park, who were in flight home from the Stewart army when the Prince turned back from Derby ; and I have heard in Burford that a man not so long ago would tell of being turned out of Cornbury park by soldiers, on guard, was it, or on the watch, to prevent the capture, or to prevent the arrival, of the " royal exile."

From Dr. Brookes,[1] sometime Rector of Shipton under Wychwood, at the western side of the forest—Cornbury is at the north-east—comes the story of 1745 :—

" So strong was the attachment of the great families about this part of Oxfordshire to the Stewarts, that if the Scotch had been able to push forward, and the French Court had sent an army so strong as that which accompanied King William, they would have thrown off the mask and taken up arms on their behalf. Lord Cornbury was the soul of

[1] See *The Monthly Magazine*, vol. xlix. pp. 25 sqq.

the disaffection in this vicinity ; next to him (he said) stood Sir Robert Jenkinson of South Lawn Lodge. He then told me that when the Pretender, as he was called, was in England, incognito, he visited Lord Cornbury. Banbury, a barber of Charlbury, who shaved the prince and dressed his wig, knew the Pretender by a word which dropped incautiously from Lord Cornbury, and by the extraordinary respect which was shown to the mysterious stranger."

The way the story is told nowadays—I have the authority of the learned Vicar of Charlbury—is that " the Pretender was once shaved in Charlbury, and never forgot it ! "

There is a visible, and perhaps significant, memorial of that time, in the Scots firs at the top of the hill midway between Cornbury and Walcot, which are said to have been planted to welcome the Scots army in 1745, and are certainly of that date. The Jenkinsons at Walcot, who gave much Church plate to Charlbury, were certainly Jacobites. These county families, it may be noted, would send their sons to Burford grammar school, and thus young Rochester from Cornbury, earlier, and Jenkinson (afterwards Lord Liverpool) from Walcot, were " Burfordians."

Dr. Brooke's information—to return to that—is said to have come from a lodge-keeper at Cornbury. There is no corroboration of it that I know of ; but it is not at all improbable. The Lord Cornbury in the early part of the eighteenth century, the friend of Pope, was the grandson of the Lord Chancellor Clarendon, and thus a " connection " at least of the later Stewarts. Though he was ostensibly a Whig, he may well have thought kindly of his royal kindred and have been not unwilling to see them on the throne.

That Charles was in England in 1750 seems certain. The best account of his feelings and conduct at that time is that of Dr. King, Principal of St. Mary Hall at Oxford, who as late as 1754 excited the theatre at the Encaenia by pronouncing with especial emphasis and pause the word " Redeat " in his Latin oration. Thus it runs :—

" September, 1750, I received a note from my Lady Primrose, who desired to see me immediately. As soon as I waited on her, she led me into her dressing-room, and

presented me to ———.[1] If I was surprised to find him there
I was still more astonished when he acquainted me with
the motives which had induced him to hazard a journey
to England at this juncture. The impatience of his friends
who were in exile had formed a scheme which was impracticable ; but although it had been as feasible as they
had represented it to him, yet no preparation had been
made, nor was anything ready to carry it into execution.
He was soon convinced that he had been deceived, and
therefore, after a stay in London of five days only, he
returned to the place from whence he came. As I had
some long conversations with him here, and for some years
after held a constant correspondence with him, not indeed
by letters but by messengers,[2] who were occasionally
despatched to him ; and as during this intercourse I informed myself of all particulars relating to him and of his
whole conduct, both in public and private life, I am perhaps
as well qualified as any man in England to draw a just
character of him ; and I impose this task on myself not only
for the information of posterity, but for the sake of many
worthy gentlemen whom I shall leave behind me, who are
at present attached to his name, and who have formed
their ideas of him from public report, but more particularly
from those great actions which he performed in Scotland.
As to his person, he is tall and well made, but stoops a little,
owing perhaps to the great fatigue which he underwent in
his northern expedition. He has an handsome face and
good eyes ; (I think [3] his busts, which about this time were

---

[1] The Pretender. [These notes are King's own].

[2] These were not common couriers, but gentlemen of fortune,
honour, and veracity, and on whose relations I could entirely
depend.

[3] He came one evening to my lodgings and drank tea with me.
My servant, after he was gone, said to me " that he thought my
new visitor very like Prince Charles." " Why," said I, " have you
ever seen Prince Charles ? " " No, sir," replied the fellow, " but
this gentleman, whoever he may be, exactly resembles the busts
which are sold in Red Lion Street, and are said to be the busts of
Prince Charles." The truth is, these busts were taken in plaster of
Paris from his face.

commonly sold in London, are more like him than any of his pictures which I have yet seen ;) but in a polite company he would not pass for a gentleman. He hath a quick apprehension, and speaks French, Italian, and English, the last with a little of a foreign accent. As to the rest, very little care seems to have been taken of his education. He had not made the belles lettres or any of the finer arts his study, which surprised me much, considering his preceptors, and the noble opportunities he must have always had in that nursery [1] of all the elegant and liberal arts and science. But I was still more astonished when I found him un-acquainted with the history and constitution of England, in which he ought to have been very early instructed."

Thus, and a good deal more of it, Dr. King writes in the spirit of one who had deserted the party. There is no doubt that the doctor, at least up to the famous Oxfordshire election of 1755, was an ardent Jacobite. He died in 1763, and had—like so many—come over to the Government side when George III became king. There is a story that it was not till then that S. John's, the most notorious Jacobite college in Oxford, became "loyal" to the Hanoverians. We have pictures of King George and his wife, when they were still quite young, which they are said to have given ; and after the death of Lord Lichfield (a rather talkative and not very sober S. John's man), the portrait of the King which he had at Ditchley was given to us.

At Oxford the failure of the '45 did not by any means crush the Jacobite interest. The Hoadleian chaplain, Edmund Pyle, whose letters to Dr. Kerrich of Dersingham have recently been published, wrote on March 24, 1749 :—

"There is no news stirring, but that there has been a most terrible riot at Oxford, on the 23 of last month, which

[1] Rome. His governor was a Protestant, and I am apt to believe, purposely neglected his education, of which it is surmised he made a merit to the English ministry ; for he was always supposed to be their pensioner. The Chevalier Ramsay, the author of *Cyrus*, was Prince Charles's preceptor for about a year ; but a court faction removed him.

is the Pretender's youngest son's birthday. King George was damned and King James blessed, in the open streets, by open daylight, and the Vice-Chancellor (who is a Jack) is sent for up to give an account of his conduct. I am in attendance at Court with a very clever man of that university, who tells me that Jacobitism at Oxford at this time wears less reserve, and cares less about the decency of the exterior than in the year '15. God save us."

Very soon after this Charles Edward formally declared himself to be a member of the Church of England. In a statement of his own (quoted by Mr. Andrew Lang) he says that he did this in London in 1750. Another statement is that he was admitted " in the new church in the Strand " in 1753. Was he ever "reconciled " to Rome ? I do not know any evidence that he was ; and it is perhaps significant that he was buried not at Rome but at Frascati, of which his brother was bishop, and thus all objections could be over-ridden. It was a long while after that his body was removed to S. Peter's.

For several years he lived a life of perpetual disguise and intrigue, and there are many gaps in our knowledge of his "itinerary." When was he in Surrey, in a house near Godalming ? Early in 1753, probably. In the previous November there was a plot brewing ; Pickle the spy tells James III that his son "did not then adventure himself at London," but was "upon the coast." Which coast ? The Oxfordshire interest perhaps comes in now. " Jemmy " Dawkins, a Jamaica planter, of the Oxfordshire family, and bred at the Jacobite college of S. John's in Oxford— whence he took the D.C.L. degree in 1749—already famous for his expedition to Palmyra, was now deep in Charles's interest. As early as 1751 we find Charles sending compliments to him. He assisted in the published books on Palmyra in 1753 and on Baalbek in 1757 ; and, while to the world he might seem a rich and leisurely antiquary, he was really deep in plots for the return of the Stewarts.

In March or April 1753 " Pickle the Spy " reports that " Dawkins went lately over and brought money for the Prince. Pickle believes upwards of £4,000." Probably nothing like that amount came ; and Dawkins at any rate was a little later at Berlin negotiating, as one of the heads of an English party, including Dr. King and the Earl of Westmoreland, with Frederick the Great. Frederick was very ready to make use of the plot and the plotters. " I can pay the English King back," he wrote, " by means which perhaps he knows nothing of and does not yet believe in." Dawkins acted at first through Marshal Keith ; then Frederick saw him himself, but it seems did not think much of the plans in detail. The English government all the while knew about it. " Mr. Dawkins," says a report of Lord Albemarle's to the Secretary of State at the end of the year, " as well as his uncle, who lives in Oxfordshire, is warmly attached to the Pretender's interest." He came to Paris in the spring of 1753, and has been watched ever since, and now a warrant is out for his arrest.

The uncle was James Dawkins, born in Jamaica in 1698, the son of Richard Dawkins, one of the earlier settlers in the island. He had come to England early in life, bought the estate of Over-Norton, and sat as M.P. for Woodstock from 1734 to 1741. He died unmarried in 1776, and a monument is erected to his memory in Charlbury Church. Near it is an inscription to another Jamaican, William Morant, who died after " three not unfruitful years of study at S. John's College, Oxford."

Meanwhile, Charles's relations with Clementina Walkinshaw had become notorious and caused great scandal among his supporters, and danger too, it was thought ; for her sister was, " and still is," says Dr. King, " housekeeper at Leicester House," and thus very likely to betray all she could learn. On January 4, 1754, Henry Goring, one of the most famous of all Charles's friends, wrote a serious remonstrance. At the same time Charles had dismissed one of those who had long served him, Dumont, and Goring protested that he was very likely to betray Charles's " secret." It was likely to come, through him, to Dawkins among others ; and it was likely enough he would tell the names of the English Jacobites, Dawkins among them. It was not long after this that Dr. King describes another friend, MacNamara, as warmly pressing Charles to dismiss the lady, and finding him unmovable, saying, as he left him, " What has your family done, sir, thus to draw down the vengeance of Heaven on so many branches of it through so many ages ? "   Now, in my copy of Dr. King's *Anecdotes*, a former possessor has written, " This is a mistake. It was Mr. James Dawkins who went over to the Pretender." And the writer is evidently well informed, for when Dr. King asked how the envoy came back and reported the Prince's refusal, he has written at the side, " The parties held their meetings at Mereworth Castle in Kent, then the seat of John Earl of Westmoreland. The then castle is now pulled down and a House built after a plan of Palladio, and is the property of Earl Le De Spencer." The evidence no doubt is late, for my copy is the 1819 edition. But it is very likely that James Dawkins was the envoy, and that it was from Charles's obstinate refusal that he now turned from him and became reconciled to the Hanoverian government. But this may well not have been the only reason for the Oxfordshire man's secession. By all he had seen Jemmy Dawkins was bitterly disappointed. A report of 1756 shows that he had found out what was at the root of the difficulty. Poor Charles could not be depended on. He had told the English Jacobites that the prince was " entirely abandoned to an irregular debauched life, even to excess, which brought his health, and even his life, daily in danger."

The report, there seems every reason to believe, was true. It is only an anticipation—by twenty years, though, and more—of the account, bitter but probably veracious, that we hear of the Prince's later life in Italy.

Sir Nathaniel Wraxall noted " among the objects of mingled curiosity and compassion which Florence presented in 1779 to the view of an Englishman," the Chevalier de S. George. Reduced indeed he was, for Clement XIV had withdrawn both money and honours, nor had Pius VI restored them. He had about £5,000 a year, which Wraxall thinks quite enough to maintain a fit establishment at Florence. But he " exhibited to the world a very humiliating spectacle." There was Alfieri, "a Man singularly eccentric in his Mind, Habits, and Manners," always in attendance on his wife ; and Charles could never be seen (by non-Jacobite Englishmen, at least) except across the theatre, " where he appeared almost every evening . . . led in by his domestics, who laid him down on a species of sofa, in the back part of his Box ; while the Countess d'Albany, his consort, occupied the front seat during the whole performance." Wraxall waited to see him one night as he came out of the theatre, and Charles, seeing the English uniform which he and his friend wore, stopped, gently shook off the two servants who supported him, and, " taking off his hat, politely saluted us."

Still Charles wore the garter, still he simulated royal state, but " his whole figure, paralytic and debilitated, presented the appearance of great bodily decay." All was due to " an unhappy propensity to wine," which Wraxall tells had shown itself at the most critical moment in 1770 when Choiseul was prepared to make an attempt in his favour had not poor Charles come to him to plan it " in such a state of intoxication as to be utterly unable even of ordinary conversation."

So the sad story ended ; and before it ended the surviving Jacobites had become few indeed. Yet in Oxfordshire, if tradition is to be trusted, Jacobitism lasted as long as anywhere in England. It is said that there was a Jacobite meeting at Burford about 1780, at which one of the Dawkins family was present ; the Crown got wind of the meeting, and Dawkins and others fled the country. Which Dawkins this was I do not know, and I cannot as yet trace the meeting, the date or the persons. It is, however, interesting as a tradition, and there are hints that in an out of the way place like Burford opinions may well have survived which elsewhere had died out.

If there were not Jacobites there may at least have been Nonjurors. Dr. King is very bitter against the party and especially against one Bettenham, "a printer, a sanctified member of Gordon's congregation, but one of the greatest knaves I have ever known." Bishop Gordon and his

IN THE GREAT HOUSE, BURFORD.

followers lingered on very late, after there was any real Jacobitism in England. The Great House at Burford has a room in which the panels are decorated with religious emblems, which may very well have been a Nonjuror's chapel. There is a crucifix painted, with an angel pointing to it from a skull, and the word *Memento*. Below are the lines :—

> Nec prius obducat mollis tua lumina somnus
> Exacti quam ter repetisti facta diei,
> Quid lapsus feci quid recte quidque remisi,

and on the other side of the room, on a little door leading to a small closet lighted by a window looking on the stairs (which may have been a vestry or a powder-closet), a tower, with the legend round it, " Fidei per scutum castrum fit tutum." In the window seats are " Si Christum noscis nihil est si caetera nescis " ; and " Christum noscis nihil est si caetera noscis " ; above the windows, " Mens sana in corpore sano. Influentia entis ornamenta mentis" and "praeter propter vitam vivimus Credenda, agenda, petenda "—these three words exactly under the others. It may be that here a faithful remnant, which would take no oaths to the Hanoverians, met and worshipped, using the old Prayer Book or the revised Liturgy, with its beautiful reminiscence of ancient sources, wearing the vestments of the rubric, and longing for the days when the Church should be in communion at least with the East, and when a Stewart, no longer pledged to Popery, might sit on the throne of his fathers.

I am not sure that I cannot tell who the Nonjuror was who lived in the house. Traditionally it is said that the house was built for the Fettiplaces, whose chief seat was at Swinbrook, quite near, and this the dower house. In 1745 was published a list of the Nonjurors who refused to take the oath to George I. drawn up in 1715, with their estates and the value thereof. Among these is Margaret Fettiplace, who is stated to have "an annuity out of Swyncombe £150." The list of place-names is not very exact, and thus " Swyncombe " may well be a mistake for " Swinbrook." I do not find the name Fettiplace at Swyncombe.

It is quite possible then that this Margaret Fettiplace who was a Nonjuror lived in the Burford Great House.

But, after all, this is mere guess work. Thomas Castle may have built, and John Castle have lived in the house. It may be the portrait of one of them that we see there on a panel. But, do you say, *they* may have been Jacobites and Nonjurors? I wonder.

Gloucestershire and Oxfordshire, indeed, are reported at this time as being swarming with " Jacks," and " the cause was constantly and secretly speeded," says Mr. Albert Hartshorne in his book of the Pyle and Kerrich letters, " and the sentiment kept alive by the ever popular practice of pledging ' the King over the Water ' in the *Fiat*, the *Radiat*, the *Redeat*, or the Virgilian-mottoed and rose-engraved glasses, over the glittering bowl." And thus it is that relics of the Jacobite days still linger where memories have faded. At the beautiful seventeenth century Chastleton House, just on the borders of Oxfordshire, there was a famous Jacobite, Henry Jones, who belonged to a club the members of which had a special set of glasses made for them. " On the decanters was a spray of roses, a compass pointing to a star, and the word *Fiat*. The glasses have only the roses on them. There are only two or three sets of this glass in England, and that at Chastleton is the most perfect, consisting of two decanters and eleven glasses," says Miss Whitmore Jones, the owner of Chastleton.

Such memorials still preserve the tradition of perilous days when Charles Edward was a serious pretender ; and it was thus, in sentiment and conviviality, that " the Cause " came to its end.

A SPANISH COURT PAINTER

FEW reputations are so ephemeral as those of court painters, for the personages who choose them do not usually know much about art ; and posterity has no subservience to the opinions of departed kings. Only an historical interest will preserve most of the portraits of the Victorian age. Many of the works of artists great in other fields, but diverted from their true field of labour to paint the amusements of royalty, are doomed to neglect and decay. " Landseer," wrote Burne-Jones when he saw the Academy of 1854, " has drivelled his time away on another group of the royal family in Highland costume. Will he ever learn that the subject is not remarkable for conception, or capable of a counterbalancing beauty of execution, that it should be repeated every year ? " Who remembers now von Angeli or Winterhalter ? Who is surprised that a Beechey was preferred to a Reynolds ? We need not wonder that the fame of many a court painter is writ in water.

But, on the other hand, there can be few more enduring titles to fame than those of the great artists who have pre-served the visible impression of great leaders of men in thought or action. Holbein makes us know Erasmus as by books alone we could never know him ; Velasquez, Innocent X. ; Vandyke, Charles I. ; Reynolds, Garrick ; Lenbach, Bismarck. There are many great heroes whose outer form, through which, as it thinks, the spirit can be seen not obscurely to express itself, the world would not willingly allow to perish ; and if a great artist has not preserved them, the world is content with inferior work, because some record at least is essential. Such is the justification of the picture, I feel, when I look at the portrait of " Carlos III., rey de España y de las Indias," which Carmona engraved in 1783 from the painting by Antonio Raffaello Mengs.

Charles III., once said the most eminent English historian of the nineteenth century, was the greatest king Spain ever had. He was indeed a benevolent despot whose benevolence overruled his despotism, a reformer who left work that was enduring, not revolutionary, a genuine lover of his country and his people. Born in 1716, established as an independent sovereign at Parma in 1731, but within a very few years King of the Two Sicilies, he succeeded his father, Philip V., in 1759, as King of Spain. As with so many kings of his house, the influence of a wife supplied the most enduring motives of his reign. Elizabeth Farnese, who had ruled Spain when her husband lived, expected to rule also under her son, but Maria Amalia, King Charles's wife, determined that the power of the old lady, whom she regarded as intriguing and untruthful, must end. Two hours a day, when he first came home to Spain, did the dutiful son give to his mother, and his wife wrote bitterly to the trusted minister and friend of their Neapolitan days, Tanucci, of " la incomodidad de las dos horos de visita a la anciana." The wife triumphed, partly because she was able to represent " the old lady " as incompetent and senile : " llega á tal extremo su incapacidad, que no sabe el valor de los monedas." Charles was an able and industrious man, thoroughly trained in the work of government, but his wife, so long as she lived, was an admirable helper to him. Together they were the initiators of every wise measure for the reformation of Spain, as they were the acutest critics of the social and political evils of their time. But their fellow work lasted only till 1760, when the Queen died ; and for nearly thirty years Charles pursued his course of beneficent public service alone. Ministers helped him ; he wrote still to the faithful Tanucci, who directed his anti-papal policy with a keen zest ; he was well served by Aranda, Floridablanca, Wall, badly by others whose names are no less famous in Spanish history ; but till the end, in 1789, when the shadow of the French Revolution was already beginning to cast its blight on Spain, the King was the most faithful, the most understanding, of public servants, the truest guardian of the interests of the nation he loved. Schemes of colonization, education, economic reform, ecclesiastical change, were pressed on, and—after the first disaster of the "motin" at Madrid—wisely and with success. Charles, if he could have lived, might perhaps have brought his country safely through the storms that fell upon her, for he was an enthusiastic nationalist and a conservative reformer ; and if the ineptitude of his successor destroyed his reforms and checked all further development, what he had himself accomplished left a great and enduring mark on the history of Spain. Charles III. was a wise man and a good King ; he was worthy to be preserved by a great painter.

But Mengs was not a great painter. Ford's immortal handbook, the first edition of 1845, makes him the herald of low commonplace art—" Mengs, the incarnation of the academical mediocre." The judgment is too severe, at least when we view him as a portrait painter. In the palace at Madrid are rooms full of extremely interesting portraits from his hand. There are in our own National Portrait Gallery two of his pictures. One is among the charming portraits of the later Stewarts, and is not improved by the contrast with some of the French artists' work. It is James " the old Pretender,' wearing the blue ribbon and star of the Garter and the jewel of S. Andrew, with a crown on a table at his side— a hard, affected, unsympathetic picture. The other is equally uninspired. It is the diplomatist, Sir Charles Hanbury Williams, a man not without fame in the middle of the eighteenth century, but, for all Mengs shows of him in his brown coat, wholly uninteresting. There could hardly be two persons less like each other than these two, and yet, for all you could learn from the artist, there might be no difference between them. The character has not appealed to him, or he has been unable to catch it. On his canvas they are mere smiling clothes-props.

But the portrait of Charles III. has at least the real dis-

tinction of *vraisemblance*. Pass away from the details of
burnished armour, in the style of that which Titian gave
to Charles V., of lace ruffles, collar and jewel of the Golden
Fleece, mantle embroidered with the fleur-de-lys, the lion,
and the castle, the cognizance of his race and his possessions,
to the thin, sharp, lined face. It is the face of a Bourbon,
but it has, too, the humour and the keenness of the witty
Italian. No one could doubt that here was a man above
his fellows, active, alert, intelligent, discerning. The portrait preserves Charles to us as not one of those commonplace men who carry out good resolutions with persistency
yet without enthusiasm, but as one whom life amused as
well as instructed, one who could gauge interests, estimate
capacities, penetrate into problems of policy and conduct.
It is the work of an artist, too, who clearly felt himself
unfettered ; there is no attempt to make the King a courtier : if the sharpness of the chin which the coins show is
avoided, there is no concealment of the fact that the features
are not classic, that the face is no more than that of a clever,
laborious, humorous man. " Primero Carlos que Rey,"
says the Spanish proverb about him ; and that—his
humanity even more than his kingship—is what the artist
has managed to express.

Mengs indeed deserves to be remembered for such a picture as this, not for the acres of ceilings in the Spanish
palaces, the Annunciation at Aranjuez, or the conventional
Holy Families which the Spanish princes sought and pre-
sumably admired. "Crowned heads contended for his
works " ; and, what was more remarkable, the critics of
his day regarded him as the greatest artist of his time.
Mengs, says his friend Azara, " venne al Mondo per ristabilire
le Arti." His own writings show in what way he thought
he could build up again the house of beauty that men had
lost. The *Opere*, edited by Azara and published at Venice
in 1783, four years after the painter's death, show that he
studied his art, according to his lights, as Reynolds studied
it, historically and with attempt at science. The works
had a certain vogue in England. Even so late as 1796 they
were published at London as a translation. But they

scarcely influenced English art. His worship of the antique was without real understanding. His heroes in the art of more recent days were Raffaello and Coreggio ; but he fancied that he could discover and reproduce the art of a much earlier time. The classic statues seemed to him to embody the same principles as the lost paintings of antiquity. He thought it possible to unite the beauties of sculpture and of painting. Coreggio, with his canvasses crowded with pink-fleshed nymphs and goddesses, seemed to him to have accomplished the task : but it is impossible. Angelica Kauffmann, who was his imitator, tried it, but the influence of Reynolds had made her see that colour must be the dominant feature in the painter's art—an obvious fact which Mengs seems persistently to ignore. For himself, indeed, he was no colourist ; and his works have paid the penalty. We see him, as in the portrait of Charles III., at his best, perhaps, in engraving.

In that curious repertory of the bitter and the unauthentic —though it is more than that, too—the *Memoirs of Richard Cumberland written by himself, containing an account of his life and writings, interspersed with anecdotes and characters of several of the most distinguished persons of his time, with whom he has had intercourse and connexion* (2 vols. London, 1807), the author explains that the only reason for publishing them in his lifetime was that the copyright brought him £500. In these vivacious pages there is much about the art of the painter as well as that of the dramatist. In Spain there is much more too. There is the account of how the author lived at Madrid, fed by " a Milanese traiteur " and served by lacquies at two shillings a day, having a " round table of low Pope Joan " every afternoon at the same minute, and a house of fourteen rooms on the principal floor and but one fireplace. But he bitterly complains, which is the present point, that his views about Mengs and Reynolds have been quite misunderstood, and that it was not he but Azara reporting Mengs who said that the English artist's academical lectures were calculated to lead young students into error—" que puede conducir los juvenes al error." And indeed, he adds,

Azara himself says that Mengs was "of a temperament colerico y adusto."

But of Mengs Mr. Cumberland had but a very poor opinion—"he was an artist who had seen much and invented little " ; " he was as capable of painting Rubens's Adoration as he was of creating the Star in the East." "Mengs loved the truth," says Cumberland again, " but he did not always find it out." His lectures, in which he followed the fashion set by Reynolds, that the great painter should himself teach the principles of his art, confirm Cumberland's view. He perversely directs the attention of students to an art of which they can discover no survivals : he imagines what the ancient painters' merits were from the survivals of their sculpture. He follows Winckelmann, but he had not that great critic's true appreciation of antiquity. Winckelmann, he says, in his letters to M. Falconet of S. Petersburg, "non è un guidice infallibile, nè era della nostra Professione " ; but of his own infallibility he seems to have had little doubt. In truth, he was wholly of his own century, an honest craftsman enough, but an indifferent critic. His treatise on Beauty and Taste is intended to explain the meaning of the terms, and especially for painters, " in order that they may discover whether they have taste or not." His work is naturally a criticism of other painters, and I am forced to say that I do not find it at all interesting. Again and again we find ourselves brought back to Coreggio ; " everything painted by that great man has all the enchantment of the art." Titian and Raffaello are commended, but with so many exceptions that one is surprised that Mengs paid them any attention ; and as for Velasquez and Murillo, though he had so long lived among their pictures, he seems quite unable to appreciate them. The Spanish School, he says, " had not the exact ideas of the merits of the Grecian works, either in beauty or the ideal," and so " they imitated one another, and the greatest of them imitated truth, but without choice, and were pure naturalists." So in the same way, when he admired Raffaello, or Coreggio, or Titian, he admired without understanding ; and when he endeavoured to reproduce the classic spirit in his decorative art, he failed because he lacked just that touch of genius which makes Tiepolo memorable. The full brush and fluent colour which the last of the Venetians possessed were denied him. He was to Tiepolo as West to Reynolds. To the vivacious Cumberland belongs the credit of assigning him his true rank.

The association between Charles III. and Antonio Mengs had its source in the neoclassicism with which the latter was infected. Charles, an antiquary and—in the sense of his day—a dilettante, had been stirred and delighted by the discoveries at Herculaneum and Pompeii, in his own Kingdom of Naples, was proud of the great art of his native land but did not understand it, and thought that, on classic principles, it might be surpassed. Nature, said Mengs, did not provide perfect models : there was an ideal type which the study of the classic survivals would make it possible to reproduce. The view became orthodox : it was the King's and the Court painter's, it must become that of the Academy now founded and named after San Fernando. The works of Mengs were the first to be published in Spain that reduced æsthetic ideas into practical maxims, which attempted to teach method and analyse taste. They came at a time when art was at its lowest, and at least they made men think when they painted. If they thought on wrong lines so long as they were led by Mengs, there was a Goya to come in the next reign who should lead them back to the true and characteristic excellencies of Spanish art, vivified as was that of Murillo by continual contact with common contemporary life.

Mengs was a typical court painter. With something of a genius for portrait painting, which can be seen at its best in Dresden as well as at Madrid, comparable—as Sir William Stirling Maxwell well said—to that of Mignard and Rigaud, he was led away by his own want of judgment and the ignorance of his patrons, to work in which his performances were very inferior. If only he had remained content to paint the extensive royal family of the King of Poland and Elector of Saxony, the Spanish and Neapolitan Bourbons, and the entourage of Clement XIV., his fame would have stood far higher with posterity. But the delusion that a court painter can paint everything is undying, and Mengs was suffered to delight himself with intolerable illustrations of antiquity and religion. " Pictor philosophus," he delighted to be called, and his friend Azara, who as Spanish Envoy to the Vatican had helped him in many a difficulty, set the words on the monument he placed in the Pantheon beside that of Raffaello. But if his philosophy did not spoil his painting, his painting was but a mediocre tribute to the excellence of his philosophy. His contemporaries asserted that he combined the merits of the great masters, and he seriously thought it possible himself ; but to us he is little more than a journeyman of intelligence, whose wits are in advance of his education, and whose modesty has been eclipsed by his success.

MEMORIES OF SIR WALTER SCOTT

WE often think, when we have time to encourage idle dreams (which yet have their use in withdrawing us from the anxieties and sorrows which surround and which, because we cannot remedy them, go far to weaken our power of work, and even our instincts of benevolence), how great would be the joy of discovery and taste and analysis if an unknown but certain play of Shakespeare were given to the world, if we could unearth a chapter of autobiography from his pen, or come upon a lost canto of Dante, a new play of Sheridan, or a new essay of Charles Lamb. Something like this pleasure comes to us when we find ourselves in the presence of fresh and delightful records of one of the most beautiful characters in all the history of letters, and, under guidance of a new friend, revisit the familiar scenes and recall the unforgotten memories of Abbotsford and Scott.

It is no idle dilettantism which makes us thus rediscover our happiness in the past and link it to the names that are great in letters or in art. Our feeling may not be unlike that which made his friends mock at young Dapper in the *Alchemist* :—

> That's heir to forty marks a year,
> Consorts with the small poets of the time,
> Is the sole hope of his old grandmother,

in that we idly use our idleness and linger over records of deeds that were never more than trivial, set down by people who were, and are, of no importance in the world.

So I think when I go again over the records of that

131

Warwickshire coterie which gives me so much pleasure. Do others care for them ? Are their memories worth recalling ? Certainly I think they are. But of others I have no doubt at all, for the closer the ties that bind us to those who have enriched the life of man, the truer and richer may be our own witness and the happier our own lives. So it seems, at least, every time we turn the immortal pages in which Lockhart tells, often in the hero's own words, the story of how the great and gentle spirit of Scott met, and, in unselfish and self-sacrificing labour, triumphed over the misfortunes that would have overwhelmed a character less strong and less generous than his own. Any new record of the life of Scott, its simplicity, its humanity, and its genius, must be cherished by those who are capable of learning from man at his best. And such a record, little though it may add to the incomparable memorial of Lockhart, is before us in the letters and recollections of Mrs. Hughes, of Uffington.[1]

It is a relief to turn to such a book from the hurries and distractions of to-day. For with it, indeed, we are in a leisurely world. Almost do we feel ourselves back in the company of my Warwickshire friends and in the company of that quite forgotten book, a colloquial tale, indeed, which the author of *The Spiritual Quixote* called *Columella ; or the Distressed Anchoret*. We move slowly, if not so slowly as the two learned friends in that most quaint story, along the Bath road ; we travel through England and Scotland in easy stages by post horses, or even, if need be, in a chance gig. Mrs. Hughes is a delightful, because she was so easily a delighted, traveller. She drives from Berkshire through Oxfordshire, with her comfortable clerical husband, past the old-world town of Burford, which she does not tarry to describe, past Shipton Court, the beautiful Elizabethan house of Sir John Reade, which her editor—and the warning is not unneeded by those who travel now by railway—mis-

---

[1] *Letters and Recollections of Sir Walter Scott.* By Mrs. Hughes, of Uffington. Edited by Horace G. Hutchinson. Smith, Elder & Co.

names Shipston, or past Bruern Abbey (which he calls Boncon), now indeed transfigured and transformed, and so up into the land of Wordsworth and Southey, and at last to Auld Reekie and Abbotsford itself. A leisurely journey it is, and a leisurely time.

We have the inconvenience, it is true, of having to pay incredible sums, like poor Sir Walter, for the postage of repeated supplies of undesired and undesirable rubbish, and we remember with sympathy the Duke of Wellington's indignant repudiation, in similar circumstances, of the lady's black box and the charlatan's pills. But we are more than content with the fact that the journey to Bath from London, which used to take three days, can now be accomplished in twelve hours, and that—

" The interval between London and Edinburgh has been contracted in my lifetime to one-sixth part of the time which it formerly occupied."

And, when we do not travel, we walk about our gardens, or sit beside our fires reading our old books with the insatiable enjoyment of indestructible content. Even our sport is leisurely ; we do not go to the meet in motors, and the whole countryside is gratified when Sir Walter provides it with a mild coursing meeting. Amused though we are at the strangeness of foreign manners, really, if we rub our eyes, we are not sure that we ourselves do not make as much of little things as did the old *noblesse* in the story we hear at Abbotsford :—

" Sir Adam Ferguson's father was visiting at a French *château ;* being a great lover of field sports, and seeing much game, he was much rejoiced to hear in the morning a flourish of horns and a summons to the Chasse. Out he went full primed, and saw his host and all his visitors armed with crossbows and shooting the frogs in the castle ditch, the horns sounding all the time to inspirit the Chasse."

We are glad to take up our crossbows again and to hear the horns, which, if they have lost some of their power to inspirit, at least do not warn us to get out of the way.

And Abbotsford, when she gets there, what a delightful

description of that strange Gothic medley! Here are pinnacles and turrets and towers, old oak and old armour and old pictures, relics of Claverhouse and Rob Roy, glass, glittering light, great folios, and then the Wizard himself, whose talk was to her "like swallowing draughts of champagne without being intoxicated." The good lady, the "clever, active, bustling friend," had a genius for description; and thus she described Scott at home :—

"The brilliant imagination, the vivid description, the quick perception and happy delineation of character, the sterling good sense and acuteness of remark, the magic power over the feelings while he leads you from grave to gay, convulsing you with laughter, thrilling you with horror or melting you to tears, and above all the sweet spirit of benevolence, candour, and charity in its fullest sense, which breathes in every word and action of this extraordinary man are all precisely what you would expect from the author of the Scotch novels."

She was on the look-out everywhere for clues that would connect the author and the man. Not so thorough as young Adolphus, who made the discovery certain, yet she was sharply acute to mention names and tales, and sites, which helped to identify. This is but one example :—

"Tom Purdie made the speech given to Andrew Fairservice during a continuance of rainy weather in harvest time. 'If there is one day in seven, Sunday is sure to come and lick it up' : this Sir Walter told us after tea yesterday, and Dr. H. was so struck that he exclaimed involuntarily, 'Oh! that is in *Rob Roy!*'—it was curious to see the arch smile at the corner of Sir Walter's eye and the beam from under his overhanging brow as he carelessly answered, 'Oh! I dare say it has been often said in a wet season.'"

Mrs. Hughes, whose letters and memories have so delightfully brought back the old and peaceful days, was Mary Ann Watts, of Uffington, on the Berkshire downs, "the only child of the last of a line of clergymen who had, for several generations, succeeded one another in the cure of souls in that delightful place." She married the Rev. Thomas Hughes, D.D., Canon of S. Paul's, who had endeavoured

" to bring up the younger sons of George III. as Christian gentlemen." Her son John was the father of Tom Hughes, whose memory is green in Berkshire still, and one of his children had for godfather the Wizard of the North. Dr. Thomas Hughes did not die till 1833, and his widow survived him for twenty years. She must have been a charming, kindly creature, officious, bustling, and a little dictatorial, but always full of the sentiment which made her bring tears to the eyes by her singing of the old ballads, English and Scots, and of the humour which made " her gay talk and amusing stories " delightful to the end.

From 1806, and through Miss Hayman, a lady-in-waiting to Caroline, Princess of Wales, Mrs. Hughes became acquainted with Sir Walter Scott, and the first link between them was the lady's kindness to a dog. They soon became real friends, and Dr. Hughes also was in many respects congenial to the great writer as antiquary and man of cultivated taste in art. Among the earliest letters that passed between them are two in which he denies pretty roundly the authorship " of the novels which the world ascribes to me so pertinaciously ; " and on her side there is a delightful description, in no very kindly spirit though, of Dr. Parr, " the old original lion, which cannot be tamed by the hand of man," among " the very respectable Menagerie of Leamington Lions (to use the Oxford term)." The friendship was cemented by two visits to Abbotsford ; and it was at Amen Court that Scott, for the last time in England, accepted any invitation—a touching scene, described by Mrs. Hughes, when he came to breakfast a few days before he sailed on his last journey.

This last occasion, it is worth noting, as recorded by Mrs. Hughes, enables one to observe that, earlier, in 1828, Scott had breakfasted in Amen Court, and met William Blackwood. " Worthy Mrs. Hughes," says the publisher (*Annals of a Publishing House*, vol. ii. p. 85), " was, I daresay, as happy as it was possible for her kind heart to be." This breakfast is not recorded in Scott's diary, nor is the last sad one, on October 8, 1831, when again the Bishop of Llandaff (Copleston, also Dean of S. Paul's), came to meet him, but not Blackwood now. He seemed hardly able to crawl across the hall, she tells, and he said that he was a broken man. But he was pleased with some Yarmouth bloaters, and this led to a touching incident. Mrs. Hughes went to Billingsgate to order some for him, to be sent to Sussex Place, where he was staying. He did not send so far, said the fishmonger. Mrs. Hughes said she was sorry, for " it was for Sir Walter Scott."

" The rough fishmonger started back, and pushing forward to me through his piles of fish, cried out most loudly : ' Sir Walter Scott—did you say, Madam ! Sir Walter Scott —God bless my soul !—he shall have them directly if I carry them myself.—Sir Walter Scott !—they shall be with him to-night '—then pausing—' No, not to-night—for to-morrow morning at 7 o'clock a fresh cargo comes in, and he shall have them for his breakfast—Sir Walter Scott ! ' "

It is but one instance, and the volume overflows with them, of Scott's universal popularity. Another is more personal and less literary. It connects the great writer with the Hetman of the Cossacks :—

" When Sir Walter was in London in 1814 he was introduced to Platoff ; they had some conversation, if so it may be called, in dumb show, for they had no common language, but they contrived to be pleased with each other. Afterwards, when Sir W. was in Paris, and walking on the Boulevards, he heard a galloping of horses, and, turning round, saw the Hetman dashing along, with his long spear in rest, and followed by six or seven wild-looking Cossacks ; as soon as he came near he reined his horse so tight that he stood on his hind feet, threw himself off, gave his bridle to one of his attendants, ran to Sir W., embraced and kissed him on both sides of his face, and, almost instantly remounting, rode off like a whirlwind."

Full of illustration like this of the charm of the Wizard is Mrs. Hughes's book. She was herself one who could fully appreciate it.

The memorials of the congenial association of these two are several letters from Sir Walter Scott and several extracts from the diaries of Mrs. Hughes. They give a picture, as intimate as it is delightful, of the unstudied friendliness of the greatest of Scotsmen. As might be expected, whether he writes or Mrs. Hughes records all she could remember— with bitter regrets that she cannot remember more—the pages overflow with humour. Some of the stories are old, some new, and I do not know which are the better. Let me mention a few, though I cannot tell them at length. One of the first and not the least funny is that of one of the children of the Marquess of Lothian, who had a trick of calling everybody " old fat goose," and was only by his father's resolution prevented from addressing the appropriate but scarcely complimentary appellation to George IV. Another is of an eccentric servant who wore an oxhide dressed with " the horns so fitted as to be worn on the head," and, when he was one day walking along a road reading, caused astonishment to a gentleman and lady, who saw, seemingly, an ox on his hind legs reading a book. Mingled with the stories are descriptive passages of considerable interest. Of course, most notable are the descriptions of Scott at home, with his children and his friends and his dogs and Tom Purdie ; but Mrs. Hughes has also a talent for sketching scenery or recording impressions of houses and of company.

I hardly think that the passionate attachment of Scott to his children has ever been so clearly shown as in these letters. Lockhart's restraint is most marked when he speaks of the family affections ; we do not forget the admirable letters which he prints from the father to his sons ; but nothing shows so plainly how Scott's life was bound up in theirs as the constant unstudied references he makes to their doings when he writes to Mrs. Hughes. Indeed, no happier picture of Scott in his domestic relations has been given than that which Mrs. Hughes's memories and his own letters show us in this book. Our admiration and love, if they could not be increased, are justified at every point.

Insensibly we digress, from the stories we were at least to tell of, to the man himself, so much more charming than the tales he so charmingly told. But we shall not soon forget the story of the two Irish gentlemen who fought a duel because one would not believe that the other had seen anchovies growing in a garden, and was killed, his opponent thereupon exclaiming, " Oh ! what a pity—I just recollect I meant *capers ;* " or the Highland chief, who after his second marriage, comparing his napkins with a list and finding it wrong, said to his bride—

" I now weel remember me there are but eleven : the twelfth was lost at my first wife's funeral : I'll behove to be more careful on the next occasion, my Doo " ; or Scott's description of a meeting with Coleridge, which I will give in Mrs. Hughes's words :—

" At a dinner given by Mr. Sotheby a large number of the Literati were assembled : of Mr. Coleridge's behaviour Sir Walter gave us the following account :—

' After eating as never man ate before, and drinking with every person with whom he could possibly make an excuse to take wine, thrusting himself besides as thirdsman whenever he saw two people drinking together ; at last, when the cheese was brought on the table, he began in a most oracular tone, and, without the least thing having been said which could have led to it, an oration, which lasted three-quarters of an hour, on the Samothracian mysteries.' "

Scott appears in these pages without disguise. It would be difficult, indeed, to disguise him from eyes so keen as those of Mrs. Hughes—though he could keep his own secrets, and rightly, when he wished. But, in all the affairs of life, in all that makes character and stamps influence, he had nothing to disguise, and he was incapable of the attempt. In his serious moments, which come not rarely in this book, when he speaks of sorrow, of relations with the other world, of poverty and suffering and Christian faith, he is as genuine as when he works and feasts and laughs and shows his friends the sights of his county and his home. Every new record of him fixes him more securely in his sincerity and greatness.

THE DUKE OF WELLINGTON AS A LETTER WRITER

ROBERT LOUIS STEVENSON congratulated the British people that their famous admirals were not only great hearted, but big spoken. It has been as clear a characteristic of our generals that they have been good writers. Occasionally, as in some recent instances, a tendency to magniloquence has been prominent, and that without much relation to the operations to be commemorated, but as a rule no men have written more straightforward English than our chief soldiers ; and the plain tale of the Indian service of our most successful general has been almost the greatest literary success of recent years. I do not know that any one has thought to criticise despatches in any detail as literary compositions. Were such a book essayed, I have no doubt that it would be found that historians have learned much as to the telling of a story of war from those whose exploits it has been theirs to record. It is of course to be observed that a despatch is a very different thing from a letter. The object, the circumstances of composition differ widely. But the qualities which make a good despatch are those which give their effect to the best letters of the best letter writers—vividness, point, the definite expression of definite ideas, clear statement, and an entire absence of affectation, rhetoric, or ornament.

There was never a more conspicuous example of these excellencies, or indeed of the corresponding defects very naturally associated with them, than the correspondence, official and private, of the great Duke of Wellington. It may prove not uninteresting to observe the characteristics of his despatches and his letters, and to illustrate them by extracts which are worthy of attention more close than they have already received.

139

The two great brothers Wellesley—and, I believe, the same distinction belongs to a third, Lord Cowley—were eminently impressive as writers of public documents. The style of the Marquis was superbly dignified, stately, moving like a solemn pageant, unsurpassed in defence of a policy of masterly venture or in indictment of lukewarmness. Lytton's once famous lines explain the characteristics of the letter writer as well as they do those of the politician. Few know them now ; they are worth quoting :—

> Accomplished Wellesley, equally at home
> In Ind or Europe, Westminister or Rome,
> Vigorous in action, eloquent in speech,
> Scholar and statesman, Laelius-like in each,
> Supreme in that which Cicero called the urbane,
> Graceful as Canning, and perhaps as vain.

The charm which Hoppner's beautiful portrait gives him he was fully conscious of ; and he was industrious to retain it throughout life. Partly it was a literary charm—in which he was entirely unlike the Duke of Wellington, who had probably, if he would have admitted it, a very poor opinion of books and those who wrote them. Lord Stanhope illustrates this literary interest very well by a note he made on October 4, 1839, of a conversation with Wellesley's niece at a dinner party at Walmer. He says :—

"Lady Burghersh told me that lately calling on Lord Wellesley she had seen upon his table a print of Sir Joshua Reynolds's Ugolino, and the conversation turning upon this, Lord Wellesley repeated several lines from Dante's description. She expressed her surprise at his powers of memory when he answered that he really thought, if he tried, he could repeat nearly the whole of that canto ; and on trying he really did repeat to her above fifty lines of it. She was struck too, she said, at his pure and classic pronunciation of the Italian, and of that there could not be a more competent judge. I observed to her that what enhanced the merits of these accomplishments was that they never could have proceeded from business or ambitious objects, as he never had any Italian mission to fulfil or Italian negotiation to conduct, so that love of literature must have been his only motive."

The literary interest was prominent in his conversation. Mr. Charles Gore, son of the Earl of Arran and father of the present Bishop of Birmingham, who was in his youth a notable figure in society and was with Wellesley in both his viceroyalties of Ireland, remembered much of the charm that belonged to the talk at his table, and started from himself. In reminiscences he kindly gave me some years ago, Mr. Gore pointed out the contrast between the two brothers, and told me some sharp sayings about the younger by the elder. I respect his wish that these should not be made public ; but he allowed me to say this from him : " My belief is that Lord Wellesley had a very small opinion of the Duke as a politician." It was a view, no doubt, very like that which Disraeli expressed so clearly in *Sybil*. Rogers put the difference between the two brothers very distinctly when he said, at breakfast with Lord Stanhope, " I think that the most remarkable contrast that history affords is between the Duke of Wellington and Lord Wellesley, the one scorning all display, the other living for nothing else." " Yes," said Macaulay, who was present, " no two brothers, to be both eminent men, were ever so unlike."

" Living for nothing but display " was no doubt far too harsh a judgment. Wellesley really had a warm and affectionate heart, but he had so strongly the talent of expression that at times it almost seemed as if he could rival Pecksniff or Digby Grant in his use of it. For comparison with the Duke's letters, this one of the Marquess to his niece, Lady Burghersh, is worth quoting. Her daughter in publishing it added the caustic comment : " He wrote beautifully expressed letters, full of kind sentiments, to his relations, but rarely put himself out for any one." This letter is dated February 25, 1818 :—

" MY DEAREST PRISCILLA,—

" Your very interesting and affecting letter produced mixed emotions of pleasure and pain in my mind such as I have seldom experienced. It is a great satisfaction to perceive that you remember me with so much tenderness and affection, and it is with heartfelt grief that I read the relation of your sufferings and afflictions. You possess, however, a source of consolation in every sorrow—an honest and affectionate heart. This great advantage was always your principal recommendation to my affection and esteem, and I am sincerely gratified in finding that you retain it. Be assured that I take the most warm interest in all that regards you, and although my retired habits and your health have prevented our meeting for some time past, my regard for you is undiminished, and I trust you will always consider me as one of your most attached friends." A few more equally pleasant words, and he ends, " believe me ever, dearest Priscilla, yours most affectionately."

This was one style. The manner of the Duke was different. It was above all things explicit, fully explanatory, regardful of details. It had the military, rather than the political, tone. In the enormous number of the published despatches of the great general there is practically no change of style. There is growth—the growth which comes naturally from intimacy with public affairs, increasing in importance as years go on. But the same chief aim—to be explanatory and explicit—is still prominent in 1832 as it was in 1794, at the end as at the beginning of Colonel Gurwood's laborious collection. There are no despatches in the world like them, so full, so detailed, so clear. One marvels, with Sir Herbert Maxwell, " at the cool head and iron frame " which enabled the writer to compose so well in the midst of circumstances so agitating, so tremendous, as beset him on many of his campaigns. The Duke himself noted in the earlier ones, when he re-read them after thirty years, " the same attention to details—to the pursuit of all the means, however small, that could promote success," that marked his after work as statesman and minister. They were, he said, " as good as I could write now." And he supplied us also with the clue to the excellence which belongs to his despatches as well as to his letters : " My rule always was to do the business of the day in the day."

WELLINGTON AS A LETTER WRITER

It is impossible, indeed, to go beyond that statement. It is the one explanation of the really good letter as it is of the valuable despatch. There must be no elaboration, no after-thought, no art ; whether or not the truest lover be the most feigning, there can be no doubt that the best letter writer is he who, like Polonius, can swear that he uses no art at all.

I do not forget elaborate letters like those of Pope, or some modern writers whose laboured compositions are a source of keen satisfaction to themselves ; but, to my mind, the excellence of the true letter is that, like those of R. L. Stevenson, it is red hot ; and that too is the excellence of the despatch.

This, however, is far from meaning an avoidance of trouble. Wellington, to the end of his life, took immense trouble with everything that he wrote. His last biographer has told us that in 1800, when he was placed by his brother in command of an expedition that was intended to act against the French, "long lists of provisions, from beef, flour, and rum, down to raisins and vinegar, specifying the amount required for each, are appended in his own hand-writing to letters addressed to various officials." In 1846 his letter to the landlord of the "Norfolk Arms Inn," at Arundel, shows in deliciously absurd exaggeration the same extraordinary care for the details of preparation. The letter cannot too soon be read by those who do not know it ; and I am sure those who are already acquainted with its beauties will rejoice at the opportunity of studying them again.

"Strathfieldsaye,
November 24th, 1846.

"F.M. the Duke of Wellington presents his compliments to the Landlord of the Norfolk Arms Inn. The Duke has been invited to Arundel Castle during the period of the visit of H.M. the Queen to His Grace the Duke of Norfolk. He will arrive at Arundel by the Rail Road on Tuesday, the 1st of December, by the train which will quit the Station London Bridge at eleven a.m. and reach the Station Arundel at 1.39. He will bring his Carriage with him, and he requests the Landlord of the Norfolk Arms Inn to give order, and if necessary to take Measures, that he may find a pair of Horses at the Arundel Station at half-past one on Tuesday, the 1st of December, to draw his carriage from thence to the castle.

" The Duke will have with him two Saddle Horses, and he requests the Landlord of the Norfolk Arms Inn to give orders that Stabling may be ready for them at the Norfolk Arms if possible ; if not, in the Town in the immediate Neighbourhood.

" If the Landlord of the Norfolk Arms Inn should have occasion to write to the Duke of Wellington, it is requested that he will address the letter to Piccadilly, London."

This precious document was not only written by the Duke, but was copied by him in his own hand and endorsed by him thus :—

" To the Landlord of the Norfolk Arms Inn, Arundel, desiring him to have a pair of horses to take the Carriage to the Castle."

The mention of this letter irresistibly draws one to the more humorous aspect of the Duke's correspondence. It is in that, indeed, that his true characteristics as a writer are most evident. The desire to be fully explanatory, to convey exactly the feeling of the writer's mind, and to give full effect to the sentiment or rebuke that inspires the letter, is what always marks the Duke's epistles. It is the result, one cannot doubt, of a long training in the value of detail, added to a severe conscientiousness. He would, when he was sixty-eight, write fifty letters in a morning. " I declare that I dread," he said to Lady Salisbury, " going into my own house, from the heaps of letters that are ready to receive me there." And yet he answered them all, even down to a washerwoman who begged him to pay his son's bill, a quack who desired to advertise a pill, and an impudent lady who sent a mysterious box to Apsley House.

It is a distinct addition to the literature of the country

that is gained by the decision, which we may now regard as final, of the authenticity of the Duke's correspondence with Miss Jenkins. From this brilliant collection I venture to reprint a few gems. The lady, it will be remembered, was anxious to convert the Duke to her own Evangelical opinions, and was not averse to completing her work by becoming Duchess of Wellington. In his replies, extending over seventeen years, to the warm epistles of the beautiful damsel, the Duke is, as Mr. Michael Finsbury said of his didactic uncle, "incredible." If it seems unkind to laugh at the great man's weakness, it must be remembered that it is laughter which, as an old Lothario, he richly deserved. Here, first, are two specimens which illustrate the excellences of his method as well as establish what has already been observed above.

"LONDON, *July 24th*, 1835.

"MY DEAR MISS J.,—

"I received your Letter by the Post written on Wednesday ; and have this day received that written in London to inform me that you was about to go to Harrowgate. I am much obliged to you for both.

"It is true that I am in the habit of writing Answers to all Letters. But I feel great satisfaction in writing to some ; to those in particular from whom I am desirous of receiving Letters, and who express a Desire to hear from me.

"I am very glad that you corrected your first Impressions respecting your Preacher. I believe that we cannot too frequently pass in revision our opinions upon what passes before us. We shall find ourselves frequently in Error.

"I sincerely hope that the Waters of Harrowgate may have the effect of restoring Your Health entirely.

Believe me Ever Yours most sincerely,

"W."

A week later came the following :—

"MY DEAR MISS J.,—

"I have received your letter of the 31st, and I am really much concerned to learn that I have again created a feeling of displeasure in your Mind by having omitted the Inconvenience which you felt from your Journey to Harrowgate.

"There is always Inconvenience in travelling in a Stage Coach. It cannot be otherwise. Indeed, it is wonderful that there should be so little ; and I must observe that there is less of a physical and personal Nature in travelling in this Manner in England than elsewhere. The inconvenience felt in England is of a moral and mental description. It is formed of the trash and nonsense which a traveller is condemned to hear in these vehicles ; because everybody talks ; and says not what he thinks but what the fancy of the Moment suggests. For this which was the particular Inconvenience which you suffered upon this Journey, there is no remedy, but *Patience ;* and I would add *Silence.*

"You would practice neither. You would not sit *patiently* and hear the stupid Irreligion of the Talker ; you would reply to Him ; and this occasioned much of the Annoyance which occurred.

"I find that I am again taking your part instead of my own. I do so in my own satisfaction. If you are not satisfied with my observations, you will at least perceive that I had read, nay, more, reflected upon your Letter and the account you gave of yourself.

"But why should you torment yourself by thinking that I did not read, and did not care for what you represented that you suffered. You must be aware that you are mistaken !

"Believe me Ever Yours most sincerely,
"W."

The Duke was very careful, in another letter, to explain that he was far from meaning that Christians should not defend their faith, but, in one of those happy phrases which often come as an unconscious inspiration to those who are unaccustomed to literature, he added that he did not think it a lady's duty " to answer every wandering blasphemer."

These letters are very deferential, and to the verge of

affection. Here he is in his weakest vein ; now we may read one decidedly sharper.

> "WALMER CASTLE, *Novr.* 3, 1835.
>
> "The Duke of Wellington presents his Compliments to Miss J.
>
> "He received only this morning Miss J.'s Letters of the 28th and 31st October.
>
> "The Duke returns his thanks to Miss J. for her kind Enquiries about his Health. The Duke was unwell for one day ; of which the Newspapers obtained Intelligence : and, as usual, misrepresented and exaggerated the facts.
>
> "The Duke is much concerned that Miss J. is not satisfied with the formal style of His Notes. She was not satisfied when he wrote to her in a form more consistent with familiarity. Such form was considered disrespectful.
>
> "The Duke assures Miss J. that he can reply to any letter which she may think proper to address the Duke in one form as the other."

Side by side with this may be placed some words of advice from another letter.

> "Prudence and Discretion would appear to require that Miss J. should not rebuke a gentleman for Words spoken not to Her ; not even in her Presence ; but to her Landlady in the relation of a Lodger in the House. The Duke may be wrong. But he considers the exercise of Prudence and Discretion in this not unbecoming to any character however exalted."

It is tempting to continue, but the temptation is one which would be as dangerous as the Duke's own conscientiousness. Let me conclude with one more letter, written when the great soldier's patience was exhausted.

> "STRATHFIELDSAYE, *Dec.* 21, 1850.
>
> "Field-Marshal the Duke of Wellington presents His Compliments to Miss J.! He understood from a former

letter ; that it was Miss J.'s desire never to hear from the Duke again.

" Therefore he did not write ! nor should he write now ! excepting as a mere matter of Courtesy ! He thus finally takes His leave !

" WELLINGTON."

And this was not the last letter !

In all this the Duke appears very characteristically, but not at his best. There is a touch of the chivalrous politeness which marked him conspicuously. I remember that I used to be told as a child by my mother that she had often seen him come out of Apsley House, and when the crossing sweeper saluted him, take off his hat in reply. It was an old-fashioned courtesy that we were brought up in, after his model, just as we were taught to like a hard mattress, such as he had at Walmer, and to abhor a feather bed. There is in these letters a touch of this old-fashioned and universal courtesy, punctilious alike to relations and to inferiors ; but there is nothing of the deeper feeling, equally or even more genuine, which is shown in the letters to Lady Burghersh. There the Duke shows himself a really affectionate and thoughtful kinsman, constantly looking out to give pleasure to others and with that kindest of all forms of thoughtfulness, the memory of the little troubles or little joys of children, and uninteresting spinsters, and poor people. The letters too on Lord Mornington's illness and death show how ready he was to take pains to comfort others, to be assiduous in sitting by their sick beds, and thoughtful in everything that would cheer their last hours.

The features in his character which it is most pleasant to recall are his consideration and charity. " The kindness of his heart," wrote Lady Westmorland (the Lady Burghersh of earlier days) in 1852, " showed itself in his love of children from the earliest age, the delight he took in their prattle and remarks, and his dislike to any severity being used towards them. He liked to praise them, and always said the best way to make a child good was to show him that he was considered a good child. He was considerate to his servants, and did not like his carriages and horses to be used at the hours of their meals. His charities were extensive, but mostly secret. He did not like putting his name to subscriptions, but often sent large sums privately." And there is a charming story, which is Lady Burghersh's too, of his begging a footman's pardon. " Yes, I was wrong. I am very sorry, William, and I beg your pardon."

Perhaps the reaction was inevitable which has made men criticize the great Duke sharply during the last few years; but his letters, if they allow us to laugh at him, give us cause to admire and respect him too.

servants, and did not like his carriages and horses to be used at the hours of their meals. His charities were exten-sive, but mostly secret. He did not like putting his name to subscriptions, but often sent large sums privately. And there is a charming story, which is Lady Burghersh's too, of his begging a footman's pardon. "Yes, I was wrong. I am very sorry, William, and I beg your pardon." Perhaps the reaction was inevitable which has made men criticize the great Duke sharply during the last few years, but his letters, if they allow us to laugh at him, give us cause to admire and respect him too.

A Warwickshire Coterie

A WARWICKSHIRE COTERIE

AMONG the figures which cross the stage like dim, ghostly apparitions in Johnson's *Lives of the Poets* there are some here and there whose pleasant memories it would not be an unhappy task to revive. A few thin volumes preserve such of their lucubrations as themselves, or their friends, thought worthy of print ; and the albums of eighteenth-century bluestockings or dilettante clergymen often contain some other odes or elegies which achieved no public fame. Among these memories it has often seemed to me that there is one coterie which deserves resurrection, and that with some touch, not too elaborate, of homage.

The Warwickshire circle of the reign of George II. has some pleasant associations, and I should like nothing better than to search among the dwellings and the churches with which it was connected for some surviving memorials of its kindly and not ungraceful existence. It has left works in modest abundance, poems of different degrees of artificiality, and letters of a charm which seems to us to-day curiously old-world, quiet, and complacent. The names which are most naturally recalled are those of Shenstone and Jago, Somervile and Lady Luxborough, and Richard Graves. But there are others, whom the curious may discover among the letters of these constant correspondents, who might, perhaps, be traced with difficulty and prove to have some interest beyond that of the shadows which await on the glimmering lights we know. Among such are Outing, and Wheatley, and Lord Stamford, and Mr. Whistler, not to forget those two gentlemen, Mr. Nixon and Mr. Tracey, who wrote verses to Mr. Somervile " on his poem *The Chase*." Of Mr. Whistler, I like to remember that he dwelt in the southernmost part of Oxfordshire, in " a very small box " in the village where his mother, now married to a clergyman of fortune, resided in the manor-house, that "he lived in an elegant style, and was visited by all the genteel families of the neighbourhood." There were the Duchess of Somerset, too, widow of Duke Algernon, James West, the Antiquary, of Alscot Park, about three miles from Stratford-on-Avon; and Mr. Miller of Radway; and if we go a little farther, or more into the world, we come to the Lyttelton family, with their connexions the Grenvilles and the Pitts. It is a circle that widens continually.

One word, by the way, as to this Duchess of Somerset, for if you penetrate into this coterie, you are like to hear so much of her. She was Frances, eldest daughter and co-heiress of Henry Thynne, the only son of Thomas, first Viscount Weymouth. In 1713 she married Algernon Seymour, Earl of Hertford, who had fought under Marlborough. He became Duke of Somerset in 1748, and died in 1750. She was something not far removed from a blue-stocking, and poets fluttered round her like bees. Thomson dedicated his " Spring " to her in 1728, and Shenstone's verses are full of her. It was she who won Savage's pardon, when he had been condemned for murder. In the later years of her life she gave herself almost entirely to books and bookmen. [1]

After the Duke's death she " lived retired at her seat near Colnebrook, which they had purchased of Lord Bathurst and called Percy Lodge (its common name being Richings); and this is the place so often mentioned in the works of Shenstone and other poets of her time, by whom she was most deservedly admired and celebrated for her fine taste, distinguished genius, amiable manner, and exalted virtues."

[1] Mr. Coldicott kindly helps me by saying: " It is quite true that in ' Rural Elegance,' written in 1750, and elsewhere, Shenstone refers to the Duchess of Somerset, but on 20 Nov., 1753, the Duchess declined the dedication, and requested Shenstone, whenever her name or that of Percy Lodge occurs, to fill the blank with ' stars, dashes, or any other mark you please.' [Hull, page 182.]"

Her first connexion with Lady Luxborough brings in the
name of " the ingenious Dr. Dalton, to whom the stage is
indebted for the revival of Milton's *Comus*," and on whose
account it was—Horace Walpole says—that Lord Luxborough sent his wife into retirement. Dalton was the
tutor of Lady Hertford's boy, George Seymour, Viscount
Beauchamp, who died of smallpox at Boulogne in 1748.
The Duchess lived till 1754, and lies in Westminster Abbey
beside her husband. More about this good lady can be
found in Hull's *Select Letters between the late Duchess of
Somerset, Lady Luxborough, Miss Dolman, Mr. Whistler,
Mr. R. Dodsley, William Shenstone, Esq., and others* (1778),
a book I have hitherto been unable to procure.

The literary interest of the coterie is to be found in two
directions. They wrote very good letters ; not at all
stilted, very slightly artificial, concerned, perhaps, with
very small interests, but very kindly, good-humoured,
gracious, and charitable. Shenstone's letters are quite
charming. They touch quite the high-water mark of
middle-aged complacency. He wrote, for the only reason
which should ever cause people to write to their friends,
because he knew that those he wrote to cared to hear from
him and wanted to know about all his petty activities, just
as if they were living in the same house with him and could
watch him, out of those plain strait windows at the
Leasowes, planting and trimming and draining and inscrib-
ing epigrams on classic urns. " Pray, is laziness an excuse
for not writing ? " he says. It is not one he will accept
for himself, if he delays inditing a letter :—

" I have indeed," he says, " been pretty busy at home
raising a pool-dam, and have interchanged a few visits with
such of my acquaintance as live within three miles. What
then ?—I abominate all excuses that are grounded upon the
business or amusements of an idle man—as if such a person's
time was so wholly filled up that he could not find half an
hour to write a line to his friend. It is best to acknowledge
laziness at first, and that there are particular intervals
when one is much less disposed to write even a few lines
than at others ; and then, as to laziness, one has nothing

to do but to plead human frailty, which, if a person has not too many frailties besides, may, perhaps, be indulged him."

In comparison with the laborious ineptitudes of many busy men, of course Shenstone's ways were not lazy at all. He piped a tuneful note, he made a beautiful garden ground—alas! that it is destroyed; yet it was well worth the pilgrimage I made to Hales-Owen to see it, "ruinated" though it be—and he was a most agreeable, kind writer of letters. Lady Luxborough again was delightful as a correspondent: just a little timid, poor lady, as was natural in her state; but a kind, gracious, affectionate friend, with the nice manners, which are backed by real kindness where they do not mean real personal interest, that belong to good breeding. Not only that uncommon volume of her letters which was published after her death is worth reading, but also her correspondence with her famous half-brother, my Lord Bolingbroke. Of the others, one may say that people generally forget what they wrote. The innumerable works of the Reverend Richard Graves are, I find, very difficult to obtain, but only because they lie undisturbed on old bookcases and no modern man of letters has tried to give them a vogue. Yet in its time *The Spiritual Quixote*—a very delightful book—" had an enormous vogue," as Mrs. Humphry Ward says (I wonder how she knows) had the Book of Daniel. *The Chace*, by William Somervile, you find on old bookshelves in country houses; it is high time it were reprinted, with coloured prints of its own day. And *Hobbinol, or the Rural Games*, which also had its sixth edition in 1773, is not to be forgotten. Perhaps it is the Dover games he commemorates, as did the poets a hundred years before him and more in *Annalia Dubrensia*, and Mr. Ashbee has done just now in his delightful *Last Records of a Cotswold Community*. He dedicated the work to Mr. Hogarth, saying, amid pretty compliments, " In this, at least, let us both agree, to make vice and folly the object of our ridicule ; and we cannot fail to be of some service to mankind."

Not many people know anything of the Rev. Richard Jago's " pleasing elegy, *The Blackbirds*." The fact is that these people did not write for money ; still less did they write, as a delightful old Yorkshireman in humble life, an antiquary and *raconteur* at Knaresborough, said to me disparagingly of certain antiquaries whom he contemned beside the great Bishop Stubbs, " for writing's säake." They wrote to amuse themselves and their friends, and so they wrote easily and happily. To borrow what Dr. Johnson said of Somervile, for really it is applicable to them all, though, perhaps, they did not in any kind of literature reach such excellence as to raise much envy, it may commonly be said, at least, of any one of them, that " he writes very well for a gentleman." Of Somervile says the light-handed *arbiter elegantiarum* who wrote the *Lives of the Poets*, " his serious pieces are sometimes elevated, and his trifles are sometimes elegant ; " and again :—

" His subjects are such as require no great depth of thought or energy of expression. His fables are generally stale, and therefore excite no curiosity. Of his favourite, *The Two Springs*, the fiction is unnatural and the moral inconsequential."

The *habitué* of Fleet Street was not quite at home in field sports, so we may accept with no great seriousness the faint praise that he gives to *The Chace ;* but we delight in the way he turns the subject :—

" With still less judgement did he chuse blank verse as the vehicle of *Rural Sports*. If blank verse be not tumid and gorgeous, it is crippled prose; and familiar images in laboured language have nothing to recommend them but absurd novelty, which, wanting the attractions of Nature, cannot please long. One excellence of the *Splendid Shilling* is that it is short. Disguise can gratify no longer than it deceives."

Some such ingenious way of departing from strict relevancy seems desirable for all those who would embark upon a criticism of the works of these gentlemanly people—for I insist that they were not genteel, they were gentlemanly —who dwelt on the borders of Worcester and Warwick, or—not to be too strict as to county boundaries—in the district round about. Solihull, which is not, I fancy, quite the same sort of a place now as in 1725 or so when they went to school there, was probably the first link between Shenstone and Jago. Then they and Graves were friends together at Oxford, a time described in quite delicious manner by the last in his *Recollection of Some Particulars in the Life of the late William Shenstone, Esq.* (Dodsley, 1788), a rather rare book about which I should like to say a great deal, but have now " nor time nor place." Jago was of University College, where, I am afraid, Shelley has eclipsed his fame, but Graves and Shenstone were of Pembroke, and there, in their happy undergraduate days, they made friends with Mr. Whistler, spent a " morning's lounge," and almost every evening " read plays and poetry, *Spectators* or *Tatlers*, and other works of easy digestion ; and sipped Florence wine." I cannot forbear to tell how Mr. Graves describes the third member of the Pembroke trio :—

" Mr. Whistler was a young man of great delicacy of sentiment ; and though, with every assistance at Eton, he had such a dislike to learning languages that he could not read the Classics in the original, no one formed a better judgment of them. He wrote great part of a tragedy on the story of Dido ; printed a mock-heroic poem, called the Shuttlecock ; and left other MSS. which would be no discredit to his memory."

When the not too industrious days at Oxford were over, the literary coterie in the Warwick lands began. Beaudesert, by Henley-in-Arden, where Jago's father was parson, is not far from Barrells, the home of Henrietta Luxborough. A few miles further south is Snitterfield, where Jago was vicar from 1754 to 1781, and on the way there was Edstone Hall, the residence of William Somervile, Esq., not only the poet of the Chase, but also " a useful justice of the peace." A little farther off, in an opposite direction, was the Leasowes, by Hales-Owen, but it was not beyond a drive, and Shenstone was glad, indeed, when he journeyed to see " Asteria, Queen of May," the lady of Barrells :—

> When lo ! in happier hour,
> I leave behind my native mead,
> To range where Zeal and Friendship lead,
> To visit Luxborough's honoured bower.

A WARWICKSHIRE COTERIE

And then, again, on the other side of Stratford, but in Gloucestershire, is Mickleton, the ancestral home of Graves. The district gives one many fine places of pilgrimage, and I wish for nothing better than the chance to visit those I have not seen. People tell that a Bishop of Worcester in the last century said that Wootton Wawwen, between Edstone and Beaudesert, had the "most delightful church in the whole of his diocese." There William Somervile is buried. Thus they translate his epitaph, which Shenstone wrote : I have not seen the original :—

HERE LIES BURIED

WILLIAM SOMERVILE, Gentleman,

WHO DIED 17 JULY, 1742.

IF YOU DISCERN ANYTHING GOOD IN ME IMITATE IT.
IF YOU SEE A FAULT IN ME, AVOID IT WITH YOUR UTMOST
STRENGTH. TRUST IN CHRIST, FOR KNOW THAT
YOUR LIFE IS UNCERTAIN, AND DEATH IS SURE.

It could not be, for the man, more kindly or more happily penned. These men certainly had the art to tell in Christian spirit each other's failings and their own ; and it is a pleasant savour that they leave behind them. It was Shenstone's lot to commemorate Somervile, and Jago's, in his poem of "Edgehill," to regret the loss of Shenstone. For Graves there was a much longer life of recollection. In his old age, as rector of Claverton, he walked into Bath almost every day, and belonged to a new literary society, vastly inferior to that of his youth, which gathered round a bluestocking at Bath Easton, the Mrs. Leo Hunter of her age. Of this *The Festoon* (1766), and *Euphrosyne, or Amusements on the Road of Life* (1776), contain part of the record. But the author of the *Spiritual Quixote* was a writer of much more skill than these little jokes of the poetaster would suggest. Of him I shall have more to say.

Several of these personages, it will be seen, were clergymen. Perhaps some will say when they read their books that they might have been better employed ; perhaps Crabbe would have said so, because he wrote better. So they might, or worse. But I cannot think that the country clergy in the eighteenth century, who wrote so kindly as these men did, and belonged to so kindly a society, were bad parish priests. Certainly they knew their parishioners and their ways, to the life.

Shenstone, in 1741, wrote thus to a friend—probably it was Graves—when he took Holy Orders. It does not represent a high ideal, but it is probably very much what country gentlemen would have thought fifty, or a hundred, or even a hundred and fifty years later :—

"I want to be informed of the impression you receive from your new circumstances. The chief aversion which some people have to Orders is, what I fancy you will remove in such as you converse with. I take it to be owing partly to dress, and partly to the *avowed profession* of religion. A young clergyman that has distinguished his genius by a composition or two of a polite nature, and is capable of dressing *himself*, and his *religion*, in a different manner from the generality of his profession, that is, without formality, is certainly a genteel character. I speak not this with any sly design to advise, but to intimate that I think you are very capable of *shining* in a dark-coloured coat."

Advice or not, it was a course that Shenstone's friends generally followed. They did not give up Letters though they continued to wear their black coats.

Graves passed away from the Warwickshire party ; but a survivor of the brother clergy of Jago was the famous Dr. Parr. He affected quite a different style of literature, and he was an outrageous Whig to the verge of Radicalism. But then he was linked to Walter Savage Landor ; so the ghosts of the older poets might welcome him to their company. And I do not think that, as a representative of Warwickshire parsondom, even Shakespeare would have turned his back on him.

With the Lytteltons in politics and society, and Dr. Parr in politics and religion, there might be connecting links for this Warwick and Worcester assembly of cultivated people down to the present day. I remember an old man who kept a curiosity shop in the High Street of Warwick, who had been, I think, a page-boy to Dr. Parr. He recalled a good deal about him, his good humour and his bluff politics; but chiefly, I observed, that when he went out to dinner there were always placed beside him *two* plates from each of his favourite dishes.

But I must stay my pen, or I shall sink into mere garrulity; and I would not forget the words of Mr. Shenstone, that—

" Every single observation that is published by a man of genius, be it ever so trivial, should be esteemed of importance; because he speaks from his own impressions; whereas common men publish common things, which they have, perhaps, gleaned from frivolous writers."

Now, that is just what I have done; but these common things, I confess, interest me. They link the new country life to the old; and I cannot help thinking that it were worth tracing, in a literary history of Warwickshire, the links between William Shakespeare and Walter Savage Landor, through such common persons as Drayton and Somervile and Jago and Parr.

A PILGRIMAGE ACCOMPLISHED.

" I SHOULD like nothing better than to search among the dwellings and the churches with which it was connected for some surviving memorials of its kindly and not ungraceful existence "—so I wrote of " a Warwickshire Coterie " some months ago ; and now I have been able to make the pilgrimage I then suggested, and I should like to suggest it to others, too. Indeed, there is nothing more delightful in all England than the leafy lanes and homely villages of Warwickshire, the heart of our island. A summer's day in Arden—then and there you can see, if ever, how England, as the poets have known her, still remains. New houses are building everywhere, and you cannot go very far away from the railway, for you are within but a few miles of Birmingham, from which everything among the Middle English radiates ; but still the country is pure country, pastoral, woodland, sweeps of yellow corn and green pasturage, and it even keeps something of the forest that is forest no more.

When you begin to look more closely into the lives of the eighteenth-century writers of whom I have been thinking, you see that, with some eliminations, they belonged all to the Forest of Arden. Graves, the Gloucestershire man, who was once the vicar of Great Malvern, but for much the greater part of his life lived at Claverton, near Bath, we may put aside, for he comes only casually into the records of the others ; and with him might go Shenstone on the other side, because the Leasowes is not strictly in our forest land, save that Shenstone came so constantly into it—for he was really within a short drive—was so close a friend of Lady Luxborough's and Somervile's and Jago's, that we must rank him with the rest.

Lady Luxborough is really a subject by herself, but perhaps the best way to treat of her in this collection of memories is to make her the centre of the quest—her *Letters* illustrate the scenes better than any other book, though the others come for example and comment. It is her letters, indeed, that lead me to get out of the train at Lapworth on a very hot August morning and make my way to Broom Hall. Is it there, down in a valley amid a grove of ash-trees, in this rebuilt little farmhouse, certainly not a *ferme ornée*, but with a piece surviving of the old red brick at its best and topped by red tiles, with a grand sixteenth-century chimney, such as Warwickshire often shows, coming from a sloping roof, and one dear dormer which Lady Camper forbids me to call " sweetly pretty "—is it there that Miss Dolman lived, and the kindred of Shenstone ? Now that I have come all this way, and looked at the house, and photographed it, and gone back again, and read many pages of my Lady Luxborough's writing, I do not think that it is. Their Broome is probably a small parish now in Worcestershire—a skilled antiquary tells me—near Hagley. It is the place, then in Staffordshire, on whose parish clerk Shenstone wrote an epitaph.

Still, this Broom Hall is within the radius, and Lady Luxborough and her friends must have known it. We will go, with them, nearer home.

A delightful ride it is, but quite the most complicated I have ever taken. Every lane seems to have fifty turnings, and if you go the way you ought it is sure to be in just the opposite direction to where you think you should be going. There are trees overhanging our road wherever it turns, but now and then there is a free space, when you have mounted a hill and look over a wide expanse of rich pasture. Woods there are every mile or so, shrunk into mere copses, or sometimes with the rough ground around them seeming to belong to the old days when the poet's eye saw his Banished Duke there, among his co-mates and brothers in exile, in life more sweet than that of painted pomp. Such a view of park and woodland is before you when you stand on the brow of a hill which overlooks Umberslade Park. A tall obelisk of grey stone, without a word of inscription, surmounted by a star, points the spot where you should take your place ; and then you stand on a champaign country such as only England can show. The Park was, in the eighteenth century, the home of Lord Archer, and it was he who set up (in 1751, I fancy) this curious monument of nothing in particular. He designed for it, it would seem, a more curious completion, for Lady Luxborough says to Shenstone, " Lord Archer's copper Globe and Cross, gilt, are coming by the carrier from London, for the Obelisk." A poet, too, commemorated the scene :—

> See, how the pillar'd Isles and stately Dome
> Brighten the Woodland-shade ! while scatter'd Hills,
> Airy, and light, in many a conic Form,
> A Theatre compose, grotesque and wild,
> And, with their shaggy Sides, contract the Vale
> Winding, in straiten'd Circuit, round their Base.
> Beneath their waving Umbrage FLORA spreads
> Her spotted Couch, Primrose and Hyacinth
> Profuse, with Ev'ry simpler Bud that blows
> On Hill or Dale . . .
> . . . Such UMBERSLADE !
> In the sweet contest join'd ! with livelier charms
> Intent t' illumine ARDEN's leafy gloom !

So the Reverend Richard Jago, in his *Edge Hill ; or, The Rural Prospect Delineated and Moralized* (to which the Right Hon. Lord Archer was a subscriber). Lord Archer, however much or little his handsome house deserved this far from brilliant panegyric, was one of Lady Luxborough's few neighbours of her own rank who were also friends. They dined and supped at each others' houses without ceremony, and my lord was so good as to inquire after Mr. Shenstone and to add " that a gentleman had told him lately that yours "—says Lady Luxborough to her friend—" was the prettiest and most elegant place in all these parts ; " and when he was told it was but a *ferme ornée* he said, " What is more agreeable ? It is the very thing one would choose ; and what I have heard Lord Bolingbroke made Dawley."

In that famous lampoon " The Abbey of Kilkhampton or Monumental Records for the year 1980," Lord Archer is thus described :—

" On a plain stone, almost concealed from Observation—

A PILGRIMAGE ACCOMPLISHED

"HERE LIETH LORD A——
WHOSE INSIGNIFICANCE PROTECTED HIM, WHILE LIVING, EVEN FROM CONTEMPT,
HIS MIND WAS UNACQUAINTED WITH ANY SENTIMENT THAT MIGHT HAVE DIGNIFIED
THE MEANEST OF HIS COMPANIONS,
WHOM HE SELECTED FROM THE MOST WRETCHED CLASS OF MORTALS.
HIS CONVERSATION PARTOOK SOMEWHAT MORE LIBERALLY OF
THE BOORISH VULGARITY WHICH DISTINGUISHED HIS ASSOCIATES,
THAN THE EXCESS OF HIS OWN NATURAL STUPIDITY;
HE PASSED THE YOUNGER PERIOD OF HIS LIFE IN A BARN,
MARRIED IN A FISHING-SMACK,
AND DIED, UNLAMENTED, IN THE HONOURABLE EXERCISE OF
BASKET-MAKING."

How the poor man deserved all this I do not know.   He seems to have been capable at least of politeness to Lady Luxborough and in regard to Mr. Shenstone.   Umberslade, with its great, well-timbered park, was certainly nothing like the humble acres of the Leasowes : it was, and is, a fine " place ; " but there is no Lord Archer now, and I do not know if the family has left any descendants.[1]

A few miles' ride, up and down, through a land thickly wooded, and we come to Ullenhall.   A large new church— locked, I regret to say—has superseded the old, small chapel of which Lady Luxborough writes, but in what remains of the older edifice lie the Knights, moved from Wootten Wawen.   For a time the remains of the Knights, after the removal, rested in a mausoleum in the Park, which Lord Catherlough built for himself.   It was taken down in 1830 (at a cost of £23 6s. 2d.) and the eleven bodies were re- moved to Ullenhall Chapel.   Barrells itself has been almost entirely rebuilt.   One wing, a few rooms only at most, on which the arms of the Earl of Catherlough appear, belongs to the time of our Warwickshire coterie.   A word about the persons who lived there.   Robert Knight, son of the cashier of the South Sea Company (as Horace Walpole noted in his copy of Lady Luxborough's *Letters*—a copy, by the way, which fell into the hands of

[1] Mr. Coldicolt kindly writes to me : "The last Lord Archer, who died 25 April, 1778, aged 41, left four daughters by Sarah, daughter of James West, of Alscot.   Umberslade came by marriage to the Earl of Plymouth, who sold it to Bolton King, who disposed of it to G. F. Muntz, the father of the present owner.   The Park in its present dimensions is comparatively modern."

the late Dr. John Taylor Brown, who described it in his *Bibliomania* (1867) : it was sold for an absurd sum last year at Sotheby's), married Henrietta St. John, the daughter of Lord St. John, Bolingbroke's father, and Angelica Magdalen, daughter of Georges Pelisary, Treasurer-General of the Marine under Louis XIV. As to his separation from his wife, the cause of which Horace Walpole seems to consider certainly to have been her grievous fault, I need say nothing. Mr. Sichel, in his exhaustive *Bolingbroke*, rightly discounts Walpole's slanders, and Lady Luxborough does not write like a bad woman. Her husband was certainly not a good man. Knight was created Lord Luxborough —the name of his house near Chigwell—in 1746, and, after his wife's death, Earl of Catherlough. He left no heirs to his titles. It was at Barrells that Henrietta lived after her separation from her husband. There she made friends with her literary and clerical neighbours, with Jago and Shenstone and Somervile, with Mr. Outing, who seems to have been a sort of secretary, or steward, as well as a friend, with one good country parson, Mr. Holyoake, and with another, Mr. Hall, who is described as " round, fat, and oily." Her only son died quite young, her daughter, Mrs. Wymondsold of Lockinge in Berkshire, whose house is " sung " in Pye's wonderful Thames poem, (sometimes spelled Wymondsell—Mr. Sichel has curiously misread it Wymondfold), ran away from her husband, was divorced, and married again. Lady Luxborough was under bond, on the separation from her husband, not to go within twenty miles of London, or on the Bath-road ; but she might, strangely, go to Bath itself, and did. Her only distractions seem to have been a very genuine affection for Shenstone —whom in her letters she treated as an idol of poetic and literary excellence—and a keen interest in the manufacture of a landscape after his model. The letters are full of avenues, and views, and hermitages, and arbours, and waterfalls, and seats, and urns. Almost every trace of the poor lady's industrious efforts was swept away by the Knights who succeeded her. You can only find the remains of one of the walks and hardly any objects she speaks of

in her letters—so an antiquary, full of all local lore, tells
me. But there is the ruined semblance of a ravine, not
far from the house, which irresistibly recalls a similar
piece of ingenuity at the Leasowes, and in it the ruins of
a hermitage. You see the resemblance at once, if you have
been to both places—as few have. And there still survives,
in its last days, the " great double oak," of which she writes,
where she would place an urn, by " the new entrance at
the corner of the Pit "—that Pit the ravine I speak of.
There a soldier from Worcester played the German flute
to her ; " it sounded so well as I walked among the trees."

Shenstone was, no doubt, the focus for both her interests.
Her letters to her brother, the famous Bolingbroke, are not,
to my mind, half so fresh and natural as those to the poet,
yet, perhaps, it was from the first that she learned the love
of gardening, which was developed by the instruction of
the second. She is perfectly happy when she is speaking
of planting trees and modelling urns, of narrow, winding
paths, of venerable trunks, of " reserving glades for the
prospects, but hiding the house and gardens, and of placing
the urn there, as much surrounded with evergreens as
possible, and having a small entrance from the field, in the
nook near the corner of the Pit." She scrawls upon bits
of rumpled paper. She protests that she has no power to
draw the French horn that she designs for Mr. Somervile's
urn, and then she draws it very well indeed, and after she
has told all the little news of her little circle, asked for new
books and pamphlets, mentioned as new the lines in a
Country Churchyard, and put in a few words about the
oddness of full-bottomed wigs on a tomb, she must add a
second postscript—" One word more about Urns."

It is all very gracious trifling, and as one sees the park
of Barrells in the bright August sun, one does not think
with unkindness of the poor lady who bore such a brave,
kindly heart, so ready to amuse and be amused, in the
dark days of her waning life. It is pleasant to remember
that her first welcome in her banishment to Barrells was
from the country parsons and their wives. Of this more in
another paper.

A PILGRIMAGE ACCOMPLISHED—II

IN the eighteenth century the country clergy certainly had the characteristic note of charity, which I do not think that in England they have ever lacked. It was not kind of Lady Luxborough to write to Shenstone—" I like your fancy of making your parson Bishop of Nova Scotia, which would be making him of some use." Their quarrel was only about gardening ! :—

" I have not," she continues, " experienced the good luck you wish me with ecclesiastics ; so cannot say anything in their favour ; though I wish I could, because of their function, which puts it in their power to do good or hurt, and they generally choose the latter."

This is a mere fit of ill nature; for, as I have said, nobody was so kind to Lady Luxborough as her clerical friends. They and their wives were her most constant companions ; they certainly had the charity which she for once lacked ; they were eager to see the best in their people.

At Henley-in-Arden, in 1739, lived the young Mr. Richard Jago, son of the rector of Beaudesert. " You, sir," wrote Lady Luxborough to him, " have the art to describe the most simple things with the nicest elegance (as appears by your Pastoral)." The Pastoral is " Ardenna," an eclogue with the beloved forest for subject. Did Lady Luxborough, or Shenstone, or Jago, think that her ladyship was, perhaps, remembered in the lines :—

> Escap'd from all the busy world admires
> Hither the philosophic dame retires ;
> For in the busy world, or poets feign,
> Intemp'rate vice and giddy pleasures reign ;
> Then, when from crowds the Loves and Graces flew,
> To these lone shades the beauteous maid withdrew,
> To study Nature in this calm retreat
> And with confed'rate Art her charms compleat.

The beauteous maid was, of course, Ardenna herself ; but then there may have been a polite intent to personify her for the moment in the guise of the lady of Barrells.

Henley-in-Arden is still a delightful place, such as might inspire a better poet than Mr. Jago. A local guide-book complains that it is not " vivacious," for which, at least, we may be thankful. It has an entirely peaceful, decorous street of beautiful half-timbered houses, quaint, respectable, dignified even, a fit centre for the forest of which it is the capital. It is not too rustic to be a town, and certainly it is not too urban to be in the heart of the country. One church it has, of late Perpendicular style, good and solemn enough ; but only a few yards away, across the little Alne, is the church of Beaudesert, which Jago's father served, and where there is a tablet to his memory. A fine Norman church it was originally, the chapel, it may be, of the Mont-forts' castle hard by. Still there remain fine Norman doorways, and an exquisite little chancel, a noble arch, pure Norman—the whole sanctuary, with so few compeers left in England, most like, perhaps, of all that remain, the chancel of Hampnett, on the Cotswolds, but, unlike that, free from modern confusion of decorative addition. The admirable fourteenth and fifteenth century work at Beau-desert is no bad setting for the Norman. There is fine Perpendicular ornament on the outside of the tower, and there are many other happy curiosities of design here and there—a beautiful church, well kept, if not unharmed by restoration. Thus early the Warwickshire forest was penetrated by the Church. The lords who came into its fast-nesses did not forget the people's needs, and when their castles perished they left happier memorials of their work in the land where lay, in the words of that notable treatise the *Dialogus de Scaccario*, " eorum maximae deliciae."

The district of Henley-in-Arden, " exempt from public haunt," finds not its only " tongues in trees," for the churches that Shakespeare saw, and, it may be, worshipped in, still survive to connect the modern life with the older time. Beautiful though Beaudesert is, a few miles further on is a still more interesting church—that of Wootten

Wawen. I will not enter into the controversy as to the open door, or wonder if it were not possible to find an old woman for custodian so that there might not be an hour's delay, perhaps, before one could see within. They speak of outrages from trippers, and I know there are sad instances of desecration ; yet surely a church open and well cared for is the best protection against such outrages. However, we entered the church ; when we were inside we did not wonder at the praise of Bishops and antiquaries. As to the Saxon origin of it, and the Saxon work, if such it be, here and there, we may leave that for the archæologists to dispute about. The fine Perpendicular woodwork, the modern glass, will have their admirers ; the wonderful sanctuary, belonging to remote days, and the worship that S. Wulstan himself may have joined in, sets its seal of antiquity and reverence on the whole. On the south side of the chancel, and stretching as far eastwards, is the damp, neglected chapel where the family of the Knights was laid to rest. There is no record of Lady Luxborough, but others—her unsympathetic kindred, and her son and daughter—are there commemorated. Too much memory there is of the stern and selfish husband, the first and last Earl of Catherlough. If Henrietta Luxborough has no claim to be remembered here, he, at least, might be passed by with less of pomp and eulogy. But the monument of which I am in search is another, and I find at last the Latin inscription, which books have preferred to translate.

H. S. E.

GULIELMI SOMERVILE ARMIG.

OBIIT 17 JULIJ, 1742.

SI QUID IN ME BONI COMPERTUM HABEAS IMITARE.

SI QUID MALI TOTIS VIRIBUS EVITA.

CHRISTO CONFIDE.

ET SCIAS TE QUOQUE FRAGILEM ESSE

ET MORTALEM.

It is good in the English, but really much better in the Latin. We part with the author of *The Chase* in a very kindly spirit. His wife's death—she was Maria, daughter of Hugh Bethell, and she rests beside him—spoiled his breezy, out-of-door life ; but he was a sportsman to the last, and he bore till the end, through all his errors, the friendship of good men. It is impossible to read *The Chase* or the other rural diversions of his muse—insensibly one writes in the style of his intimates—without feeling an affection for the author.

It is this feeling which has made me collect what books I can about him. There is that pleasant copy of *The Chase* with Mr. Hugh Thomson's illustrations : there is the early edition with Walker's clever drawings—one " when the hunt's afoot " really delightful : and there is the 1796 with drawings by Stothard, and a critical essay by Aikin. Aikin says very truly of Somervile : " He is strictly and almost solely a descriptive poet ; and his talent lies in delineating actual scenes with fidelity and spirit, adorning them with the beauties of diction, but leaving them to act upon the imagination by their own force, without aid from the creations of fancy."

I have another and unique Somervile relic. It is a copy prepared for publication in Waldron's *Collection of Miscellaneous Poetry* (London 1802) of the first draught of *Hobbinol*, then first printed from Somervile's manuscript. It is called *The Wicker Chair, a Burlesque Poem in blank verse,* and it begins with a curious and interesting preface, explaining the origin of the verses. The author " a passionate lover of field sports," tells that he would go each winter in the hunting season to Gloucestershire for the pure air and good hunting country. The place was the Somerviles-Aston so often mentioned in Lady Luxborough's letters ; the place of residence was the house of a tenant, " a dry, drolling, subtle old fellow." Of this worthy Somervile writes that, " He knew very well how to keep up the dignity of a British freeholder abroad, and was a petty tyrant among the villagers at home. A majestic stately carriage, and an ardent passion for the fair sex, were the most distinguishing marks of his character ; two qualities the natural effects of health, ease and plenty. He was, it seems, remarkably fond of an old wicker chair, the legacy of his forefathers. Here he repos'd himself after the fatigue of visiting his flocks abroad ; here he smoak'd his pipe, regal'd himself with his toast and ale, and then very regularly fell asleep. This was his constant custom morning and afternoon, and in this favourite wicker, he often spent the greatest part of the night."

Dull, indeed, for Somervile, especially as the farmer's library was half dissenting theology and half books of farriery and the like. So he set to work, on the model of Phillips's *Cyder*, to describe the wicker chair and the adventures of its owner. The original version, which follows differs in many respects from the later *Hobbinol*, but the interest of both poems is now so slight that it is not worth while to particularize : the special feature of my copy is that the editor has profusely annotated it in MS. with references to Phillips and to Milton, showing how closely Somervile copied and parodied. In the volume is inserted in MS. the copy of a letter from Somervile to his kinsman, Lord Somervile, dated June 29, 1731. It compliments Lady Somervile's poetry, and talks of business and debts light-heartedly. Then, no doubt of Lady Hertford's son, George Seymour, " As for our friend George and his flaming equipage, let him blaze forth, if such is his will and pleasure, but he must give me leave to say that he wants no tinsel to set him off to advantage. How well it may become an Horse officer I will not presume to determine, but it is not very consistent with the gravity of a Justice of the Peace, and I soon expect to hear our noble squire at Combe has obtained the additional post and has deserted Pastor Fido and the works of Signor Maggi, for Dalton and Baker's Chronicles. A red coat, perhaps I shall allow, and it may be a gold button, but the devil a bit of lace or embroidery. When a man has two stations he must dress between both. He may pay all due regard to his Military Honours, without putting a slight upon his Civil Employment. Thus, merry I am to entertain your Lordship, but must assure you I am at heart, melancholy enough upon account of the condition of my poor wife, who continues very ill."

A PILGRIMAGE ACCOMPLISHED

The letter has never been printed, and no doubt there is little in it but a kindly view of the best English poet of sport. Edstone Hall was pulled down nearly a hundred years ago. The park is well wooded, and outside it the roads are sheltered by tall trees, the way is by pleasant, leafy lanes till you come to Snitterfield, where the third poet of the triad lived in his later days, he from whom during these last paragraphs I have parted, the ingenious and kindly Mr. Jago. On the brow of a hill climbs the village of Snitterfield, with prosperous, new houses dotted among the old. At the summit is the church, Decorated and Perpendicular, restored to the uttermost, but with a good deal of holland wrapping about, because there are bats there, they tell me. There are good Laudian rails; but the glory of the church is the Perpendicular woodwork in the choir, saints and mermaids, a Bishop and a boy angel, shields and standards, beautiful decorative panels, the best in all this district. It was at Snitterfield that Richard Jago, the poet of *Edgehill* and *The Blackbirds*, spent the later years of his life. He was given the vicarage in 1754, worth about 140*l.* a year then. He had been curate, but non-resident, before. He now lived in the vicarage for nearly thirty years, " both by his doctrine and example a faithful and worthy minister of the parish over which he presided," says the gentleman who wrote the account of his life for Mr. Dodsley in 1784, when he had been dead but three years. In the vestry is a simple stone, of which the inscription has never been completed :—

TO THE MEMORY

OF THE REV. RICHARD JAGO, M.A.

HE DEPARTED THIS LIFE

MAY 1781.

Jago's fame, such as it is, is due not to a few slight pieces which are very pleasant writing, but to the more ambitious efforts of *Edgehill* and *The Blackbirds*. The former has a certain interest still, because it preserves the names of the chief personages of the district in which he lived, and the illustrations show what the Warwickshire antiquities were

173

like in the middle of the eighteenth century. As to its style, almost any one could write like that who had a fair acquaintance with the classics and knew something of English verse.

But *The Blackbirds* still less deserves the eulogies lavished on it. It is an outrageous example of the audacity with which poets, or aspirants to poetry, will write of things about which they will not take the trouble to learn. How many people, I wonder, when they have read Matthew Arnold's glowing apostrophe to the " Elms of Great Tew," in his eulogy of Falkland, have known that there is hardly an elm in the village, that for a mile or two round, as well as in the famous hamlet itself, the characteristic tree, seen everywhere, in churchyard and by hedgerow, is the ash ? When Jago kindly says to the blackbird :—

> For thee the plaister'd nest I'll make

has he forgotten, or did he never know, though he lived all his life in the country, that the words might be appropriate if addressed to a thrush, but are out of all sense in regard to a blackbird, which never " plaisters " its nest ? When he speaks of the goldfinch as drawing " the pond'rous stick " to make his nest, and making that nest, too, in a currant bush, " an airy seat," he had taken leave of Nature, or never studied her. It is better than this when he writes a verse, about the man who shot the blackbird, which would have made his friend Somervile smile :—

> At him the gunner took his aim,
>   Too sure the volley'd thunder flew !
> O had he chose some other game,
>   Or shot—as he was wont to do !

But, after all, these are innocent amusements for the country parson. Jago was a good clergyman, and if he amused his friends by his verses, he amused himself, at least when old age came on, " at his leisure, in improving his vicarage-house and ornamenting his grounds, which were agreeably situated, and had many natural beauties."

These are trivial memories of people who were not very

important. "What numbers," said one of the party, "live to the age of fifty or sixty years, yet, if estimated by their merit, are not worth the price of a chick the moment it is hatched." I would be far from applying this epigram of Shenstone's to his friends. They were kindly people who did good in their generation, and they made country life for one particular district—and that a most delightful one, in the heart of Shakespeare's England—very happy, very interesting, and at least tinctured without affectation, with the love of letters and the arts. "Perhaps boors, rusticks, and esquires, make a principal figure in the country, as inanimates are always allowed to be the chief figures in a landskip." So said the same observer. The memories of the poets of Warwickshire and their friends that come down to us from the eighteenth century are not impressive or didactic, perhaps, but they are gracious and pleasant, like the three silver birches which Jago's daughter planted in the vicarage garden at Snitterfield, and which still wave their graceful boughs over the trim lawn.

A FORGOTTEN POET.

THE Cotswolds, I have often been tempted to say, have
no poet. I have been often contradicted ; and, indeed,
I am not eager to defend myself. There have been many
since Robert of Gloucester looked on the battle of Evesham
and saw the storm—'grisly,' as he calls it—sweep over
the hills, who have set down their thoughts in verse. I
certainly do not forget some charming lines of Mr. Norman Gale. But now I am inclined to think rather of one
who is forgotten—William Shenstone, who sought some
of his first subjects among the Cotswolds.

Though his chief fame circles round his own house of
the Leasowes, near Halesowen, he belongs not a little to
the country which lies between Stratford and Campden
and Cheltenham, as pretty a wooded hilly land as you may
see. It is near here that William Morris thought of settling before he went to Merton. Broadway, the too hackneyed resort of artists and Americans, a place far inferior
in picturesqueness to Campden, or to Willersey, its nearer
neighbour, is hard by. Shenstone himself knew all the
attractions of the district, and he did not forget that it was
Shakespeare who had given immortality to them all. Indeed, he was almost at his happiest when he wrote those
quaint lines that he called "Slender's Ghost." They begin :

> Beneath a churchyard yew,
>   Decay'd and worn with age,
> At dusk of eve methought I spy'd
> Poor Slender's ghost, that whimp'ring cry'd,
>   "O sweet, O sweet Anne Page."

176

Certainly we none of us doubt that Slender walked the streets of Stratford, and he may well have stepped out a few miles to where the yews grow round a church that Shenstone knew well,

> Where Avon rolls her winding stream,
> Avon, the Muse's fav'rite theme !
> Avon, that fills the farmer's purses,
> And decks with flow'rs both farms and verses.

So Shenstone wrote when he told a scandalous tale that happened " in Evesham Vale or near it." It was from Mickleton, where his close friend Graves (best remembered as the author of *The Spiritual Quixote*) lived, that he chiefly saw the Cotswolds. At Mickleton there is still the manor-house of Graves, built perhaps by the Porters and lived in by that peerless Endymion, the associate of all the Jacobean wits—a fine Elizabethan " mansion," as they call it. The church has the more abiding memorial of Shenstone. It is a fine Decorated building with some earlier work about it, a priest's chamber over the north porch, a large south aisle, and a fine spire. It is filled with monuments—of the Graves family and of earlier folk—but its most interesting memorial is that which Shenstone's friend put up " in memory of an extraordinary young woman, Utrecia Smith, the daughter of a worthy and learned clergyman who, on a small living of about fifty pounds a year, a curacy of thirty pounds, and a lifehold estate of about the same value, bred up two sons and two daughters in a genteel manner, and died at the age of ninety, without any other preferment. This daughter, Utrecia," said Mr. Graves, " at a time when the ladies did not so generally rival our sex in learning and ingenuity, from the books with which her father supplied her had formed to herself so good a taste of polite literature, and wrote so well in prose (and sometimes in verse), that a very ingenious clergyman, bred at a public school and a Master of Arts in the University, often said he was afraid to declare his opinion of any author till he previously knew hers."

The inscription runs thus:

BURFORD PAPERS

UTRECIAE SMITH
PUELLAE SIMPLICI, INNOCUAE, ELEGANTI
R. G.
UNA ACTAE MEMOR PUERITIAE
MOERENS POSUIT.
MDCCXLIV.

It is on this that Shenstone wrote his first elegy, which he called " Ophelia's Urn."

> Sure nought unhallow'd shall presume to stray
>   Where sleep the reliques of that virtuous maid ;
> Nor aught unlovely bend its devious way
>   Where soft Ophelia's dear remains are laid.

He was himself, so a manuscript note of an ancestor of mine tells me, an elegant writer of epitaphs. " Shenstone's epitaph on his amiable Relation," wrote my great-uncle in his copy of Johnson's *Lives*, " Miss Doleman, who died of the small-pox at the age of twenty-one, is one of the very rare modern Productions, that not only resembles, but rivals, the dignified and affecting conciseness of the Ancients in their sepulchral Inscriptions. It is worth volumes of his pastorals :

PERAMABILI SUAE CONSOBRINAE
M.D.
AH ! MARIA,
PUELLARUM ELEGANTISSIMA,
AH ! FLORE VENUSTATIS ABREPTA,
VALE !
HEU QUANTO MINUS EST
CUM RELIQUIS VERSARI,
QUAM TUI
MEMINISSE."

But to return. As it was the memory of Utrecia Smith that gave a subject for his first elegy, so it was in this neighbourhood that Shenstone was inspired by the mild passion of his life, the delight in the artifices of a garden maker. Mickleton, wrote the brother of the squire, " though in an indifferent country "—a statement which it is hard to forgive—" has many natural beauties ; of surrounding

178

hills, and hanging woods ; a spacious lawn, and one natural cascade : capable of great improvement, though, from various circumstances, the place is to this day in a very unfinished state." It was his friend's design that set Shenstone to work at the Leasowes, and there he wrought the mimic wonders which brought him so much fame and the tepid eulogy of Johnson—" that to embellish the form of Nature is an innocent form of amusement ; and some praise must be allowed by the most supercilious observer to him who does best what such multitudes are contending to do well."

Johnson's inimitable description of the foibles of this ingenious gentleman—" nothing raised his indignation more than to ask if there were any fishes in his water," and " in time his expenses brought clamours about him that overpowered the lamb's bleat and the linnet's song ; and his groves were haunted by beings very different from fauns and fairies "[1]—concerns us as little as Mr. Graves's serious defence. Shenstone has the artificiality of his age most of all when he strives to be natural, and we care but very tepidly for his waterfalls and groves, and not at all, when they are described in verse, for his hermitages and statues and urns. It is as a poet and a lover of country life that we think of him when we wander over the Cotswolds, for they were his first inspiration.

It was at Mickleton, where it would seem that he was first brought into a society above that in which he had been born, that he formed that delightful idea of the rich man's country paradise which is so characteristic of the ideals of the century and of the man :

" Had I a fortune of about eight or ten thousand pounds a year, I would, methinks, make myself a neighbourhood. I would first build a village with a church, and people it with inhabitants of some branch of trade that was suitable to the country round. I would then, at proper distances, erect a number of genteel boxes of about a thousand pounds

---

[1] There is a quaint little poem in the first volume of Shenstone's works (ed. 1765), pp. 217–18, called *The Poet and the Dun.*

apiece, and amuse myself with giving them all the advantages they could receive from taste. These would I people with a select number of well-chosen friends, assigning to each annually the sum of two hundred pounds for life. The salary would be irrevocable, in order to give them independency. The house of a more precarious tenure, that, in cases of ingratitude, I might introduce another inhabitant."

The picture needs no emphasis. Genteel boxes, at proper distances, would make an eighteenth-century Elysium ; and indeed the millionaires of the twentieth are likely to make a worse use of their money. But Shenstone adds, " How plausible however this may appear in speculation, perhaps a very natural and lively novel might be founded upon the inconvenient consequences of it, when put in execution."

He himself had certainly no chance to carry out such a design : he was obliged to be content with " the peace of solitude, the innocence of inactivity, and the unenvied security of an humble station," which, however they may have satisfied his modest ambition—and they hardly seem to have done so—can fill, as Johnson says, but a few pages of poetry. A few pages, and those perhaps artificial in every line. Yet the inspiration was natural, and it was only the trammels which convention placed upon a mind most submissive to such a despotism which prevented the heart of Shenstone from speaking freely. He is hampered by the absurdities of his day. The shepherdesses are too dainty for life. There is an air of Watteau in the background. And yet Shenstone is not nearly delicate enough for the style of the prince of Court painters, though he is not ready to advance to the robust naturalism of Crabbe. Here are some lines from one of his Cotswold elegies. Colin is " a discerning shepherd," and he laments the state of the woollen manufacture :

Near Avon's bank, on Arden's flow'ry plain,
A tuneful shepherd charm'd the list'ning wave ;
And sunny Cotsol' fondly lov'd the strain.
Yet not a garland crowns the shepherd's grave.

A FORGOTTEN POET

The shepherd—and indeed he was but Mr. Somervile in disguise—must needs die, and as he departs he advises his brother-shepherds to arouse the British statesman to arrest the craft of Gallia, and again procure for Britain the markets of the world. Then

> Britons for Britain shall the crook employ ;
> Britons for Britain's glory shear the fold.

It was a plaint that he learnt on the hills beside Mickleton :

> Where the wild thyme perfumes the purpled heath.

And as he walked through those pleasant lanes that run by Weston-sub-Edge he may well have written the lines :—

> And you, ye shepherds, lead my gentle sheep ;
> To breezy hills, or leafy shelters lead ;
> But if the sky with show'rs incessant weep,
> Avoid the putrid moisture of the mead.

The neighbourhood of Mickleton remained for many years full of attraction for Shenstone. It was there, says his friend Graves, that " he seems to have felt the first symptoms of that tender passion, which appears so conspicuous and predominant in most of his lyrics, and at length produced his much-admired *Pastoral Ballad* " ; and in 1743 he paid a long visit to Cheltenham, where he became attached to Miss C——, of whom the biographer " can hardly believe, as her sister was married to a baronet of considerable fortune, that " she, " in her bloom, would have condescended to marry a man, however deserving, of so small a fortune as Mr. Shenstone." On his way to Cheltenham once he " missed the road, and wandered till ten o'clock at night on the Cotswold Hills." It was this which brought out his seventh elegy, which comes as near perhaps to a description of the Cotswolds as anything else he ever wrote :—

> On distant heaths, beneath autumnal skies,
> Pensive I saw the circling shades descend ;
> Weary and faint I heard the storm arise,
> While the sun vanish'd like a faithless friend.

181

No kind companion led my steps aright ;
No friendly planet lent its glim'ring ray,
Ev'n the lone cot refus'd its wonted light,
Where toil in peaceful slumber clos'd the day.

Then the dale bell had giv'n a pleasing sound ;
The village cur 'twere transport then to hear ;
In dreadful silence all was hush'd around,
While the rude storm alone distress'd mine ear.

There is not much description here, certainly ; but he has caught and conveyed the chill that is felt so keenly on these high downs, and one may imagine him then writing the reflection that he afterwards set down : " How melancholy it is to travel late, upon any ambitious project, on a winter's night, and observe the light of cottages, where all the un-ambitious people are warm and happy, or at rest in their beds ! Some of them (says *Whistler*) as wretched as princes, for what we know to the contrary." But there is more perhaps of the Cotswold air in the " Irregular Ode after Sickness, 1749," in which he sings his return to " catch the verdure of the trees " :

Come, gentle air ! and, while the thickets bloom,
Convey the jasmin's breath divine,
Convey the woodbine's rich perfume,
Nor spare the sweet-leaft eglantine.
And may'st thou shun the rugged storm
Till health her wonted charms explain,
With rural pleasure in her train,
To greet me in her fairest form ;
While from this lofty mount I view
The sons of earth, the vulgar crew,
Anxious for futile gains, beneath me stray,
And seek with erring step contentment's obvious way.

These pictures that came to him as he stood on the Cots-wold slopes prepared at least, it may be thought, the sensitive delicate touch which shows itself in the best poem he ever wrote, the charming " Hope," the second part of his *Pastoral Ballad*, which came, Mr. Graves tells, from the inspiration he gained at Cheltenham, and is set in scenery that may be the happiest Cotswold :—

My banks they are furnish'd with bees,
  Whose murmur invites one to sleep ;
My grottoes are shaded with trees,
  And my hills are white over with sheep.
I seldom have met with a loss,
  Such health do my fountains bestow :
My fountains all border'd with moss,
  Where the hare-bells and violets grow.

Charming though that is, it is hardly the best stanza. It sounds easy enough, but really the tunefulness of it is inimitable. And it comes, like so many other sweet things, from the Cotswolds.

But though a lover of this " sea of rolling hills and dancing air " may try to claim Shenstone as a Cotswold worthy, it were idle to deny that his fame, such as it is, belongs to the land of Hagley and Halesowen. How changed it is now ! Hagley is still beautiful, and Halesowen has her fine church unspoiled ; but all else is altered. Pits everywhere, and slag hills and rows of grimy cottages replace the " glass-house not ill-resembling a distant pyramid " in the " romantic well-variegated country " which enchanted the sober mind of Mr. Richard Dodsley, the publisher and the poet's friend. Yet the memory of Shenstone still lingers, though the memory is akin to neglect. A plain tomb, worse than that of many a yeoman of his day, still stands in the churchyard, near his brother's (as Graves tells us), but touched by another tomb still meaner than his own. The plain inscription is repeated on an urn inside the church, and below the urn are the lines Graves wrote for memorial. Thus they end :—

Reader ! if genius, taste refin'd,
A native elegance of mind ;
If virtue, science, manly sense ;
If wit, that never gave offence ;
The clearest head, the tenderest heart,
In thy esteem e'er claimed a part ;
Ah ! smite thy breast, and drop a tear,
For know, *thy* Shenstone's dust lies here.

Near it is the magnificent monument which Lady Jane

Halliday erected to the memory of her husband, who bought
the Leasowes after Shenstone's death, and who seems to have
made his chief and modest approach to fame in the boast
that he was the poet's successor :—

> What tho' no more (alas !) allow'd to rove,
> With learned ease, thro' *Shenstone's* classic grove ;
> Tho' spar'd no longer to protect that ground,
> Which the *lov'd Poet's* genius hovers round ;
> Tho' the fine *form* by a too early doom
> Be left to moulder in this votive tomb,
> Th' unfettered *Spirit* sooner wins her way
> To higher joys in scenes of endless day.

Halliday preserved the " delightful scenes which persons
of taste in the present age are desirous to see "—the walks
and grots and rivulets ; but the house he replaced by a
larger one. Shenstone had " a mere farmhouse of modest
dimensions," in which the utmost he could do was to give
" his hall some air of magnificence, by sinking the floor an
altitude of ten feet instead of seven." The house that Mr.
Halliday built still stands. He had the good taste not to
attempt to replace the *ferme ornée* by any extravagant
mansion. The gardens remained the attraction of the
Leasowes, and so they remain to-day.

Mr. Dodsley wrote a description " intended to give a
friend some idea of the Leasowes," and the description is
still useful to the visitor. Mr. Dodsley himself was for a
time celebrated there, " in a natural bower of almost circu-
lar oaks, inscribed in the following manner " :—

> Come then, my friend, thy sylvan taste display ;
> Come, hear thy Faunus tune his rustic lay ;
> Ah, rather come, and in these dells disown
> The care of other strains, and tune thine own.

Whether the kindly publisher accepted the invitation and
disowned the care of Mr. Shenstone's strains he does not
inform us. Certainly he published them in a very friendly
fashion after the author's death. And, for his own, he
tuned them in prose quite prettily when he told of the happy

valleys so cleverly planned to afford a *visto* again and again, and here and there some openings " to the more pleasing parts of this grotesque and hilly country."

The Leasowes is approached now, as in 1763, by a green lane, " descending in a winding manner to the bottom of a deep valley finely shaded." It was there that the worthy Mr. Wildgoose, the Spiritual Quixote, discovered his old college friend, " a gentleman in his own hair, giving directions to some labourers, who were working beyond the usual hour in order to finish a receptacle for a cataract of water, a glimpse of which appeared through the trees on the side of the road." With Mr. Dodsley's description in your hand you identify the " ruinated wall," you walk on by the slopes of a narrow dingle, past the Priory—a delightful piece of eighteenth-century Gothic, which seemed to be a hermitage, but really sheltered a labourer and his family —to the little lake at the bottom of the hill. Alas ! the *visto* hence is now closed by a slag hill, so you gladly turn away to seek by the " pleasing serpentine walk " a " common bench, which affords a retiring place secluded from every eye, and a short respite, during which the eye reposes on a fine amphitheatre of wood and thicket." The common bench is gone, and the fine canopy of spreading oak has followed it, and there is no cast of the piping Faunus or urn to William Somervile. Yet still through the glade you may trace, as you ascend, where once the " irregular and romantic fall of water " rushed " very irregular one hundred and fifty yards in continuity." It was only upon reflection that Mr. Dodsley found that the stream was " not a Niagara, but rather a waterfall in miniature." The language need not excite any tremendous emotion to-day. A toy Niagara indeed it must have been at best ; but now it has ceased even to flow, choked, like so many of these pretty fantasies of the gardener, by the leaves and saplings that time has strewn over the glade. The trees of Shenstone's day, except here and there a group of firs or elms or beeches, have perished, and are replaced by thin straggling shoots. The urns have long been destroyed, and no inscription survives to illustrate the poet's piety or friendship. Yet still you can follow the path as he made it, with the plan that Mr. Dodsley drew for your guide, by thickets, across broken rustic bridges, past sloping lawns, on the verge of " wild shaggy precipices." From the higher ground the distant views may still be seen—the Hagley obelisk and the hill of Clent. " Virgil's Grove " is still " a beautiful gloomy scene," with an " ingenious succession of cascades " and " a dripping fountain, where a small rill trickles down a rude niche of rock-work, through fern, liverwort and aquatic weeds."

A pathetic sight, neglected, overgrown, despoiled, is the scene to whose beauties " it was Mr. Shenstone's only study to give their full effect." But even now it shows, as do few other places in England, how in the beginnings of the art the principles of landscape gardening were developed. It was Shenstone's idea " that a landscape-painter would be the best English gardener," and Mr. Graves, in his charming *Recollections of Some Particulars in the Life of the Late William Shenstone, Esq.*," makes comparison between the work of his friend and that of Gainsborough. The poet himself very pleasantly expounded his system in prose, and indeed he has some claim to be regarded as one of the earliest masters of that craft. He had no sympathy, it is clear, with some of the later affectations, such as those which Thomas Love Peacock makes mock at. He endeavoured always to minister to Nature, not to thwart her. Yet his statues and urns were little better than an intrusion, though he could defend them thus : " Art should never be allowed to set a foot in the province of Nature otherwise than clandestinely and by night. Whenever she is allowed to appear there, and men begin to compromise the difference, night, Gothicism, confusion and absolute chaos are come again." Artifice must have been, if not obvious, yet easy to expose, if we may believe Johnson's suggestion that the Lytteltons, when they became jealous of their neighbour's success, delighted to take their visitors to the points of view from which the disguises were patent, and maliciously to destroy all the deceptive steps of gradual allurement designed by the poor owner of the Leasowes. It seems as if he found no great comfort in his art, or his simple country life, at the best. Winter seemed to him an intolerable season. " To see one's urns, obelisks and waterfalls laid open ; the naked-ness of our beloved mistresses, the Naïads and the Dryads, exposed by that ruffian Winter to universal observation ; is a severity scarcely to be supported by the help of blazing hearths, cheerful companions, and a bottle of the most grateful—Burgundy."

All did not, indeed, go well with him. His aphorisms, often witty, have a tinge of unhappy bitterness about them. There is that most charming verse, among the best he ever wrote :

> Whoe'er has travell'd life's dull round,
> Where'er his stages may have been,
> May sigh to think he still has found
> The warmest welcome at an inn.

And about it, by the way, there is a keen controversy. It is claimed to have been written at Henley-on-Thames, and Boswell speaks as if it were written at the *White Swan* in Henley-in-Arden ; but Graves, in his *Recollections*, is quite explicit. He says the lines were penned in a summer-house at Edgehill, where Shenstone was about 1750, on his way back from Whitchurch, where he had been bored beyond patience by a visit to Whistler. The account of the visit, and the quarrel, are quite in Graves's best style : one laughs, yet half cries, at the remarkably silly disagreement—but how natural it is ! " His whole philosophy," said Gray a little unkindly of him, " con-sisted in living against his will in retirement, and in a place which his taste had adorned, but which he only en-joyed when people of note came to see and commend it." A letter of his which was for sale in London the other day seems to make only a show of contentment. It was written to his friend Graves ; and it is worth quoting as it stands, for it does not seem to have been printed till now. There is no date to it, but evidently it was written while he was not at enmity with his other friend, Mr. Whistler, with whom he had the silly quarrel Graves tells us of. Thus it runs :—

MR. GRAVES.

DEAR SIR,—I did indeed give you up for lost, as a correspondent, and find by your letter y^t I am to expect but very few future ones. I will endeavour all I can to avoid any suspicion of your Indifference for my own satisfaction. But I don't know for certain y^t I shall be able, unless ᶠyou assist my Endeavours, like my good Genius, by a course of suitable Epistles at certain distances. I myself correspond but very little now, so you will meet with the more Indulgence. I don't find by your Letter y^t you have much more Philosophy y^n me. I can't tell indeed what ye situation of y^t House is. I own mine gives me offence on no other consideration y^n that it does not receive a sufficient Number of polite Friends, or y^t it is not fit to receive 'em, were they so dispos'd. I wou'd else cultivate an Acquaintance with about Three or Four in my Neighbourhood, y^t are of a Degree of Elegance, and station superior to ye common Run. But I make it a certain Rule *Arcere profanū vulgus*. Persons of vulgar minds, who will despise you for ye want of a good set of Chairs, or an uncouth Fire-shovel at ye same Time y^t they can't taste any Excellence in a mind that overlooks those things ; or, (to make a conceit of this sentiment) with whom 'tis in vain that y^r mind is furnish'd if y^r walls are naked. Indeed one loses much of one's Acquisitions in virtue by an Hour's converse with such as Judge of merit by Money, &c. Yet I am now and then impell'd by ye social Passion to sit half an Hour in my Kitchen. I was all along an Admirer of S^r. Thomas Head's Humour and Wit, And I beg you wou'd represent me in y^t light if occasion happens. 'Tis not impossible y^t I may penetrate this winter as far as y^r neighbourhood, connecting a set of visits which I have in my Eye. Tell Mr Whistler when you see him that if he must have *some* Distemper, I cannot but be pleas'd y^t it is one which is a Forerunner of Longevity. Don't tell him so neither, for ye compliment is trite. From ye " Birmingham Gazette " : " We hear that on Thursday last was married at Halesowen, in Shropshire, Mr. Jorden, an eminent Gunsmith of this Town, to a sister of ye R^t Honble Ferdinando Ld Dudley." I was yesterday at ye Grange, where his old

Father (wth a number of People) was celebrating ye Nuptials
of his Son ; when in the midst of his Feasting, high Jollity,
and grand Alliance, the old Fellow bethought him of a Piece
of Timber in ye neighbourhood y^t was convertible into good
Gunsticks, and had some of it sent for into ye Room by the
way of Specimen ! *Animæ nil magnæ laudis egentis !*
Pray, is y^r Sister at Smethwick ? For I have not heard.
You said you wou'd give me y^r Picture, which I long
earnestly for. Cou'dn't you contrive to have it sent me
directly ? I am quite in y^r debt with regard to downright
goods and moveables, and what is ye proper subject of an
Inventory—*neque tu pessima munerū ferres divite me scilicet
artium quas aut Parrhasius protulit aut Scopas—sed non
hæc mihi vis !* I will, however, endeavour to be more upon
a Par wth you w^{ith} regard to presents, tho' I never can with
regard to ye Pleasures I have receiv'd from y^r conversation.
I make People wonder at my Exploits in pulling down walls,
Hovels, cow-houses, &c. ; and my Place is not ye same. I
am, that is, with Regard to you a Faithfull Friend, and h^{ble}
servt, W. S.

Mr Whistler and you and I and Sr T. Head (who I should
name first, speaking after ye manner of men) have just
variety enough, and not too much, in our Charct. to make
an Interview, whenever it happens, Entertaining—I mean,
tho' we were not old Friends and Acquaintance.

It is the letter of a good-humoured, if a disappointed man.
And disappointed Shenstone certainly was. " The School-
mistress " should have won him more fame than it did. He
had few friends. Percy, the Lytteltons, Pitt, Lady Luxborough (Bolingbroke's charming sister), and Spence were
only acquaintances for whom he had a tepid liking ;
and after his brother's death he lived a lonely life.
Horace Walpole seems never to have heard of him
till he was dead, and in his pretty little essay on *Modern
Gardening* printed so daintily at the Strawberry Hill Press,
with a translation into French by the Duc de Nivernois, in
1785, studiously ignores his existence. Of his poetry all the

exquisite could find to say was that he was " a water-gruel bard " ; and unkindness could go no further than the cruel words in which he summed up his aims : " Poor man ! he wanted to have all the world talk of him for the pretty place he had made, and which he seems to have made only that it might be talked of."

Talked of, the Leasowes and its " landskips " are no longer ; but those who visit them can still trace the ingenuity in their ordering which friends called genius. Long enough ago Mr. Graves unkindly observed that the place was called " Shenstone's Folly " ; and he added, " this is a name which, with some sort of propriety, the common people give to any work of taste, the utility of which exceeds the level of their comprehension." Those who turn over the pages of prose and verse that Dodsley collected and eulogised may raise even now a real affection for their author. Shenstone has some of the marks of the true poet, and certainly not a few of the kindly and amiable man.

A City of the Eighteenth Century

BATH IN THE EIGHTEENTH CENTURY

IT is a delightful experience to rediscover the charm of
an English town through the enthusiastic appreciation of
a foreigner. How can we ever have forgotten that Bath
was so beautiful ? Perhaps we never did ; and yet the
history of English literature seems to show that for more
than fifty years the beauty was ignored. At least, we may
be grateful to Monsieur A. Barbeau [1] for the pains and
industry and enthusiasm which he has bestowed on a
subject which should be as fascinating to us as it is congenial
to him. Why, asks Mr. Austin Dobson, has no one ever
been clever enough to hit on so promising a subject before ?
Why, indeed ? Why have the men of letters who have
never ceased to be among the dwellers in the ancient city,
ceased to tell us about it, except in fugitive papers or brief
special studies ?

Never mind ! We need not trouble to inquire why what
is now done so well has never been done at all before. Here
is an admirable summary of Bath history as we find it in
the literature of England from the seventeenth century till
the middle of the nineteenth—from the time, let us say, in
history when Charles II brought Catherine of Braganza
(and other ladies too) to profit by the waters, till the time
when Queen Victoria's name was given to the new park
which so delightfully completes the city to the westwards ;
or, let us say, in literature, from Goldsmith's *Life of Beau
Nash* till the immortal chapters in *Pickwick* which tell of
Angelo Cyrus Bantam, of the Dowager Lady Snuphanuph,
Mrs. Colonel Wugsby, and Miss Bolo.

[1] *Une ville d'eaux anglaise au xviii. siècle.* Paris, Picard, 1904.

Bath, whether we read of it in fiction, or explore its contributions to the history of the nation, or simply look at it to-day, in all the brightness of a clear January morning, is remarkable, at the very first moment of our survey, for two things—the unique dignity and charm of its architecture, and the quaint and altogether unconscious frivolity of its life. It is quite true that writers have imagined that people went to Bath determined to be frivolous : nothing could be more untrue. They went to try and be healthy, or happy, and they sometimes fancied that either of these things involved frivolity, or even that there was frivolity in the air of the place they went to be cured in :—

> Haste then to Bath, for there you'll find
> Amusing scenes of every kind,
> Suited to every different stage—
> The fire of youth, the frost of age ;
> What joyous groups in every street,
> Where beauty, rank, and fashion meet ;
> Yet ah ! my friend, how much I fear
> You'll not meet happiness e'en there.

So said the Rev. Richard Graves ; but then he was a clergyman, and also he was an " octogenarian scribbler."

M. Barbeau has much to say about this Mr. Graves, the diverting author of the *Spiritual Quixote*, and, indeed, he derives not a little of his information as to the Bath of the fifty years between 1760 and 1810 from the same writer's very pleasant little book, *The Triflers*. We need not follow him there, for the memory of Mr. Graves can hardly yet be said to have died out in Bath, since it was preserved not so very long ago by the amiable Mr. Kilvert, a clergyman and tutor at Claverton, whose memorials you may still pick up in Bath bookshops,—and indeed I have more to say of him myself.

But let us begin with the medical side of Bath life, for there is one book, which M. Barbeau has neglected, that has a quaintness of its own. It is a serious medical work, published in London by Loundes in 1782, and sold at Bath by Tennent in Milsom Street and at Crutwell's printing office. The title is, *An Essay on the Bath Waters, in Four*

BATH IN THE EIGHTEENTH CENTURY

Parts : containing a Prefatory Introduction on the Study of Mineral Waters in General. Part I. An account of their possible impregnations. Part II. The most approved Means to be used for the discovery of their Contents. Part III. Experiments on the Bath Waters, with an Application of the foregoing Rules to a Discovery of their Contents. Part IV. On the Effects of the Bath Waters on the human Body, and the Propriety of their Use in Medecine, with an Application of the Experiments to Medecine and Pharmacy. Long enough, in good sooth. The author was William Falconer, and I cannot but suspect that it is he who was the early patron of Sir Thomas Lawrence, the " learned and cultured " man to whom M. Barbeau gives the Christian name of Edward. I do not know of any Edward Falconer, but William (1744–1824) was in his day a famous man. In January, 1770, he came to Bath on the advice of the noted physician, Dr. John Fothergill—to whom this book is dedicated as " to one of the first Names in the Science and Practice of Medecine." The friend and correspondent of Edmund Burke and Dr. Parr, he was a man of wide interest and wide culture. He wrote on subjects theological and geographical as well as medical, and he is one of the early authorities on a common enemy of us all, witness his *Account of the Epidemical Catarrhal Fever, commonly called the Influenza, as it appeared at Bath in the Winter and Spring of 1803.* The treatise I now speak of was his earliest work, but he never wrote better. He begins by wondering that among all the books that have been written upon mineral waters so many " are filled with the grossest ignorance or misrepresentations." Among the many causes he mentions for this, after dwelling upon " desire for gain," he tells us, in truly humane fashion, that " another reason, and perhaps a more justifiable one, is, that since a Patient's good opinion of the efficacy of his medecines is, in many cases necessary, and at all times favourable to his cure, by keeping up his spirits, and securing his obedience to the Physician's directions ; should many of these boasted arcana, however efficacious in practice, be at once developed, and discovered to be no more than the most common and simple substances, it might diminish his confidence in the remedy, and by that means deprive him of many of the advantages otherwise to be expected from it."

The " boasted arcana," it would seem, are the properties of mineral waters ; and much remains in darkness because practitioners are idle and will not indulge in experiments— whether at the expense of their patients or not. I heard the other day, by the way, of a surgeon who proposed an " exploratory operation " on a lady who had had a bicycle accident. So the courage of surgeons seems to have returned. Now, I do not feel at all inclined to give an analysis of Dr. Falconer's stout book, nor do I suppose that it has very much interest even for doctors to-day, though some of the experiments detailed are quite diverting. To some readers the merit of the book would doubtless lie in the freedom with which the Bath waters are recommended for many ailments, many of them most strangely named ; but more seriously it may be noted that, far though he wanders, the writer brings himself down eventually to gout and rheumatism in their different forms as the chief ills benefited by the internal use of the waters. Of the external use we will say more later. It was not so popular a subject. Entertaining all this, no doubt, to some, and instructive at the time to many. But one must not dwell too long with those bold, good men, the doctors.

Let us rather take another source of illustration of the manners of Bath in the eighteenth century, since it chances to be the only literary book we know that M. Barbeau has neglected—the memoirs, so well edited a few years ago by Mrs. Clementson, of Mrs. Lybbe Powys. Mrs. Powys was first at Bath in 1759, and employed her morning—

" As is usual, in going to the Pump, the Abbey Church, and the rooms, tho' each were but little frequented, there being but two or three families beside that of the Duchess of Marlborough. The heat of the water," the good lady adds, " is very extraordinary, and the people attribute it to different causes, but most to its passing thro' certain sulphurous veins of the earth."

In 1784 Mrs. Powys went for three months with her

mother to the city, and had a house in Gay Street. Twelve years later her brother-in-law came over to preach at the Octagon, which was then at the height of its fame—he was afterwards Dean of Canterbury—" whose sermon was so generally admir'd, he was much desir'd to print it."

This is the period of Bath's greatest glory. The Duke and Duchess of York had bought a house—the centre one— in the Royal Crescent, and were visited by the Prince of Wales. They, or rather the Duchess, had a seat in Queen Square Chapel—(what has become of that chapel now ?)— attended the theatre, and were the great feature of the balls at the Upper Assembly-rooms. The water-drinking was so fashionable that, Mrs. Powys tells us, " the pump-woman gives £1,000 a year for the place," and the traffic was so great that " to mend the road two miles the London way costs £22 a week." But wine-drinking, if we may credit her, was much more fashionable ; for when the Prince of Wales came, in 1799, he seems to have been remembered chiefly for the bad company he kept and for saying he would make one of them " Lord *Cinque* Port." Even more notorious was the gambling. In 1804 (the year of the estimable Graves's death) at the Upper-rooms, reopened in February, there were twenty-five tables, and a few days after twenty-seven. To such an extent did this grow, that O'Beirne, Bishop of Meath, came and preached a sermon against card-parties and Sunday-evening concerts, to the great indignation of the old ladies, who declared they would have their parties " for all the Bishops." And the number of card-parties was said quite to spoil the balls, " as 'tis fashionable to attend five or six before you go to the room." There were 16,000 strangers at Bath in the season of 1805.

Such a book as Mrs. Powys's enables one to see how persons of fashion, and even of intelligence, used Bath as a place for the cure of their real or fancied ills, amused themselves, and saw their friends, without knowing any- thing whatever about the real interests which seem to us to have given the city its fame. A word on these.

Bath, though it was visited—another microscopic fact M. Barbeau has not noticed—by Robert Cecil, Earl of

Salisbury, in James I's reign, did not really become famous till the time of Charles II and Grammont, when it was compared to the French springs of Bourbon ; and even then it waited for the rule of Nash to achieve its fullest glory. How great Nash was, how "immense" in his ostentation and conceit and dictatorial skill, M. Barbeau shows us from Goldsmith's immortal *Life*, and from many corroborative sources ; and if we want a concrete proof we cannot do better than look at the picture of his vast, impressive house, now, alas ! fallen indeed from its high estate, but preserved for our wonder in a charming series of reproductions published recently by that true Bath-lover, Mr. Meehan, of Gay Street. It rivals the greatest "town houses" of noblemen in eighteenth-century London, and some idea may still be obtained of the opulence of its owner by any one who will penetrate to the heart of the old city and find it —part absorbed by *The Garrick's Head* and part by the Theatre Royal.

The first interest of historic Bath is Beau Nash, whose florid picture still adorns the Pump-room and seems to set the tone to the whole scheme of elaborate decoration—glass, and gold, and paint—which makes them recall, more exactly than anything else, the setting of the Bath we read of in the novelists. His is the interest of a really great organiser, though it were only of amusement, and to some extent of a moral reformer. Bath scandals died down, or were private only, in his day. He taught English people to amuse themselves reasonably and without vulgar social distinctions, and M. Barbeau is probably right in thinking that Bath in his day did a great deal for the unification of classes in England, and so, we may add, indirectly, for the suppression of any such antagonisms as were so largely responsible for the social revolution in France at the end of the century. Cards in his day were in the background, decorous dancing and decorous drinking of the waters were the two *pièces de résistance*. It was an easy and familiar life, and no one was very much the worse for it. Certainly it was a distinct elevation from the taste and manners of the Restoration age.

With the growth of the passion for play, the fetters being removed after Nash's death, Bath began inevitably to degenerate, and the degeneracy was completed by the period of Evangelical supremacy which destroyed rather than ameliorated the amusements. Bath really was a very respectable place. M. Barbeau very fairly says that in the contemporary literature the surprise is the very small quantity of scandalous anecdotes or allusions. And this is due very largely to the tone set by Nash at the first.

The episode of Sheridan's marriage adds another interest to historic Bath. It is very well told by M. Barbeau. We feel the charm and goodness of Miss Linley, and we delight to know the dear young Irishman when his heart was full of romance and humour, and before success had spoiled his life. And Sheridan is almost insignificant among the writers who for sixty years made Bath, it might be said, the literary centre of England. Their period begins with the patronage of "low-born Allen," the friend of Pope and Fielding and Warburton, and of the worthy Graves, who seems to belong to quite another generation. M. Barbeau singles out for special mention Smollett, Jane Austen, and Dickens, and he does well, for each, in a very different way, preserves the indefinable aroma of a distinct period, with its special interest and characteristics. Smollett is of the time when low-bred people made vigorous efforts to get "into society" by way of Bath; and his account of the "rooms," highly coloured though it is, shows the difficulties out of which a highly organized English civilization was at last evolved. With Jane Austen all is smooth and polite and kindly. Bath is the rendezvous not of gamblers and upstarts, but of lovers and matronly ladies and gentlefolk who want to make their small incomes and their petty interests go a long way.

Between Jane Austen and Dickens there is an intervening step, the view of a fashionable foreigner. That curious book, *The Tour of a German Prince in England in 1828 and 1829*, contains a pleasing account—among its many amusing pictures of English life—of Bath in the earlier year. "Since the day on which I communicated to you that the sun had shone," says the writer on December 22, 1828, " I have not seen his beneficent face. But in spite of fog and rain, I have wandered about the whole day long in this wonderful city, which, originally built in the bottom of a deep and narrow hollow, has gradually crept up the sides of all the surrounding hills. The magnificence of the houses, gardens, streets, terraces and semicircular rows of houses called ' crescents,' which adorn every hill, is imposing, and worthy of English opulence. Notwithstanding this, and the beauty of the surrounding country, *fashion* has deserted Bath, and fled with a sort of feverish rage to the unmeaning, treeless and detestably prosaic Brighton. Bath is still much resorted to by invalids, and even the forty thousand opulent inhabitants suffice to enliven it ; but the fashionable world is no longer to be seen here. The once celebrated King of Bath, the formerly ' far-famed Nash,' has lost more of his ' nimbus ' than any of his colleagues. He who now fills the office, instead of driving through the streets with six horses and a retinue of servants (the constant *cortège* of his august predecessor), goes modestly on foot. No Duchess of Queensbery will he send out of his ballroom for not being dressed according to rule." This master of the ceremonies seems, by the way, to have been a Colonel Jervoise, who ruled from 1828 to 1849. He is not at all to be regarded as the original of Angelo Cyrus Bantam ; and perhaps for his very sobriety of tone he did not attract the interest of the lively German. In all his tour it is smartness that he seeks. Cheltenham, a dead-alive place at best, seemed to him not so deserted as Bath ; and Bath charmed only for its abbey,—which he thought beautiful because he believed it to be in the German style,—and the mysterious seclusion of Beckford.

When the author of *Vathek* became replaced in the literature of the Bath neighbourhood by the author of *Pickwick*, there was a change indeed. With Dickens the decay has set in ; there is too much of the " genteel " and too little of the old world of fashion, but, perhaps, that is because Dickens, at the date of *Pickwick* at any rate, had no idea of what "society" was. Anyhow, as M. Barbeau says :—

"The great novelist drew a picture of Bath in its decline, prim, narrow, and languid, just as another great novelist three-quarters of a century earlier has painted it in its turbulent and scandalous vigour, and as several others had sketched its most curious aspects in passing."

But, after all, the literary memories of Bath, or the records of the somewhat trivial personages who "made" the city's history, are less durable in visible effect than the labours of the great architects who built the unique city. From about 1728 begins the era of building which created that wonderfully harmonious whole which we now behold, if we have the least intelligence, with admiration, and marvel that the architects of to-day are utterly unable to rival. Prior Park, under Ralph Allen, was a nursery of architecture, and the elder Wood was, with Nash, the true founder of Bath :—

"Nearly every building in Bath owes its existence to the first Wood, or to the second, or to contemporaries and successors guided and more or less inspired by them."

Some may think with Landor that the Circus is the most splendid thing in the city, and a thing that no foreign architect has equalled ; but to most the Crescent, set in greensward with a glorious view before it, with its magnificent sweep and subtly calculated combination of dignity and elegance, is the finest collection of houses in the world.

The Circus was finished in 1765, the Crescent a few years before ; Queen Square before that ; and afterwards the imposing Pulteney Street, Laura Place, the New Pumproom, and the Town Hall. But all up the hills, from Camden Crescent to Lansdowne, ascend the ingeniously simple buildings, which combine a certain impressiveness with undeniable solidity and comfort, and which give to Bath its unique place in England as a city of one age, beautiful in its soft grey colouring, in its quiet, sober air of past homeliness and calm. Mr. Swinburne caught the wonderful charm, which still escapes so many eyes, when he wrote those beautiful lines which M. Barbeau makes the Envoy to his most interesting book :—

Like a queen enchanted that may not laugh or weep,
Glad at heart and guarded from change and care like ours,
Girt about with beauty by days and nights that creep
Soft as breathless ripples that softly shorewards sweep,
Lies the lovely city whose grace no grief deflowers.

A BATH EVENING

AN admirable book, I said, as I closed the volume. The most beautiful town in England is brought back to us, as she lived in the days of her greatest pride, when those stately streets, the creation of the Woods and their pupils, were still new and glittered in the sun, which never in England, surely, is so bright as here. In the mid-eighteenth century, when Nash was king, Bath was truly in her glory. There was a city organized for health and pleasure, and how complete an organization it was! Within the cup that lies below the tree-crowned hills, the genius of a consummate architect planned a town which should be all the expression of a single idea, the adaptation of classic style to modern life. He gave the very perfection of comfort and dignity combined. Nowhere are rooms so lofty or well proportioned, walls so thick, passages so conveniently designed, decorations so simple yet so fine, as in this unique city; and that not for a house here and there, but for the streets and squares and crescents which stretch over the whole place, and fit into each other, with spaces of grass and trees, as neatly as the bricks with which a child lays out the buildings of her toy design. So cool in the hot sun Bath lies as you look down on it in August from the hills, so warm in winter as it catches the brief sun of a January noon. Is the art lost which made this city so fair and so complete?

But it is not so much of this that M. Barbeau tells me, though he has seen the charm of these English architects' work and knows what an achievement it was to build such a city : he tells me more of the men and women who made the fame of those streets and those rooms. There is Beau Nash, so pert and dictatorial, with the air that overawed royal duchesses and provoked country misses to smart rejoinder. There is Gainsborough in that charming house of his, number 24, The Circus, thronged with visitors ; fortune, they said, taking up her abode with him, and the lovely ladies and the gentlemen of wit and fashion crowding to be painted. Richardson and Sterne and Burke and Garrick are there, all painted by the skilled hand of the most charming of English artists .There is Sheridan, witty and romantic, carrying off the fair Eliza from under the nose of her unworthy admirers and fighting a duel on Kingsdown hill to preserve the fair fame of the lady whom the world did not know to be his wife. There is Chatham, stately and attitudinizing, and Pope before him, scornful of the gaieties of a watering-place, and " low-born Allen," who was the Maecenas of the rising city, Fielding scrutinizing human nature, and Smollett girding at its follies and its vice. Not a man there is, as the eighteenth century passes, in the roll of famous English worthies, who has not come here and left some memory behind him. And all this M. Barbeau embalms in his crisp French prose. I shut my eyes, and the streets fill with gentle-folk carried in their sedans to the baths or to the pump-room, or to the nightly card parties, Selina Countess of Huntingdon looks gravely upon the frivolous Mr. Nash, who was " orthodox in his toasts and well content with the state of religion amongst his subjects," and Anstey watches, out of the windows of that fine house you may see to-day if you will, in the Crescent, the fashionable mob that shows itself airing on the finest sweep of promenade in an English town.

When you begin to count, or recount, the memories of Bath, you cannot tell where to speak, where to cease speaking. It is the mirror of Eighteenth-Century England. Every interest that Englishmen had sooner or later found its expression here. Here, though M. Barbeau forgets it, Wolfe drew his sword and swaggered before Pitt of the things he would do in Canada. " Heavens ! that I should have intrusted to such hands the fate of this country and of this administration ! " exclaimed the Prime Minister when he had said good-night to the future conqueror of Quebec.

A BATH EVENING

Here Sheridan saw the types that he made immortal in *The Rivals*, and Smollett the blustering bullies and discredited women who, he will not let us forget, were to be found even in the city which Mr. Nash had made so correct. Here Wesley preached, and Burke meditated, and Anstey satirised, and every person we have ever heard of—except Hannah More—gambled. Austere and tender-hearted, the Methodist rubbed shoulders with the gambler and buffoon.

> Where gambling and graces
> Each other embraces,
> Dissipation and Piety meets ;—
> May all who've a notion
> Of Cards or Devotion
> Make Bath their delightful retreat.

Bath, wrote Gibbon, was the city of all others where he would live if he ever left Lausanne, and Landor set it by Florence in his heart. Fanny Burney and Jane Austen were equally at home. Shall we ever forget the immortal chapters which make the great Assembly Rooms live again ? Do not the sound of horses' feet in Pulteney Street still make us look up involuntarily for the egregious Mr. Thorpe ? " Here all the year round, there is always the town at command and always the country for prospect, exercise and delight," said the sensible Fanny Burney. That charm remains, though the Pump-room has lost its glory, and the " cure " has become a science, and the glittering chandeliers of the Upper Rooms light up frigid concerts more often than brilliant balls.

And all this one may think as one turns the pages of M. Barbeau's delightful book. Bath has found the chronicler who will not let one episode of its history pass into forgetfulness.

So I closed the book and went out into the city of quaint romance. The stars were shining, as I stood in Orange Grove and looked up at the pinnacles of the Abbey twinkling in the cold bright night. I passed on to the terrace that turns towards the old bridge, and there below the waterfall was a boat gently, silently, passing up and down where the waters flow swiftest, while a lithe figure stood poised to throw his net or bent slowly to recover it. Night is so silent here, the streets so deserted, the lights in the windows so few, the houses so still and restful.

Dreamily I recalled these beautiful verses, of which, says Anatole France so truly, " l'accent était nouveau, singulier, profond."

> Votre âme est un paysage choisi
> Que vont charmant masques et bergamasques
> Jouant de luth et dansant et quasi
> Tristes sous leurs dèguisements fantasques.
>
> Tout en chantant sur le mode mineur,
> L'amour vainqueur et la vie opportune,
> Ils n'ont pas l'air de croire à leur bonheur,
> Et leur chanson se mêle au clair de lune,
>
> Au clair calme de lune triste et beau
> Qui fait rêver les oiseaux dans les arbres
> Et sangloter d'extase les jets d'eau,
> Les grands jets d'eau sveltes parmi les marbres.

" Nouveau, singulier, profond " indeed, and yet how the expression is in harmony with the tone of this old-world place as one sees it by moonlight !

> Jouant de luth et dansant et quasi
> Tristes sous leurs dèguisements fantasques.

I started, and yet all seemed natural : Pierrot stood beside me, wistful, pale, beautiful with a beauty that does not belong to the earth I know. " There is the theatre," he said, " where Quin and Garrick acted, and the adorable queen of tragedy. Still they act there with a memory of the old tradition. Nowhere have the actors quite that air of happy insincerity that belongs to these boards." It was a strange, deserted scene, a square close by the centre of the city and yet like a forgotten slum. Night closed on us, and sad shapes seemed to flit by, and I heard them murmur of great things which had vexed men a century ago. Was all this real ? Has Bath ever ceased to live its old life ? Are the statesmen and poets, the gamblers and artists, the beautiful ladies and insistent lovers, really gone ? I do not think so, for certainly as I stand here, with my strange companion by my side, I see a sedan come silently down Queen Square and pass into the door that is opened at its approach ; and as the clock strikes the crowd begins to come forth from the Assembly Rooms. " Is all the fashion gone, are all the loves lost, all the hates forgotten ? " says Pierrot. Such a city never forgets, and its memories are never silent to those who have ears to hear.

Strangely the scene reminds me of that fantasy, half pathetic, half silly, of Ernest Dowson's :—

> Music, more music, far away and faint :
> It is an echo of my heart's complaint.

In the deserted garden of Queen Square the shapes of past days seem to rest. There the carriages still hurry by, soundless : the link boys flash their lights a moment in your eyes : the crowd is suddenly upon you which hooted George of Wales and called at him, " Why don't you bring your wife here, as your brother does ? "—poor foolish York, soon to be discredited too. Forgotten tales of old history return. Again the hot gambling fever claims its victims, and the men with haggard faces pass by me in the streets as they fly the last time from the public tables. So up the hill through Gay Street, its gaiety stilled now, into the Circus, where the memories thickly cluster, where the great Pitt is looking out on the night as I pass, for the carriages have scarce rolled out into Brock Street, or down the hill, after the long sitting over the port and the battle plans. Brock Street is dark and tragic, the moon does not seem to light it, and the houses are gloomy and sad. At last I am in the Crescent, with the heavens clear and open above me, and we pace up and down waiting for the sunrise.

Poor frail humanity, how little remains of thy happy memories, days and nights that spend themselves in the vain pursuit of pleasure, the vain hope to forget the pain that clings close to the heart. Every stone here is a sad memorial : so many young lives squandered, so many old lives foolishly cherished, so much mockery of sentiment, cruelty of sacrifice, wantonness and childish wastefulness. What sore hearts those thronged walls of the Abbey bear record of, hearts that carried their sorrow to its resting-place here, and then decked and decorated it with pompous record of achievement and virtue. It is the tragedies of the old life, the faded hopes, the shattered careers, which come back to us here, as we pass by the silent houses at night.

"Gone is the old life I remember," says Pierrot, "gone is the life which could be so artless and at ease, which dreamed of no sorrow, nor rose at morn to combat the dark wings of care. Gone are the measures of formal stateliness, gone the modes of careless delight, gone the bright dresses, the ceremony, the etiquette that was so natural in its affectation. Gone is all that belonged to the days I knew."

"If sleep has come to all," I said, "is there not still love ? "

> Sleep ! Yet thy days are mine ;
> Love's seal is over thee,
> Far though my ways from thine,
> Dim though my memory.
>
> Love stays a summer night,
> Till lights of morning come ;
> Then takes her winged flight
> Back to her starry home.

"Love is gone," he said, "for when the years come quickly by, she too has passed, like the baseless fabric of a vision, into dim thought of that which never truly was. Idle fancy ! All is gone."

I shivered : it was dawn. The moon had shone her last beam on the pale grey houses, fringed with dark trees. The birds began to twitter round the eaves. Day surely would bring back at least the memory that once we were happy, though sorrow had tarried for the night. "There are treasures which time cannot destroy," I said as the sun rose and dispersed the blue mists, and the houses opened their windows to the new day.

A BATH EVENING

City lulled asleep by the chime of passing years,
Sweeter smiles thy rest than the radiance round thy peers,
Only love and lovely remembrance here have place.
Time on thee lies lighter than music on men's ears ;
Dawn and noon and sunset are one before thy face.

I looked round for my companion.   He was gone, and I
was awake.

THE REVEREND RICHARD GRAVES

ONE name, which to my mind has been too soon forgotten, connects the Warwickshire coterie of Lady Luxborough with the Somerset coterie of Lady Miller. It is that of the Reverend Richard Graves, whose long life lasted from 1715 to 1804.

There are many things for which he is worth remembering, so many that it is difficult to know how to arrange them. It may be best perhaps to think of him as in all probability he would have liked to think of himself, first as a man of letters, then as a parish priest, and lastly, as a friend of persons of importance in his day. A necessary prologue is a brief record of his life.

He was the second son of Richard Graves, of Mickleton, Gloucestershire (1677–1729), who lived in the beautiful manor house which remains one of the most beautiful examples of Cotswold architecture. The father, it is said, is described in the son's *Spiritual Quixote* under the name of Mr. Townsend, a worthy antiquary who is easily led aside to behold any curiosity of the past. Graves the elder, one feels when the character of Townsend is sketched, may thus be the literary grandfather of Monkbarns himself. The *virtuoso* whom the Spiritual Quioxote met, in Lord Bathurst's woods, eager after Roman antiquities, was, however, not so easily taken in as the Scottish antiquary. A woodman led him aside to inspect a treasure. " I thought," says Mr. Townsend, " by his account he had found a Roman stylus (which they used to write with) ; but, I am afraid, it is nothing more than an old skewer." Graves the elder was indeed a very considerable antiquary in his day, an authority on coins and medals, and a writer on local history among the best. Graves the younger was born the year after Shenstone, but, though Mickleton is

Rᵈ GRAVES. M.A.

RICHARD GRAVES.

not very far from the Leasowes, the two were not acquainted till the former went to Pembroke College, Oxford. There a friendship of over thirty years began, which ended only with Shenstone's death. A word from what Graves wrote of their Pembroke experiences is worth quoting here :—

" The young people of the college at that time (as I believe is the case in most colleges) were divided into different small associations, according to their different tastes and pursuits.

" Having been elected from a public school in the vicinity of Oxford, and brought with me the character of a tolerably good Grecian, I was invited, by a very worthy person now living, to a very sober little party, who amused themselves in the evening with reading Greek and drinking water. Here I continued six months, and we read over Theophrastus, Epictetus, Phalaris's Epistles, and such other Greek authors as are seldom read at school. But I was at length seduced from this mortified symposium to a very different party : a set of jolly, sprightly young fellows, most of them west-country lads ; who drank ale, smoked tobacco, punned, and sung bacchanalian catches the whole evening ; our ' pious orgies ' generally began with,—

> Let's be jovial, fill our glasses,
> Madness 'tis for us to think,
> How the world is rul'd by asses,
> And the wisest sway'd by chink.

I own, with shame, that, being then not seventeen, I was so far captivated with the social disposition of these young people (many of whom were ingenious lads and good scholars) that I began to think *them* the only wise men ; and to have a contempt for every degree of temperance and sobriety.

" Some gentlemen commoners, however, who were my countrymen (amongst whom were the two late successive lords Ch—d—s) and who considered the above-mentioned as very *low* company (chiefly on account of the liquor they drank) good-naturedly invited me to their party ; they treated me with port wine and arrack punch ; and now and then, when they had drank so much, as hardly to distinguish wine from water, they would conclude with a bottle or two of claret. They kept late hours; drank their favourite toasts on their knees; and, in short, were what were then called ' bucks of the first head.' This was deemed good company and high life; but it neither suited my taste, my fortune, nor my constitution.

" There was, besides, a sort of flying squadron of plain, sensible, matter-of-fact men, confined to no club, but associating occasionally with each party. They anxiously inquired after the news of the day, and the politics of the times. They had come to the university on their way to the Temple, or to get a slight smattering of the sciences before they settled in the country. They were a good sort of young people, and perhaps the most rational of the college : but neither with these was I destined to associate.

" In each of the above-mentioned parties, except the water-drinkers, I had once or twice met Mr. Shenstone." [1]

Thus the acquaintance began; and an early fruit of it was the character which Shenstone wrote of Graves. It is really so good that it is worth quoting entire. It makes us see the kind of man we have to deal with, for such as Shenstone drew him in most respects he remained to the end of his ninety years of life.

" He was a youth so amply furnished with every excellence of mind, that he seemed alike capable of acquiring or disregarding the goods of fortune. He had indeed all the learning and erudition that can be derived from universities, without the pedantry and ill manners which are too often their attendants. What few or none acquire by the most intense assiduity, he possessed by nature; I mean, that elegance of taste, which disposed him to admire beauty under its great variety of appearances. It passed not unobserved by him either in the cut of a sleeve, or the integrity of a moral action. The proportion of a statue, the convenience of an edifice, the movement in a dance, and the complexion of a cheek or flower, afforded him sensations

[1] *Recollections of Mr. Shenstone*, pp. 13–17.

of beauty ; that beauty which inferior genius's are taught coldly to distinguish ; or to discern rather than feel. He could trace the excellencies both of the courtier and the student ; who are mutually ridiculous in the eyes of each other. He had nothing in his character that could obscure so great accomplishments, beside the want, the total want, of a desire to exhibit them. Through this it came to pass, that what would have raised another to the heights of reputation was oftentimes in him passed over unregarded. For, in respect to ordinary observers, it is requisite to lay some stress yourself on what you intend should be remarked by others ; and this never was his way. His knowledge of books had in some degree diminished his knowledge of the world ; or, rather, the external forms and manners of it. His ordinary conversation was, perhaps, rather too pregnant with sentiment, the usual fault of rigid students ; and this he would in some degree have regulated better, did not the universality of his genius, together with the method of his education, so largely contribute to this amiable defect. This kind of awkwardness (since his modesty will allow it no better name) may be compared to the stiffness of a fine piece of brocade, whose turgescency indeed constitutes, and is inseparable from, its value. He gave delight by an happy boldness in the extirpation of common prejudices ; which he could as readily penetrate as he could humorously ridicule : and he had such entire possession of the hearts as well as understandings of his friends, that he could soon make the most surprising paradoxes believed and well-accepted. His image, like that of a sovereign, could give an additional value to the most precious ore ; and we no sooner believed our eyes that it was he who spake it, than we as readily believed whatever he had to say. In this he differed from W——r, that he had the talents of rendering the greatest virtues unenvied : whereas the latter shone more remarkably in making his very faults agreeable : I mean in regard to those few he had to exercise his skill." [1] So far Shenstone, and he adds :—

[1] Shenstone's *Works*, vol. ii. 41–43.

" N.B.—This was written, in an extempore manner, on my friend's wall at Oxford, with a black-lead pencil, 1735, and intended for his character."

The friendship thus begun was continued in the country, where Shenstone was introduced to the elder brother of Richard Graves, who lived at Mickleton, " a single man and lately come "—that is about 1735 or 1736—" with his sister, to reside in the country ; his house was the rendezvous of most of the young people, of both sexes, in the neighbourhood " ; and this was one of the foundations of that Warwickshire coterie of which there has been elsewhere something to say. Among the fair ones was the charming Utrecia Smith, whose father had been the first tutor of Richard Graves, and whose early death is commemorated by Shenstone's verse and on an urn in Mickleton Church. To Pembroke Graves had come from Abingdon school, and from Pembroke he went in 1736 to All Souls' as Fellow. There his chief friend was the great Blackstone, who " followed him thither from the same college a few years afterwards," he says, and very early Graves was impressed by his genius. In the book he called *The Triflers*, which was prepared for publication by him a few weeks before he died and published after his death in 1805, he gives a character of the great lawyer, from which two anecdotes, typical indeed, are worth quoting :—

" When he had been about two years at the Temple, on his coming down to All Souls' election, I asked him how he liked the law ? He said it was a very dry study ; ' but,' added he, ' I have made myself pretty well master of it.' ' What ! in two years,' I exclaimed with surprise ? ' Yes,' says he ; ' I have reduced it to a system ; so that I have only to read new Acts of Parliament, and the different authors who have written on our laws.' " [1]

And the other tale runs thus :—

" A no less important, though seemingly trifling economical plan, during his Bursarship, was his laying in wine by the pipe, in the college cellar, so that the sober part of the

[1] *The Triflers*, p. 54.

IN CLAVERTON VILLAGE.

college might drink a pint, or even half a pint of good wine and return to their studies, without going to the tavern across the street ; where the jovial part went after dinner, to drink bad wine ; and where they were often tempted, I fear, to loiter a good part of the afternoon." [1]

From All Souls' Graves went to London to try medicine, but illness turned back his thoughts to Holy Orders, and he returned to Oxford and was ordained in 1740. Various parochial and tutorial duties then attached him to the Fitz-Herberts, in Derbyshire, not far from Ashbourne, where the redoubtable Dr. Taylor was to live in such splendour and depress Dr. Johnson so profoundly by his worldliness. Thence he went to Aldworth, near Reading, as curate, and there he found his wife, Lucy Bartholomew, the romantic tale of whose wooing and education he tells—as of one Rivers, in the second volume of the *Spiritual Quixote*. In 1748 he received the Rectory of Claverton, near Bath, and in that village he lived from 1750, with not a month's absence together the whole time.

Claverton is a lovely village, in the lovely country of Bath. In early spring the way is one of unbroken delight. Up Bathwick hill, by houses skilfully designed and substantially built, giving views as you ascend of increasing loveliness, till gradually the city stretches at your feet, the white crescents glittering, and the houses often bowered in green. Then along an avenue of shade, with distant views now and again revealed, then a short descent, with a scene before you that can hardly be surpassed in England—trees, valley, old houses of Elizabeth's day, and you are in the village of Claverton. The rectory is transformed beyond knowledge, though it still includes some of the building Graves lived in. The church, well kept and trimly cared for, has also seen the restorer's hand. It contains the monuments of wife, husband, and daughter, the records of the events which broke the even tenor of the Rector's long life. A wreathed urn on the east wall of the vestry has the inscription :—

[1] *Ibid.* p. 56.

BURFORD PAPERS

Luciae, conjugi carissimae Ricardus Graves conjux infelicissimus fecit et sibi. Ob. Kal. Maii MDCCLXXVII. Aet. xlvi.

In the vestry also is a tablet to the daughter, Lucilla Anna Maria, who is stated to be buried in the family vault at S. Martin's, Ludgate, London, and who died March 10, 1822, aged 57. Graves himself is the subject of a long epitaph. Thus it runs :—

SACRED TO THE MEMORY

OF

RICHARD GRAVES, A.M.,

SECOND SON OF RICHARD GRAVES, ESQRE.,
OF MICKLETON IN THE COUNTY OF GLOCESTER,
FELLOW OF ALL SOULS' COLLEGE, OXFORD,
AND RECTOR OF THIS PARISH,
FROM WHICH DURING 55 YEARS HE WAS NOT AT ANY
ONE TIME ABSENT FOR THE SPACE OF A MONTH.
A GOOD AND EXEMPLARY MAN,
AFFECTIONATE, CHARITABLE,
BLAMELESS IN HIMSELF,
BEHOLDING THE INFIRMITIES OF OTHERS WITH PITY.
AT THE CLOSE OF A LONG LIFE
DISTINGUISHED BY DOMESTIC PIETY,
BY THE VIRTUOUS EXERCISE OF ELEGANT TALENTS,
AND BY THE FAITHFUL, ZEALOUS, AND TRULY CHRISTIAN
ADMINISTRATION OF HIS SACRED CHARGE,
HE CHEERFULLY OBEYED THE AWFUL CALL OF HIS CREATOR
AND MET HIS LAST HOUR WITH SERENITY—
FOR, STRENGTHENED BY FAITH,
THE UPRIGHTNESS OF HIS MIND WHICH HAD
ADORNED HIS LIFE
SUPPORTED HIM ALSO IN DEATH.
HE DIED NOVEMBER 23RD, 1804, AGED 89.

In the churchyard is the large tomb to Ralph Allen and many of his kin, including his niece, Mrs. Warburton, of whom the inscription speaks much more kindly than do the biographers. Near the church once stood the old manor house, now destroyed, where the Skrines—who now again are lords of the Claverton manor—lived in Graves's day. To-day only the charming stone steps remain which once led up the garden terraces. There is an old print of Mr. Meehan's which pictures them delightfully.

THE REV. RICHARD GRAVES

The walk from Claverton to Batheaston is delightful, along a road which in spring is bright with fresh green, with views of wooded slopes, and the sleepy canal below. Across fields you go, and through the quiet village of Bathampton, then across the river and up the slope to the villa where the dilettantes read their verses in the little circle of admirers. How often Graves in his fifty-five years at Claverton took this walk, and on to Bath, it would be a weariness to count. They say that every day his slim figure was seen on the road.

A beautiful road it is. Again there is a valley below you, with the canal running along it ; again there are fine woods, and grass fields thickly sprinkled with trees. After a while, if you are wise, you turn into the fields and so across to Bathampton, cross the canal and the river, and then mount the slope to the house that gives—or shall I say gave ?—Batheaston its fame. Here once were Sheridan, and Pitt, and Horace Walpole, and Dr. Johnson, Fanny Burney and the Thrales, and very many more ; and Graves was of the company. That was in the days of the Millers, whom surely Dickens must have heard memories of when he wrote of Mrs. Leo Hunter.

At Batheaston Villa, from about 1769 for some twelve years, " a society of friends, of whom the greater number visited weekly, upon a fixed day "—I quote from the preface to the first volume of their *Poetical Amusements*, published in 1775, and reaching a third edition in 1776—met and read the verses they had written. The object, they say, was " to naturalize a little Gallic Institution, which has been productive of much wit and pleasantry to that light and sprightly nation. Words were given out that rhymed to each other, by the French called *Bouts Rimées* (to be filled up in metre) for the following Friday ; to which was afterwards added, a *subject* at large, for those who should prefer unshackled numbers." The best description of the entertainment is undoubtedly that of Graves himself.

" A scene rather trifling, was exhibited twenty years ago near Bath, which may be worth recording. The liberal-minded Sir John Miller and his lady amused the company from Bath with regular morning assemblies at stated times, at their beautiful villa at Bath Easton.

" Lady Miller, once in a for'tnight, gave out a subject for poetical composition ; on which, when the company were assembled, those whom the Muses, or perhaps vanity, or the love of fame had influenced, produced their performances, and put them into an elegant antique marble vase brought from Rome, and placed on a pedestal in the bow window : when the company were seated, some young nymph put in her delicate arm, and took out a single poem, which the author, or some one who either had, or fancied he had, an agreeable elocution, read to the assembly. When in this manner the whole collection was gone through, the gentlemen retired into a contiguous apartment ; where amidst a profusion of jellies, sweetmeats, ice-creams and the like, they decided on the merits of the several performances ; from which they selected three, which were deemed the best ; and of course entitled to prizes ; which her ladyship distributed to the respective authors ; a pompous bouquet of flowers to the first, a myrtle wreath to the second, and a sprig of myrtle to the third. These were then usually presented, by the successful candidate, to some lady, who wore them in her hair or her bosom the next evening, to the publick rooms.

" I ought not perhaps to have spoken of this as a trifling exhibition, since it called forth some of the best poets of the age : Mr. Anstey, lord Palmerston, Miss Bowdler, Miss Seward, &c., &c., &c. But I think it was comparatively so ; in proportion to the extraordinary attention, which was paid to it : as I counted one morning about fifty carriages drawn up in a line from Bath Easton, towards Lambridge ; and was at one time present at it, with four duchesses ; the duchess of Cumberland, Northumberland, Ancaster and Beaufort." [1]

Batheaston Villa, which now belongs to Mrs. Tollemache, to whose kindness I am much indebted, is a charming place. The house has been added to, but much of the old

---

[1] *The Triflers*, pp. 11–13.

remains, notably the curious window shutters in the drawing-room, with mirrors in them, and the fine fireplace in the library. From the front of the house there is one of those beautiful views which seem essential parts of the district's character. The valley below, where the river flows, and across it the hills crowned with trees and houses, rising in slopes of gentle loveliness till they shut in the prospect of other slopes and other valleys beyond. In the garden is still the old bowling-green, with that soft turf which only England can grow ; at the end of it, among great laurels, is the classic temple, in which sometimes the famous vase was placed—at least, I think so, though the authorities are not precise ; generally it stood in the bow-window of the drawing-room, overlooking the beautiful view—a view which Horace Walpole could not choose but praise, though an anonymous scribbler disposed of it thus—

> Bless us ! what toil, what cost has been bestow'd
> To give that prospect—of the London road !
> Our admiration knows not where to fix—
> Here a cascade, and there a coach and six.

The original vase, dug up, they said, by a labouring man in 1769 at Frascati, " the receptacle of all the contending poetical morsels," was quite a small thing. The Millers brought it from Italy, and it remained in the house, I learn from Miss Layard, of Petercourt, Bath, in the time of her grandfather, when it was struck by lightning and much damaged. When it would no longer hold together it was thrown away. In the Park at Bath is a copy, much enlarged (which the Dictionary of National Biography took to be the original). Sir John Miller and his wife returned from Italy filled with " taste " and determined to naturalize another " little Gallic Institution," the salon. They succeeded better than—the wits a few years ago would have it—did a rich young minor poet in London, who tried to found a salon and succeeded only in establishing a restaurant. Lady Miller wisely relied more on intellectual than on gastronomic attractions. Lady Miller, says Fanny Burney, was " extremely good-natured and extremely civil " ;

but—" all her aim is to appear an elegant woman of fashion, all her success is to seem an ordinary woman in very common life, with fine clothes on. Her movements are bustling, her air is mock-important, and her manners inelegant." Poor Sir John was a Mr. Leo Hunter, but " his fingers are loaded with cameos, his tongue runs over with *virtu* "—those are Horace Walpole's bitternesses. Everybody who was not invited laughed heartily at the amusement, the visitors, the house, the vase. But none the less, when the first volume of *The Poetical Amusements* was published, it was bought up within ten days. Into such a scene Fanny Burney, who was fond of good company, was very glad to enter with Mrs. Thrale, who was fonder still, was admitted on Thursday, June 8, 1780, and found herself " the *ton* at Bath." But it was not " in vase time." So the admired authoress was not compelled to contribute to the medley of inferior verse which made such a stir in the little Bath world, though her friends congratulated her " very wickedly " upon her initiation.

The four volumes of artificial flowers—so Horace Walpole called them—have at least the excuse that they were written by idle people in the midst of " all the dissipations of a full *Bath Season*—alike unfriendly to contemplation and the Muses "—I cannot help quoting these egregious Millers, for they are so vastly diverting—and that they were sold for the benefit of the Bath charities. A Marquess does not always write good verses : Lord Caermarthen in volume I does not ; but really the Duchess of Northumberland is " not at all bad " in these lines :—

> The pen, which now I take and brandish
> Has long lain useless in my standish.
> Know, every maid, from her in pattin
> To her who shines in glossy satin
> That could they now prepare an oglio
> From best receipt of book in folio
> Ever so fine, for all their puffing,
> I should prefer a butter'd muffin.
> A muffin, Jove himself might feast on,
> If eat with Miller at Batheaston.

THE REV. RICHARD GRAVES

Dr. Johnson sagely answered to Boswell, "Sir, the Duchess of Northumberland may do as she pleases ; nobody will say anything to a lady of her high rank. But I should be apt to throw . . . . . .'s verses in his face." And, alas, it would seem probable that ". . . . . ." means Mr. Graves, who had, as I said, been a neighbour of Dr. Taylor's at Asbourne. Whoever he was, Johnson considered that when he wrote for the vase he was a blockhead for his pains. After buying these *Poetical Amusements* and trying to read them, I am inclined to agree with the lexicographer.

But Mr. Graves cannot be passed by without a kind word. He very happily answered the *Bath Chronicle*, which laughed at the Millers for having no meeting on Good Friday ; and really his verses are better than any one else's. That is not saying much ; though I will say a word for the lines in Volume III, called "Verses occasioned by a Reverend Dean's breaking the Bell-Rope at the Villa, while the several Odes on Hope were reading "—perhaps only because of the title itself. So much for the first three volumes, dull enough in all conscience. The fourth volume, published in 1781, remarks that it is still produced for the benefit of "the *Pauper* charity " at Bath, and that "all party in religion and in politics, all malignant insinuation and personal satire, will be looked for in vain in the present, as in the former publications." Lady Miller suppresses, she says, some lines as too complimentary to herself ; but she is not too modest to print the effusion of "the Rev. Mr. Butt of Stanford, near Worcester," which begins :—

Accomplish'd *Miller*, form'd to please
By social sweetness, graceful ease ;
Sweet tints, by Nature gently laid,
Your brighter virtue's soft'ning shade ;
For these we love you, but admire
That ardent zeal, and gen'rous fire,
Which in this cold age call you forth
To vindicate the Muse's worth ;
Thus fann'd, for ever will her flame
Reflect a lustre on your name.

BURFORD PAPERS

After this one need not be surprised that Mr. Graves, writing of the Transmigration of Souls, says that—

> Perhaps the soul of *Hyde*, or *Hamden*,
> Revives in N—rth, or B—rke, or C—mden ;
> Not warp'd by inj'ries or disgrace,
> Not hankering after rank or place,
> But much improv'd by their migration,
> With zeal to serve the King, or nation.

Christopher Anstey eulogises, amid "Winter Amusements," "*Philander's* cheerful dome." I don't know if the Villa had a dome, or if he means the "temple," or only wants a poor rhyme to "bloom."

Enough of the *Poetical Amusements*, for I seem to have forgotten Mr. Graves. He lived very happily at Claverton, poor at first, but growing richer, as time went on, through the ingenious diversion of taking pupils, a practice to which the country clergy of his neighbourhood are, it would seem, still addicted. He taught, as most of them do, or would do, the sons of a bishop and a squire, and a man or two who rose into fame in later days. Graves's famous man was Malthus, who ministered the Blessed Sacrament to him on his deathbed. The company of little pupils reached forty at one time, it would seem from a letter of Bishop Warburton's in 1766 to Hurd.

An excellent clergyman, the Rev. Francis Kilvert, memoirs of whom were published in 1876, who lived at Claverton Lodge from 1837, and also took pupils, left a very agreeable account of Mr. Graves, full of entertaining details. It is hinted that he "had family trials of a peculiarly painful nature"; if this be so, it is indeed remarkable that he preserved his cheerfulness and his health for so many years. Till within a few weeks of his death he was at Bath—so a friend of his records—every day. He wrote, scribbled, incessantly. And yet things that he wrote suggest that he can hardly have neglected his parish. Some of his poems, particularly "The Farmer's Son," suggest, like Crabbe's, a very close knowledge of the daily life of the poor. Indeed, there is a curious likeness in many respects between

Graves and Crabbe, though the latter had the genius which never visited the Rector of Claverton. He had lived among abler men than himself, and yet in facility and knowledge and breadth, and not rarely in character, he must have seemed to his contemporaries to surpass them. It is a not uncommon experience. A man so clever and so facile, so well read and so kind-hearted, left no enduring mark on the literature of his age, and is forgotten even among those who love letters, when a few lines of Shenstone preserve for him a modest place among the immortals.

Graves indeed suffered from the very excess of his power to charm. Benevolent, kindly, and witty, he was beloved wherever he was known. Says a contemporary :—

" This amiable, well-read and lively old man was known to all the frequenters of Bath . . ." and it was one of the sights of the neighbourhood " to see him on the verge of ninety walking almost daily to Bath with the briskness of youth."

" When [he was] in his 88th year, I attended with him at a visitation," says another, " sat near him at table and listened with astonishment to his uninterrupted flow of neat and epigrammatic impromptus, lively *jeux d'esprit*, and entertaining anecdotes." His peculiar humour, says Mr. Kilvert, is illustrated by the manner in which, when at seventy-eight, he had accepted the living of Croscombe to enhance its selling value (not " as a warming-pan," as the Dictionary of National Biography thinks), for the patron, he played up to his part of extreme age and pretended not to see the bell which he had to ring or hear it when he had rung it. There was " humour," too, in his walk, which was a sort of trot, and his talk, which was broken by a pleasing stutter. His writings were liked for himself and himself for his writings. To these it is high time to turn.

In the first place, I heartily wish they were republished. They give an extraordinarily good view of English life at the end of the eighteenth century, its simplicity, its amusements, its conflict of religious ideas, its relics of brutality, its philanthropy and sentiment, and—sometimes—its seriousness. The one obstacle that I see to the republication is the curiously common introduction of the idea of a " village tragedy," in plain language. Graves's experiences make him constantly recur to this topic ; hardly one of his books is without it. But otherwise, the humour of the books is their most prominent feature. It is a humour which never deserts the writer through more volumes than I have patience to count. Let us briefly run through the list.

The Spiritual Quixote is a really delightful book. To my mind the picture, which is for the most part quite consciously a caricature, of Methodism, is only a trivial part of the comedy of manners. What does it matter who sat for Wildgoose or Tugwell, whether Whitefield himself is at all commemorated, or Wesley, or any one ? There is quite enough to show that Graves had a warm affection for all the goodness of the good Methodists, and that he would have cut off his right hand rather than satirize the men who in their Master's name went about doing good. Graves could not abide a hypocrite or a silly fellow, and he is at his best when he mocks at hypocrisy and silliness. But that is not all. It is the picture of English country life which makes the book so delightful—the long walks, the scenes and sounds agricultural, the squires and farmers and milkmaids ; the Cotswold Games on Dover's hills, the Shakespeare Jubilee ; and the town sights, too ; Bath, like Jerusalem, set about with hills ; Gloucester, and the *Bell*, which no one will forget to visit for Mr. Whitefield's sake —and he was at Pembroke with Graves—Bristol, Tewkesbury, Stratford-on-Avon, and—in country again—the Leasowes, where Mr. Shenstone is found at work on his gardens, his statues, and his urns, and combats Mr. Wildgoose's enthusiastic notions, not without the aid of an amicable supper and a cool tankard. Mr. Shenstone did not always, Graves throws in by the way, rise at a very early hour ; and so his friend, having committed havoc in his cottage oriel, and thrown down his piping fawn, was off before he could be reproached. And by the way, too, my Lady Lyttelton is very warmly praised. It is the thousand and one incidents and characters and descriptions of hill and dale, and men and country houses, which give the book its charm. And it remains a book which every one should read.

I would myself say the same for *Columella, or the Distressed Anchoret, a colloquial tale*, published by Dodsley in 1779. Here again we are certainly with Shenstone, and the description of his house and gardens is to the life. There is the parish clergyman, too, whom readers of Lady Luxborough remember, who appears also, if I am not mistaken, in the *Spiritual Quixote*, the "little, round, oily man of God" who seems to have amused the whole literary coterie. Did Shenstone really fall in love with his housekeeper, as Columella does? He certainly did not marry her. Who are the lawyer and the Oxford Head? One does not very much care; but one delights with them in the country they pass through and the quaint folk they make friends with.

" The consciousness of having punctually discharged every duty of their respective stations diffused an ease and cheerfulness over their minds, and left them open to enjoyment, and at leisure to receive amusement from every object that presented itself in their way. The freshness of the morning, the serenity of the air, the verdure of the fields, every gentleman's seat, every farm-house, and every cottage they passed by, or every village they rode through, afforded some kind of pleasing reflections to persons of their happy disposition."

How thoroughly is this the spirit of the eighteenth century! I am scarcely ashamed to envy it. Yes, *Columella*, in spite of an incident or two, is a charming book. It is a rare one, too, but not so rare as *Plexippus, or the Aspiring Plebeian*—aspiring, for all Count Smorltork may say—which I have never been fortunate enough even to see. It was published anonymously in 1790, in two volumes.

An earlier book I can say something of,—*Eugenius: or, Anecdotes of the Golden Vale*, published in two volumes by Dodsley in 1785, is called " an embellished narrative of real facts." It is a simple tale enough, of a University man who goes into Wales and falls in love with the sister of his college friend. There are several other love affairs, and all of them end in marriage. There are also, as is strangely common in Graves's stories, tales of loves less simple and pure ; but the main story is very slight, and the attraction of the book really lies, as does that of all Graves's work, in the description of country life and humorous country society. There is plenty of fun in the account of the old friends who dined with each other, and called themselves the archbishop, the admiral, the governor, the chief justice, and so on. And there are a few of the characteristic subacidities which Graves's books always contain. Here is one. " We conversed half an hour with Sir Charles, and found him a very sensible, and rather modest young man, for a man of the world :—for though he had been bred, the last two years before he went to the University, at Winchester school, he had not contracted that intrepid air and petulance, which too many young men discover, who have been hackneyed from their very infancy in some of our public seminaries." A touch of contemporary interest is found in the remark that Werther's Charlotte " is said to be now a very plain old woman in Germany." Not that Graves was at all ill-natured. Far from it ; but he was easily amused, and he did not care to keep his amusement to himself. Perhaps it is for that reason that his books had the popularity they had ; certainly it was for that reason that he wrote so many of them. *Eugenius* is hard enough to get nowadays. There is no copy in the Bodleian, and the copy I read (which has an eighteenth-century label of " Calcutta Circulating Library ") was kindly lent me by a very fortunate collector of the author's works.

The prose of Graves is not all fiction. There is a volume of Sermons, which I have not managed to procure. There is *The Triflers*, from which I have already quoted, first published in 1805 and reprinted in London the next year, which has an extremely amusing description of Bath life and of the collectors of old furniture, who even then found it a happy hunting ground, and some other pieces in prose, as well as lines on Mr. Pitt and to pretty ladies. *Reveries of Solitude*, again, published in 1793, consists largely of essays in prose, in the style of an old Whig with no sympathy for Revolution. There is a great deal of very sensible writing in the book, on intemperance, on " growing old," on garrulity, and the like. " Garrulity is a propensity to be prating incessantly on uninteresting subjects " ; just the charge that might be brought against Mr. Graves, but I do not think at all justly. He might have been less garrulous if he could have kept away from verse ; but here we have verse, good, bad, and indifferent, again. Much the same is true of *Senilities, or Solitary Amusements ; in prose and verse, with a Cursory Disquisition on the Future Condition of the Sexes* (London, 1801), which has a diverting cut on the title page of a hermit blowing soap bubbles and within a paper on the consolation of neglected virgins. In this book he is severe on what one gathers to have been a weakness of his own, the unseasonable gallantry, innocent enough, of the aged, and diverting on " symptoms of self-importance," which he observed as " an idle man, living in the vicinity of Bath and spending many of his mornings in traversing the streets and public walks of that beautiful city." He has, too, a pleasant paper on Rural Felicity and the few who appreciate it, in the course of which he tells this tale :—

" I remember ' a party of pleasure,' consisting of some of the most respectable inhabitants of Bath (accompanied by a well-known Doctor in Divinity), who came to spend a day at a farm-house which commands one of the most delightful prospects in the environs of that beautiful city. As soon as dinner was ended, though in the midst of July, they shut up the parlour-windows, called for candles, and sat down to cards, till their postilion sent in word that it was almost dark ; they then hurried down to their tea and returned home, entertaining their friends for a week after, with the delightful day they had spent in the country." [1]

Graves's own pleasures were very different. They were

---

[1] *Senilities*, p. 108.

at least as much those of outdoor life as of society and verse-making. But what about his poetry ? This is what he says about the beginning of it :—

"Having been early in life intimately connected with Mr. Sh-nstone and a few more constant tipplers at the Castalian Fount ; he contracted a violent propensity to rhyming ; which (as Pope says) it is hard for the person himself to distinguish from a real genius. This by long habit became a kind of chronical disease. So that he could neither be much pleased or much displeased, without expressing his raptures in panegyrical, or his resentment in satyrical strains : and he has even suffered acute pain on those occasions 'till he had executed his purpose." [1] Verse, he could say, such as it was, " came natural to him " ; it was " as easy as lying." I would not be understood to mean that Mr. Graves was untruthful.

And more, it must not be thought that Graves could not write good verse when he liked, but really I have no time to quote it. His volume called *The Festoon* (1766), is quite a good collection of epigrams, ancient and modern ; and not the worst parts of it are his lines to Gainsborough, to Shenstone, and to his own brother in his Mickleton garden. *Euphrosyne, or Amusements on the Road of Life*, was published by Dodsley in one volume in 1776, and again in two volumes, with two charming frontispieces, in 1780. It is a really characteristic collection of the poetical amusements of the kindly creature. He has much more humour, more sense, critical and ludicrous, than he has skill in expression or originality. One is inclined to say that he knew too much, read too much, talked too much, had too many friends, to be ever really original. Yet he had real feeling : it is shown most clearly perhaps in his lines on Shenstone—" On the Death of Mr. Shenstone : to Mr. Robert Dodsley." For once he could write what he felt ; and he writes it no more sincerely than in the epitaph which adorns the urn in Halesowen Church. As to this last, one may observe that in the first edition of *Euphrosyne* he (or was it Mr. Dodsley ?) adds this note,

---

[1] *Euphrosyne*, preface, p. iii.

which was omitted in the second edition : " Though Mr. Graves could be content with the secret pleasure of erecting this urn to his friend ; we cannot but stigmatize the injustice of the gentleman who has inscribed his own name at length, on the pedestal—on account of a trifling alteration which he made in it—at Mr. Graves's expense." The volumes are not to be epitomized or selected from ; they cover too wide a field and their quality is too uniform for choice. Many people could write like that : perhaps many did ; but that is no reason why Graves should not have written and published, or why we should read.

The last book that I will name of his—there are several others that I have never seen—is *The Invalid, with the Obvious Means of Enjoying Health and Long Life, by a Nonogenarian, Editor of the Spiritual Quixote, Columella, Reveries of Solitude, etc.*, London, 1804. It was his last book published while he was alive, and it is dedicated to Prince Hoare, his old pupil, " a model of temperance and sobriety to gentlemen in your station of life." The idea of the book is that of Cornaro, that long life is due to spare eating and drinking, an idea which is very likely true, though we are told that the abstemious Graves became so thin and weak that he had not strength to combat what need not have been his last illness. He writes very wisely of the folly of Dr. Drowsy, who " insists upon it that a bottle of port at dinner and a pint at night are absolutely necessary for his health," and while he allows you when you are out to " stand upon your head and drink a bumper to the Antipodes, as Sir Wilful Witwoud says, if that be the taste of the company," he adjures you at home never to exceed the second or third slice and after the third glass of wine to thrust the cork into the bottle. The book shows what a sensible man Graves was, and accounts very satisfactorily for his length of life.

So much for Graves in Literature. I said that I would write of him as a parish priest, but now that I come to the subject, I really do not know what to say. There are very few records of him in that capacity : the only one I remember is that he continued in his office to the pain of his congregation. But the whole tone of his writing is that of an acute and kindly nature ; and thus he ought to have made a good parson. Sometimes one is inclined to say, blessed is the parish priest who has no history—when one is beset by the advertising, organising, ecclesiastic, with one ear to the telephone and the other to the drum ecclesiastic. " That ye study to be quiet," may well have been Graves's motto. He went in and out among his people ; and the last thing he would have thought of doing was to put down how many visits he paid or how much he collected for foreign missions. I am sadly afraid—I say it seriously— he said nothing about missions at all ; and yet I am bound to think that he was a good man who tried to do his duty towards his people, his neighbours, his God. The way in which he speaks of the clergy shows that the ideal of those around him was not high ; but the way he speaks of the duty of the parish priest shows that he knew its supreme importance, and, I believe, that he did not neglect it.

There is very much more that one might write about him, but short of a biography, which I doubt if any one nowadays would read, there is nothing else that would tell very much more than has been told. If a man is known by his friends, Graves was certainly a good man. Shenstone had his weaknesses, but Jago and Ralph Allen are names to conjure with among good people. Some of the most interesting pages of reminiscence that he wrote are those that tell of the virtues of " low-born Allen," his rise, his charities, his house, the company he kept. To Graves he was a constant patron. One tale of his kindness is worth quoting :—

" In the year 1758 Mr. Allen purchased the manor of Claverton, where, after having repaired, improved and built a gallery in the church ; finding that the rector had several young gentlemen of family and fortune under his care ; and a very indifferent old house for their accomoda- tion, Mr. Allen offered to build him a room, which he immediately executed ; building a room twenty-five feet by sixteen, with two bed-chambers over it, which he observed would serve for a school, as long as he continued that employment ; and might afterwards be converted into a good parlour, as it is at present." [1]

The story of Warburton's rise is another that Graves tells with spirit—how it was due to Allen's kindness in inviting the poor Lincolnshire clergyman to stay with him just because he was a friend of Pope. Mrs. Warburton, whom most writers are so bitter upon, fares kindly in his writings, and the second volume of *Euphrosyne* is dedicated to her. For the rough, overbearing, pedantic Warburton the simple, kindly Graves cannot have had much affection. Their lives were very different. The one seemed to have reached the height of prosperity. He was such a bishop as the eighteenth century produced and envied. But happiness fled from him. His wife, if the tales be true, made his days pitiably unquiet, and in his later years he suffered from the ills which Graves's temperate regimen enabled him to avoid.

" Bishop Warburton," says Bishop Newton, who tells many anecdotes of that prelate and highly approved " his capital work," *The Divine Legation of Moses,* " was in a great measure lost to the world and to his friends some time before his death, by the decay of his intellectual faculties, the body pressing down the mind that mused upon many things ; which hath been the case of many a great genius as well as himself."

With Graves the body never pressed down the mind. He lived simply and happily, and the memory of him was that of a kindly, witty, facile creature, who never had an enemy, and whose friendships have come to belong, through his own pleasant records of them, to the history of English literature.

One last word. We may not forget that Graves was painted by Gainsborough, in that delightful Bath period of his life when he was just beginning to feel the world at his feet. As Gainsborough painted him, Graves's thin, keen face and sharp nose look out from under the great wig that was still orthodox to old-fashioned clergymen. His eyes have deep hollows round, and so they stand back almost as

[1] *The Triflers,* p. 66.

if glasses were before them; his mouth is shrunk and fallen; he looks old, very old, but still unquestionably alert and energetic. One fancies him from the face as walking in the rapid way we know he had, as eager to hear and be heard, as vigorous and curious to the limit of human activity. A quaint little eccentric clergyman; there are still many of them, and the world passes them by nowadays with a smile not untinged with contempt. But Graves in his day was not contemned, or ridiculed, or ignored. And the good feeling he won I have no doubt that he richly deserved.

If we may not call him a poet, he has real claim to rank among English men of letters. He was a scholar in the old classics, and could make good "versions" of them. He loved good things, and he knew how, in his quiet way, to express the pleasure they gave him—the busy chatter of people in the streets, the sweet sounds of springtime in the country lanes, the smile in the eyes of a pretty maid, the ripe sight of a field in summer, the laughter in the heart of old friends as they sit together over the fire.

On the Religion of a Century

SOME CLERICAL IDEALS : A RETROSPECT

No class of men in any age have been more heartily abused than the clergy, high and low, of the last century. Historians and moralists have alike condemned them. Yet historically their position is most interesting, because it shows the inevitable decay which swiftly follows a religion without enthusiasm ; while morally they illustrate the utter failure of the most admirable philosophic principles to influence more than the narrowest circles. There is a general impression that, just as it is thought of the Salvation Army that their ranks are merely replenished from the masses who have already had religious experiences in other denominations, so the clerical moralists of the eighteenth century contrived to moralize none who were not moral already. It were trivial to run over the commonplaces of accusation against them, but it may be interesting to illustrate from a valuable but forgotten little book one aspect of the clerical life of the time, which is not without a bearing upon the general condition of society during the period.

We are familiar enough with the great clerical pluralist of the age of the Church's apathy. We have seen him again, perhaps more clearly than ever, in Dr. Birkbeck Hill's delightful *Letters of Dr. Johnson*. Dr. Taylor, with his prebend at Westminster, his London benefice, and his great, comfortable house at Ashbourne, in Derbyshire, with "no park but a little enclosure behind his house, in which there are about thirty bucks and does," his bullocks, and the perpetual talk of the "great bull," or of *runts*— "their talk is all of runts (a young cow")—with his valetudinarian manners, "not much amiss but always complaining," and his dinner-party on Easter Eve, which Johnson refused to attend—was just the man towards whom preferments seemed naturally to flow, and who would hurry up to London in his "large roomy postchase drawn by four stout, plump horses, and driven by two steady, jolly postilions," to urge his claim on the Ministry for a deanery. Yet he had a past which seems, in one phase at least, to have been disgraceful : he was separated from his wife, was litigious to a passionate degree, and was a man whom his constant friend, Johnson, admitted to be tedious and confined in conversation and of a quite unecclesiastical manner.

"Sir, I love him," the great man said, "but I do not love him more ; my regard for him does not increase. As it is said in the Apocrypha, 'his talk is of bullocks' : I do not suppose he is very fond of my company. His habits are by no means sufficiently clerical : this he knows that I see ; and no man likes to live under the eye of perpetual disapprobation."

Such a man was one to "go out on a country living," and to "talk of it with great pomp" like another friend of Johnson's, the Oxford don Coulson, and could preach, to boot, as Sir John Hawkins said, "with great vigour." How utterly unedifying and unspiritual such a life! How naturally such a one would sink on the least symptom of illness into a condition of melancholic lethargy with no comfort from the mind or the soul :—

"How are you," says Johnson, "to escape uneasiness ? By company and business. Get and keep about you those with whom you are most at ease, and contrive for your mornings something to do and bustle about it as much as you can."

Strange counsel for a priest. From such a one the descent is easy to Johnson's uncle Harrison.

"A very mean and vulgar man, drunk every night, but drunk 'with little drink,' very peevish, very proud, very ostentatious, but luckily not rich."

But was he a clergyman ? He is not to be confused, as

236

Dr. Birkbeck Hill with just indignation pointed out to me, with Cornelius Harrison, his " cousin german " as he calls him, who was perpetual curate of Darlington, and the only one of Johnson's relations who " ever rose in character above neglect."

Reasons for lamentable deficiencies such as these are plentiful as blackberries. You may point the moral from Bishop Butler's timorous anticipations or adorn the tale from Fielding's inimitable sketches of clerical life. Call it a reaction from the dignity of the persecuted clergy of Caroline days if you will, or a natural consequence of the " flunkeyisms and most sweet voices " of the times of the early Hanoverians. But in one point, amid a multitude of causes, is our view of this strange condition of a class both clear and instructive. It was not patronage or persecution ; it was not this controversy or the other political intrigue ; it was neither the Bangorian controversy nor the suppression of Convocation, that brought the clerical estate to such a pitch of apathy and indifference : it was the absence of all ideals of the spiritual life, or, rather, the presence of a low and comfortable standard by which life was estimated, its aims and its ends regarded, and in which its duties were undertaken.

There could be no better illustration of this than a neat little volume printed at Shrewsbury in 1791, and entitled *Letters to a young Clergyman from the late Reverend Mr. Job Orton.* This was republished in two volumes in 1805, with additional letters by Dr. Stonhouse. Mr. Job Orton was a Dissenting minister of some note. He was born at Shrewsbury on September 4, 1717, and died at Kidderminster on July 19, 1783. Educated at the school of his birthplace, he early turned his thoughts to the instruction of his neighbours, and ministered in many places, chiefly and latterly at his native town. In 1765 illness obliged him to give up preaching, but he was able to continue the writing of religious books, such as his *Sacramental Meditations* (1777), which were greatly approved by such indifferent judges of theology as Dr. Tucker, Dean of Gloucester, and Dr. Adams, Master of Pembroke College, Oxford. Mr.

Orton had already "appeared in the world under the respectable characters of a commentator, a sermon-writer, and a biographer," and the Rev. Thomas Stedman introduced him "in a new light, that of a correspondent." The letters were written between 1777 and 1779 to Mr. Stedman when he was curate of Great and Little Cheverel, in Wiltshire, under rectors either non-resident or infirm ; and they were designed to instruct and encourage the young man in the work it might be proper for him to undertake. Characteristic indeed of the times is the first of them. It begins thus :—

"Dear Sir—

"I am very glad for Dr. Stonhouse's sake and also for *your own*, that you intend accepting the curacy of *Little Cheverel*. The doctor is a genteel, good-tempered man ; truly serious, rationally Evangelical and judiciously zealous. He will treat you like a friend and a brother, and you will be pleased and improved by his company and conversation. He preaches, during his residence, twice every Sunday, and has a lecture on Wednesday evening. But *ill health* obliges him to live the greater part of the year at *Bristol*, for the benefit of the waters there."

The Rev. James Stonhouse M.D., afterwards Sir James Stonhouse, did not sink below the standard of his day. For some time at least he resided in Bath only for four months out of the twelve, that is from December 1 to March 30. Indeed it has been pointed out that nowadays some clergymen take three months "off," and several days which have a way of mounting up towards another ! Let us say the best of Sir James, for so did the kind gentleman who wrote these letters. He wrote a number of excellent tracts, and tractates, which had a large circulation.

But these at least are the facts : Dr. Stonhouse, in spite of his ill health, retained for many years the living of Little Cheverel, adding to it that of Great Cheverel, but continuing to enjoy his sojourn at Bristol, and his visits to his "patrons," Lord Radnor and the "Lady Dowager Lichfield." Mr. Job Orton, though a Dissenter, was a kindly critic of the Church, and though "an enemy to pluralities" did not hesitate to recommend Mr. Stedman to accept two curacies :—

"Your sphere of usefulness," he said, "will be enlarged ; the inhabitants of that village [Great Cheverel] and its environs will enjoy your labours, without being exposed to censure for rambling from their own fold and deserting their established pastor, who I find is very old and too infirm to officiate any longer among them."

It appears to be a question whether the curate may be permitted to take charge of two adjoining parishes ; but no censure of the non-resident rector with his many livings, genteel ill health and rational Evangelicalism, is so much as hinted at. Dr. Stonhouse enjoyed not only the preferments that have been already mentioned, but was "*Lecturer of All Saints', in Bristol,*" where he employed as curate the worthy Mr. Love, for whose monument in Bristol Cathedral Hannah More wrote an epitaph. He was eager to instruct mankind, and not only did he publish *Every man's Assistant,* but he was ready with *Hints to a Curate* and with *Prayers* and *Tracts,* which he would have distributed to every house in the parish ; and Mr. Job Orton, in no satirical humour, wished the worthy curate "some very comfortable and improving weeks with the doctor and his family during his residence at Cheverel, which you must set against many uncomfortable and dreary ones in the winter." Mr. Orton was so obliging, too, as to suggest a remedy for the doctor's disorders :—

"I wish the doctor would ride on horseback every day, as I do. *Recipe caballum* is his best prescription. Surely he might meet with some gentle easy horse, no matter how ill shaped and ugly, that might carry him safely about the fields of *Cheverel.* I remember an aged, gouty minister, who could not walk ; and, having a large garden, he used to ride often round it in a day upon an old, steady horse, who used to count his rounds for him ; and then when he had completed them, would stop and proceed no farther, though the rider tried every persuasion and pungent argument to excite him."

In fact, much of this curious and entertaining correspondence is occupied with a reverent interest in the infirmities and pieties, the pluralities and the fine friends of the holder of many rectories. Non-residence, the curse of the age, is not merely winked at ; it is accepted as natural and even beneficial :—

" I wish," says Mr. Orton on the death of the old incumbent of Great Cheverel, "you may be continued in the curacy, provided the new rector should not choose to reside. Fellows of colleges, who have been many years immured in their colleges, are not always the most fit persons to be parish priests, not knowing well how to preach or converse or behave to common people."

With such a view of the duties of incumbents, it might be expected that a peculiar method of Scriptural commentary would be associated. Yet we cannot repress some slight surprise when we are assured that Mary Magdalene " was a pious lady of quality, who had been troubled with an epilepsy." Less unexpected it is that the provision for Church services is but scanty. It is regarded as an achievement to have introduced the most meagre form of vocal music :—

" I am glad you have introduced Psalm-singing into your church. I think your best way of carrying it on in an agreeable manner will be to get some of your young men to your own house now and then, and to go over some plain tunes with them till they can sing them perfectly ; and thus by degrees the rest of the congregation will learn them. . . . . I used to take this method with my young people at *Shrewsbury* ; but I never attempted to teach them the grounds of musick, because I thought it unnecessary, and, indeed, because I was not capable of it. But they learned to sing such tune, and in such time and method, that that part of the service was honourably conducted. By degrees you and they may learn some more, though, I should think, about eight common-metre, six long-metre, and two short-metre tunes would be enough."

After this there need be no surprise that Mr. Stedman was troubled with "eccentrick singers" that had "no more religion than an organ or fiddle." One further extract will make still clearer the standing point of the writer :—

"Perhaps nothing is more necessary than frequently and plainly to caution persons, especially the sick, against *laying an undue stress on the Lord's Supper.*"

Even if we could allow for the strange lowness of the ideal which seems to be set before the clergyman in these letters, we should still probably place little reliance on the judgment of a writer who considers Blair's sermons to be "indeed judicious, lively, elegant, and Evangelical." A generation which thought Blair lively may not be expected to desire any touch of enthusiasm in its devotion. And yet we should wrong Mr. Orton, and through him the age which he so graphically depicts for us, if we did not allow that now and again among his dullest platitudes we come across, unmistakably, the "accent of high seriousness, born of absolute sincerity." No one who reads through the little book could doubt that the writer was a man of genuine religion, or that the curate whom he instructed accepted his advice in simple piety and good faith. And yet the falling short in all that we look for in the clerical profession, the absence of any definite note of self-sacrifice and complete devotion, seems to place them both far away from the standard of to-day.

Yet the moralist and the historian may wrong the age which he seeks to explain. Only the novelist, in England, at least, has seen in its many lights the "web of mingled yarn" which the characters of the clerical estate in this age display. Jane Austen sees one side ; George Eliot, in her simple picture of Mr. Gilfil, a second ; Charlotte Brontë a third. And we have learnt the lesson they taught. The religious life of one age is not, we say, in outward expression as the religious life of another ; nor do we doubt that in practical good works both Mr. Stedman and his mentor would bear comparison with the country curate and the "retired minister" of to-day. But beneath the superficial differences which may be thought perhaps only to hide a real similarity there lies surely a real divergence which explains the woeful failure of the conventional religion of the eighteenth century. For any touch of mysticism, for any realization of the immeasurable beauties of the spiritual life, for any of that Divine enthusiasm which in its different manifestations inspired Savonarola and John Wesley, S. Francis of Assisi and Nicholas Ferrar, we look in vain. Extremes meet : Religion becomes so harshly objective as, with the swing of the balance, to be at last exclusive of all but an individual and self-centred piety. External duties are no part, it might almost seem to these men, of their inner life. They have not felt the trans-figuring touch of the Divine Hand, as it is laid on every particle of life. Enthusiasm is thus a word of abhorrence. In Johnson's dictionary the first definition is " a vain belief of private revelation : a vain confidence of Divine favour." The personal experiences and the interior conflicts of the saints are passed by without regard.

There is among my great uncle's books an extremely well-written work published in 1802, entitled *A Secular Essay*. It was written by the Rev. John Brewster, then vicar of Stockton-on-Tees, and it reviews the ecclesiastical history of the century within the same limits as those of Mr. Abbey from whose book I have quoted. A passage in it— (pp. 169, 170)—so aptly illustrates the weakness of the Church during the period, that I cannot forbear to give it here :—

" It is not my intention, by any means, to apologize for those ministers of the Established Church who preach *morality* instead of the pure doctrines of the Christian Faith. If such there are, let them bear the blame of the offence they commit : but let the designs of the Church of England be acquitted. Willingly I subscribe to the opinion of many excellent prelates and pious men, that we ought to return, in our preaching, to the first elements of our faith ; that we should reject a morality without motives, and a philosophy without principle. So far have men been led away by wild and fanciful opinion in the present age of the world ; so far have they been deluded by an unsteady and deceitful meteor, that they require the direction of the *true light*, which alone can lead them to everlasting life. The Gospel of Christ is a sacred, it is an awful, deposit. It was delivered from the depths of divine wisdom, for the final salvation of mankind. Let no minister of Christ, then, betray the important trust thus placed in his hands. Let him guard it with much more than common care ; let it be dearer to him than life itself. Let him dispense it with diligence and zeal to the hungry and the naked, who are waiting for its benefits. Thus only, in the great day of accounts shall we be made to hear these joyful words : " I was hungry and ye gave me spiritual food ; I was thirsty and ye made me drink the waters of salvation ; I was naked and ye clothed me in robes of righteousness, for Jesus Christ's sake."

It was the absence of this spirit which the writer deplored, and which was the cause of the failure of the Church to retain her hold on the hearts of the people.

Turn for a contrast to those sermons of Count Zinzendorf, preached in London, which it is not impossible Mr. Orton may have heard. There the whole spirit is changed ; there is a swirl of movement fraught with Divine energy, like the sweep of angels' wings :—

" ' No man cometh to the Father but by Me.' Nobody that hath not a heart can tell what to make of this ; but he that hath the Divine Economy that rules the world in his heart, and has a share in it, he understands this. There are not two sorts of men, two sorts of souls, we are all brethren and sisters ; therefore we may look upon all the sinners in a whole city, and in half a world of men, as such, nor is there a single soul whom we may not behold with brotherly eyes. For although their signature, and their whole air and behaviour do presently discover that they are not the people whom the Father hath given to His Son as the firstfruits ; yet of this we are so certainly persuaded that we could stake our lives thereupon, that no human creature walks the streets, that no human creature is existing, let it live as it will in all manner of sins, who may not, through the sovereign power of Jesus Christ, be delivered from its sins, be laid hold of and carried home upon the arms of the God and Creator of the universe."

We are in a new world ; light and hope stream into every habitation, for it is indeed felt that the Sun of Righteousness is risen with healing in His wings. There is a great gulf between such men as Zinzendorf or Wesley and those to whom and by whom these letters were written. By the latter we judge and we condemn the eighteenth century as an age of shackling conventions and grovelling aims. But when we do so we forget the noble souls, touched in truth with the sacred fire, who handed on to the evangelists and saints of our own time the traditions in which the Divine Spirit was to them embodied and enshrined.

TWO EIGHTEENTH CENTURY BISHOPS

IT might be naturally imagined, by those who are unacquainted with the history of the English Church, that the highest level of performance among her ministers would be marked at different periods by the work of the bishops. But this is far from being the case. If statesmen and party leaders have very frequently been ahead of public opinion, have inspired as well as inaugurated reforms, have advanced the moral tone of the political arena or even of the people as a whole, much more than has been done by the rank and file among members of either house, this can rarely be said to find a parallel in the ecclesiastical world. Certain great prelates there have been who have left a conspicuous mark upon the Church, who have been leaders truly in the general advance. Such were Parker, Andrewes, Laud, Wilson, Wilberforce ; to proceed further would be invidious and indiscreet. But the list is significant ; and so indeed would be any other which might be drawn up—significant because the general work of the clergy, when once it is seriously investigated with the aid of such memorials as they have left, is found to be more deep and more fruitful in the matter of direct evangelization, or serious study, or definite pastoral labour, than that of their ecclesiastical superiors ; and significant also the list would be because it shows among bishops of the highest eminence an almost entire blank in the eighteenth century. The reasons for this are well known, and there is no need to dwell on them now, for they are, so far as the world can judge, no longer operative. Politics were too closely linked to religion, and the Whigs were in power : nowadays politics do not trouble themselves seriously—though they sometimes pretend to—with religion ; and there are no Whigs.

But none the less, if the religion of any period in English history is to be understood,it must be studied in the bishops; for if bishops do not lead, at least they reflect the current religious ideas. Sometimes they are sensitive on political matters, sometimes on philosophy or science, as their contemporary representatives expound them, sometimes on questions of ecclesiastical ceremonial or adornment ; and this is generally because the clergy are sensitive on these matters for the moment, or sometimes, but more rarely, it is because the laity are sensitive. However that may be, if a bishop be below the clerical standard of personal virtue, he will at least represent to a large extent the common view of clerical opinion. I am speaking, of course, of the eighteenth century ; and that century is one which has no very rigid time limits. In its ecclesiastical, as in its political light, the real beginning is either 1688, or 1714, and the year 1800 is in no sense an important date. The Church of Queen Anne was still the Church of the Stewarts, loyal, enthusiastic in political championship as well as in theological study, courted by the State, respected and loved by the people. The Bishops were men of learning and ability ; the lesser clergy, though often ignorant, yet possessed great influence. The leading feature of the time, indeed, was the alliance between Church and State, and the enthusiastic devotion of the Queen to the Church and the clergy to the Queen. With the accession of the House of Hanover, all was changed. A division at once occurred between the secular Latitudinarian Bishops, who were appointed for political, not religious reasons, and the clergy, who were Churchmen and Tories to the core. From 1714 dates that horror of enthusiasm, which is the distinguishing mark of the eighteenth century in England in its religious aspect. This exaggerated love of cold reason, untouched by any warmth of sentiment, and too often to outward seeming by any reality of feeling, is seen first and most completely in Hoadly, to the " deadly leaven," of whose Latitudinarianism

ON TWO BISHOPS

Bishop Wilberforce attributed all the worst features of the episcopal character which the century produced. Hoadly and too many of his successors were grossly negligent of their duties, and utterly without the missionary spirit, in which alone the Church can fulfil her vocation. Enthusiasm in their vocabulary and in that of many better men was a word to be abhorred, for it set aside the sober balance of reason in favour of excitement. It is not that many of the Bishops were not good men, but that the ideal of the age—an ideal formed by the political and religious settlement of 1714—was painfully low. Self-sacrifice was a duty of which the age seems to have had no conception. The life according to reason was that in which good was done without the loss of personal comfort, or even the sacrifice of personal inclinations. There are two admirable examples of all this to be found in the autobiographical remains of two Bishops well known in their day.

The first is the " Account of the life of Thomas Newton, D.D., Lord Bishop of Bristol and Dean of S. Paul's London, with anecdotes of several of his friends," which was prefixed to the three volumes of his works published by John, Francis, and Charles Rivington in 1782. Dr. Newton gloried in being a " moderate man," [1] a glory which has long been understood to befit his office ; he meant that he was not very strongly in favour of any political or religious movement. During the last years of his life he was " disabled by ill health from performing his duty in the pulpit, and even from attending the service of the Church," but he retained his offices and—his son says—" he was yet very unwilling to live and die altogether useless to the world." As for his autobiography, it is very largely a record of his intimates. He regards himself as " a gentleman asked to introduce better company," for indeed " truth and friendship prompted him much more than vanity or self-love. It sometimes happens that an old man's *chit-chat* is very agreeable "—I continue the son's preface—" This may truly come under that denomination ; it was amusing even in

---

[1] See his *Sentiments of a Moderate Man Concerning Toleration.*

sickness to the writer, and it may be perhaps in an idle hour not unentertaining to the reader."

Thomas Newton was born in 1703 and died in 1782. He was proud to have been born at Lichfield and to have belonged to two schools, Lichfield and Westminster, which each produced an extraordinary number of eminent persons in his day—but Lichfield the more. His father was " a considerable brandy and cider-merchant," who was " a conversable agreeable old man " and constantly attended the daily service of the Church. He made himself a sufficient fortune, and his son inherited his shrewdness. He displayed it in going to Cambridge rather than Oxford, " thinking the studies there more manly, and knowing the fellowships of Trinity College to be much more valuable than the studentships of Christ Church." And at Cambridge he learnt at least to criticise the Master of Trinity, for he remarks that the great Bentley " was indeed an arbitrary Master, attended little to the duties of his station, very rarely was seen in chapel, and set no good example but that of hard study. In his latter days he loved his bottle of old Port, and used to say that Claret would be Port if it could." When Newton went to Cambridge his friend Murray went to Oxford ; the friendship lasted to the end of the days of Lord Mansfield and the Bishop of Bristol. A very happy youth he had, for he was happy in his studies at Cambridge, and happy in his friends at Lichfield, where he remarks that " there was better society than in most country places, and at that time there were so many remarkably pretty women there that Hawkins Browne [his school fellow and friend] used to call it the Paphos of England."

As a Fellow of Trinity he was ordained. He had always intended to take holy orders, and " had sufficient time to prepare himself and composed about twenty sermons." Thus equipped at starting, he rose from elevation to elevation. He used as a young clergyman in London, a nobleman's chaplain and preacher at Grosvenor Chapel in South Audley Street, to dine with Bishop Chandler of Durham (Butler's predecessor) and sup with Dr. Pearce, afterwards Bishop of Rochester ; and before long he made the acquaintance of the great Pulteney. The first thing he records of that eminent statesman is his dangerous illness, on which he spent " about 750 guineas in physicians and his cure was effected at last by some small beer." Pitt, it would seem, was too late when he said, " I think I could eat one of Bellamy's pork pies," for, according to Lord Beaconsfield, they were his last words ; but when Pulteney was entirely given over, and was but just alive, he could be " heard to mutter in a low voice, Small beer, Small beer. They said, Give him small beer or anything." Such are eminent physicians. But to continue the story. " Accordingly, a great silver cup was brought, which contained two quarts of small beer. They ordered an orange to be squeezed into it, and gave it him. He drank the whole at a draught and called for another. Another was given him, and soon after drinking that he fell into a most profound sleep and most profuse sweat for near twenty-four hours. In him the saying was verified, If he sleep, he shall do well. From that time he recovered marvellously, insomuch that in a few days the physicians took their leave, saying that now he had no want of anything, but of a horse for his doctor, and of an ass for his apothecary."

From this time onward the *Life and Anecdotes* (as the old gentleman called his autobiography) become much more Anecdotes than Life, and Lord Bath fills the greater part. Newton certainly admired Pulteney with honest warmth, and was not inclined to blame him for any of his public actions, unless it were for refusing to be prime minister—and yet perhaps, he says even then, he chose the better part, for when there cannot be *negotium sine periculo* the next thing to be considered is *otium cum dignitate*.

To this last Newton himself was not long in coming. He did not enjoy it, as used to be said a generation or two later of Lord Eldon, working in his garden so that men might say, ." There's my lord enjoying his *otium-cum-digging-a-taty*," but he made the most of it when he became Bishop and Dean, in the beautiful house that Sir Christophen Wren built, with an occasional excursion in the summer months to his diocese, the second city in the kingdom, as he proudly styles it. In the Deanery is now a fine mezzotint from Sir Joshua's picture, with a note stating that when the picture, which was exhibited in 1774, was painted, " Dr. Newton was 69 years of age, Reynolds 50, in the midst of his fame. It was in 1773 that Sir Joshua was made Hon. D.C.L. of Oxford, and Mayor of Plympton. Considerable friendship existed between the bishop and the painter, and had it not been for the dogged opposition of Dr. Terrick, Bishop of London, Wren's design for filling up the blank spaces on the walls of S. Paul's would have been fulfilled by Reynolds."

But, for the anecdotes, they plentifully bestrew his fine quarto pages. Of Dr. Savage, who was his predecessor as lecturer of S. George's, Hanover Square, he tells that George I. once asked him at a levée how long he had stayed at Rome, when he was there with Lord Salisbury, and when he heard his majesty added, " Why, you stayed long enough : why did you not convert the Pope ? " " Because," answered Dr. Savage smartly, " I had nothing better to offer him."

Whether the English clergyman rightly gauged the Pope's interest in ecclesiastical advancement it may be difficult to decide ; but it was a subject in which, for themselves, they were keenly concerned ; and Dr. Newton speaks without a tremor of his friend's " soliciting preferment," and tells a curious tale of how George I. had to outwit his ministers to give away one of his own royal prebends. It was in the case of one of the two Dr. Thomas's, whom it was so difficult to distinguish. " It was asked, Which do you mean ? Dr. John Thomas. They are both named John. Dr. Thomas who has a living in the city. They have both livings in the city. Dr. Thomas who is chaplain to the King. They are both chaplains to the King. Dr. Thomas who is a very good preacher. They are both very good preachers. Dr. Thomas who squints. They both squint."

But the anecdotes are not by any means all witticisms. Some of them throw light upon the condition of the Church in the eighteenth century—among them the account of the introduction of what may be called the method of confirmation by railfuls, of which he says that the clergy and the people " were struck with the decency as well as with the novelty of the ceremony." Yet in this " old man's chit-chat " the conversation always turns sooner or later on preferment ; and we learn that it was from George III. and his mother that the bishopric eventually came to him, when he was fifty-nine, though the Duke of Newcastle was not above claiming some share in the matter, for " he had been so long used to shuffle and cut the cards, that he well knew how to pack them in such a way as to have the honours dealt to his particular friends."

When he is a Bishop there is hardly a word of his episcopal duties ; still the tale is of this statesman and the other man of affairs. Lord Bath was the most charming of all the great men because his address was so familiar and engaging ; he did not, like Bolingbroke, dictate and dogmatize and talk essays, or, like Carteret, overwhelm you with his dis-course and engross the whole conversation, or like Chester-field, affect quaint conceits and lay traps and baits to introduce witty sayings and stories, which he had prepared beforehand. Still the tale is of preferments, for every Bishop, if we may take Newton for example, was on the look out for translation ; and George Grenville said ingenuously that he considered bishoprics as of two kinds, bishoprics of business, for men of abilities and learning, and bishoprics of ease, for men of family and fashion. Among the first were Canterbury and York, London and Ely ; Durham, Winchester, Salisbury and Worcester among the second. And yet Cornwallis was given Canterbury, and instead of Newton, Keene got Ely, whereupon he built a new Ely house in London, which to-day is the last country bishop's official town house, and at Ely " formed a new inside and thereby made one of the best episcopal houses if not the very best in the kingdom."

Bishop Newton had many compensations, among them the Deanery of S. Paul's, but he had such a severe illness in consequence of attending the cathedral service that he gave up being present at it altogether, though in the months that he spent at Bristol he went to church " as often as his health and the weather would permit." As for Bristol, the cathedral was shamefully neglected, says Newton, for " the bishop "—he speaks of himself impersonally—" has several times been there for months together, without seeing the face of Dean, or Prebendary, or anything better than a Minor Canon." The Bishop's example, he calmly says, had no effect : no doubt the Dean and the Prebendaries and all the things better than a Minor Canon were attending to his example at S. Paul's rather than at Bristol. But the poor Bishop was much distressed by the chapter's neglect. He solaced himself, it would seem, by controversy, though he was wise enough not to print his criticisms. Gibbon, for example, he read through, which he remarks " was a greater compliment to the work than was paid to it by two of the most eminent of his brethren for their learning and station " ; and he expresses his opinion of the *Decline and Fall* with remarkable candour. " He found it rather a prolix and tedious performance, his manner uninteresting, and his style affected, his testimonies not to be depended upon, and his frequent scoffs at religion offensive to every sober mind." Johnson's *Lives of the Poets* distressed him by " the malevolence that predominates in every part." What the authors would have said had the Bishop published his criticisms may be conjectured ; but at least it must be admitted that when it was turned against Bolingbroke, the episcopal pen was not unhappily employed. Here is an example : " His lordship seemeth to take a particular pleasure in railing at pedants, at the same time that he is himself one of the most pedantic of writers, if it be pedantry to make a vain ostentation of learning, and to quote authors without either reading or understanding learning, or even knowing so much as who and what they are. ' The Codex Alexandrinus,' saith he, ' we owe to George the monk.' We are indebted indeed to George the monk, more usually called Syncellus, for what is intituled *Vetus Chronicus*, or an old chronicle. But the *Codex Alexandrinus* is quite another thing ; it is, as all the learned know, the famous Greek MS. of the Old and New Testaments, brought originally from Alexandria, and presented to Charles I., and now remaining in the King's Library, of which it does not appear that George the monk knew anything, and it is evident that his lordship knew nothing." And so on. But such a witty Bishop wearies us nowadays, and we do not discover more interest in his elaborate Dissertations, which I find profusely marked in my copy, doubtless by my great uncle. And yet he was not a bad man : religious activity seems to have been entirely absent from his scheme of life ; like the Church of his time, I think it has been said, he was sleepy but not corrupt. A man indeed who might well have been loved, who admirably edited Milton, and who very likely did a great deal of good in a humble, unostentatious way, and never thought to set it down among his Anecdotes.

A very different person from the kindly Thomas Newton was the arrogant, dissatisfied, worldly Richard Watson, who was Bishop of Llandaff—to his disgust—from 1782 to 1816, and hardly ever entered his diocese, making himself as happy as he could at Calgarth Park, " in the beautiful district on the banks of Winandermere." He was the son of a Westmoreland " statesman," one of those folk whose way of life has recently been so happily described by Dr. Kitchin, Dean of Durham. He was born in 1737, his father in 1672 : and his father, grandfather, great-grandfather, and far back were natives of the same place, Hardendale, near Shap. The bishop's father was a schoolmaster, and his brother went to college ; but it was to his mother, he says, to whom he was indebted " for imbuing my young mind with principles of religion, which have never forsaken me "—so the bishop writes in his seventy-fifth year—" in that probity of manners with which I entered into the world at the age of seventeen." His career at Cambridge was the uninteresting one of a successful don. In spite of not caring " whether Cicero would have said *fortuīto* or *fortuĭto*, *Areopăgus* or *Areopăgus*," he rose, at Trinity, from sizar to scholar, from scholar to Fellow ; and then from Fellow to University distinctions, as Professor of Chemistry and then of Divinity. They did not care much for quantity or quality at Cambridge. In neither of the subjects which he was called upon to profess did he even pretend to be an expert. He had never read a syllable on the subject of Chemistry, he says, or seen a single experiment in it ; and as for the Regius Professorship of Divinity, the best he can say is that, " on being raised to this distinguished office I immediately applied myself with great eagerness to the study of divinity." The study, he is careful to observe, was undertaken with a mind wholly unbiassed : " I had no prejudice against, no predilection for the Church of England "—of which he was a minister in priest's orders. And he was at least as idle as he was unbiassed, for—" I never troubled myself with answering any arguments which the opponents in the divinity school brought against the articles of the Church, nor ever admitted their authority as decisive of a difficulty ; but I used on such occasions to say to them, holding the New Testament in my hand, *En sacrum codicem !* Here is the fountain of truth, why do you follow the streams derived from it by the sophistry or polluted by the passions of man ? If you can bring proofs against anything delivered in this book, I shall think it my duty to reply to you ; articles of churches are not of divine authority ; have done with them ; for they may be true, they may be false ; and appeal to the book itself." This was a very easy way of discharging the duties of " the first office for honour in the University," but even this professorial duty was before very long discharged by deputy, or by an occasional visit to Cambridge when he was Bishop of Llandaff, non-resident alike in his diocese and his University. However, he busied himself with all sorts of literary work, political and otherwise, and was greatly delighted at being mentioned in the House by Mr. Fox ; he also published an *Apology for Christianity* in answer to Mr. Gibbon, who expressed " his sense of the liberal treatment which he has received from so candid an adversary."

From about 1776 onwards Watson was nothing if not a politician, " a strenuous supporter of the principles of the Revolution " ; and so he became a bishop ; but he was not pleased at his " promotion," because he thought he " owed it not to any regard which he who gave it to me had to the zeal and industry with which I had for many years discharged the functions and fulfilled the duties of an academic life," but to the opinion that he might be a useful partisan. Perhaps if he had depended on the former qualification he would not have got his bishopric. Politics, politics, politics, and some very haughty letters to Mr. Pitt asking for a move up and very angrily replying to the Prime Minister's polite answer " No," fill much of the autobiography.

Like most Whigs of his age, and like Sydney Smith, who in political matters was his worthy disciple, Bishop Watson was not a warm advocate of missions. When approached on the subject of missions to India, he did no more than send the proposal to Pitt, with the remark that he did not " presume to say whether it would be practicable to introduce a knowledge of the Christian religion amongst the natives of Indostan, nor whether the present is the fittest time for making the attempt." He applied himself rather to the support of George Prince of Wales, in regard to whose personal character he does not seem to have displayed any uneasiness, and for whose opposition to his father and mother he found no word of dispraise.

Among the strange things of which we find this strange bishop proud, perhaps the strangest is this letter to Lord Rawdon, who had been the Duke of York's second in a duel :

" MY DEAR LORD,—I know you will forgive the liberty I take in requesting you to present, in the most respectful manner, to the Duke of York my warmest congratulations on a late event. As a Christian bishop, I cannot approve of any man's exposing his life on such an occasion. As a citizen, I must think that the life of one so near to the Crown ought not to be hazarded like the life of an ordinary man ; but as a friend to the House of Brunswick, I cannot but rejoice in the personal safety, and in the personal gallantry too, of so distinguished a branch of it."

Bishop Watson the citizen would probably have very quickly ascended the guillotine if the French Revolution had had a parallel in England ; but he was very liberal where the discharge of his own duties was not concerned. He wrote an immense number of letters to statesmen of both parties, and he was ready to join with his friend the

Duke of Grafton—as to whose personal character not much can be said—in bringing in a Bill " for expunging the Athanasian Creed from our Liturgy." However, none of his good deeds brought him further preferment, though he gave many broad hints on his own behalf, and asked for advantages for his family very readily. So he retired " in a great measure from public life " to the house he built at Windermere, and when he wrote, about 1812, he was able to make this agreeable confession :—

" I have now spent above twenty years in this delightful country, but my time has not been spent in field-diversions, in idle visitings, in county bickerings, in indolence or intemperance. No, it has been spent, partly in supporting the religion and constitution of the country by seasonable publications ; and principally in building farm-houses, blasting rocks, enclosing wastes, in making bad land good, in planting larches, and in planting in the hearts of my children principles of piety, of benevolence and of self-government. By such occupation I have much recovered my health, entirely preserved my independence, set an example of a spirited husbandry to the county, and honourably provided for my family."

" Provided for my family : "and so Bishop Newton says he was able " to make a competent provision for those who were to come after him, as well as to give something to charity." Perhaps that explains a good deal, for, after all, there is no particular reason why the grandson of a Northern farmer should be provided with a colonelcy in the Guards.

However, the Duke of Grafton liked Watson, and so did other Whigs. Mr. Pitt, the incorruptible one, did not : though Lord Camden told him that " it was a shame to him and the Church that he had not the most exalted station upon the bench."

As one reads these episcopal records, dreary and unblushing, one is almost reminded of the abuses of the Church in Italy, in Germany, and in France. The electoral-bishops, and even the Bishop of Autun, did hardly more harm to the Church, though they were worse men, than Watson. Newton shines in comparison ; and when one looks at the proud handsome face of the Bishop of Llandaff, which Romney has painted so finely, one turns almost with relief to the little sharp creature, peering out of his great wig, whom Sir Joshua Reynolds has made us see so truly in his kindly shrewdness. There are bad things about them both as bishops. But perhaps what it is most difficult to forget about Bishop Watson in his quarter of a century's retirement at Windermere, is his pamphlet on "The Wisdom and Goodness of God in having made both Rich and Poor," and his confident statement: " My religion is not founded, I hope, in presumption, but in piety." Yet even Watson did many good things ; truly the world of man is indeed a web of mingled yarn. Let those at least who would condemn the parochial clergy of the eighteenth century look higher before they begin ; and those who make fun of bishops now compare them with those who lived a hundred years ago.

THE COMMEMORATION OF JOHN WESLEY AND HIS JOURNAL

IT is fit indeed that we should join in the commemoration of this great name, which our separated brothers are celebrating in our midst (1903). For no Englishman in the eighteenth century did a greater work for England, splendid though the achievements of her generals and her statesmen were : and it is good to remember that he was an ordained minister of her national Church, proud to the last of his Orders and of the links which bound him to the primitive and the Catholic Church.

And the first step in commemoration should certainly be for every one to read that wonderful Journal of his, or such parts of it as we may—for even yet the Society will not suffer it all to be printed, even in the " standard edition which the Wesleyan Methodist editor has now in hand." It is one of the most wonderful records of human activity which pen ever set down. There are few autobiographies so candid and so close in self-revelation, and there are fewer which make the reader arise from the perusal with so deep a feeling of reverence and admiration. There are not many books which tell one more exactly what the life of England was, among the middle classes and the poor, a century and a half ago.

It is a book which one would have thought it impossible to patronize, if an eminent lawyer and man of letters had not accomplished the fact. Few will follow Mr. Augustine Birrell in comparing Wesley's ceaseless activity in the cause of Christ to the efforts of a candidate in a parliamentary election for an English or Scottish county ; few will smile at a jest about his " suits in Chancery and jealous wife."

Not that Wesley himself was without humour—far from it— but his was the humour which always bears, like the finest poetry as Matthew Arnold says, " the accent of high serious- ness, born of absolute sincerity." Laugh you may here and there in the pages of the Journal, but you will laugh with Wesley : you cannot bear that any one should laugh at him. You know that he had given his life to God, that, with all his faults, there was not one thought which was not consecrated or which he did not strive to bring into subjec- tion to the law of the Cross of Christ.

When he published in 1742 the third instalment of the Journal, he explained sufficiently his object in doing so. " What I desire in the following extract is, openly to declare to all mankind, what it is that the methodists (so-called) have done, and are doing now. Or rather, what it is that God hath done, and is still doing, in our land."

The Journal leaves a profound impression on the mind. It is an impression which it is difficult to compress into a few set phrases. It is one which can be at best suggested by a few hints of the wonders the book contains. And first the wonder of activity. For many years Wesley travelled eight thousand miles. He almost always preached twice a day, generally three times, very often many more : it has been said that he seldom in a year preached less frequently than five thousand times. Part of this extraordinary energy depended no doubt on an extraordinary strength of body ; more on strength and concentration of mind. Wesley was not a man who thought little about his health. On the contrary, his Journal is full of references to it. But he was one who allowed his health very little to influence his actions or interfere with his activities. He had work to do and he did it, well or ill. If well, so much the better : if pre- cautions would secure health without interfering with his activity, very good. But anyhow the work must be done. When he was seventy-nine, on his birthday, he wrote these words :

" I entered into my eightieth year ; but, blessed be God, my time is not ' labour and sorrow.' I find no more pain or bodily infirmities than at five-and-twenty. This I still impute : (1) To the power of God, fitting me for what He calls me to. (2) To my still travelling four or five thousand miles a year. (3) To my sleeping, night or day, whenever I want to. (4) To my rising at a set hour. And (5) To my constant preaching, particularly in the morning."

I think medical men, not to speak of all persons of common-sense, will agree that there was a great deal of truth in this explanation. Open air and exercise continually, combined with temperance and mental activity, make as good a prescription as the best physician can write. Two years later, in 1784, Wesley wrote : " I find myself just as strong to labour, and as fit for any exercise of body and mind as I was forty years ago ; " and a year later still, " It is now eleven years since I have felt any such thing as weariness.' And he adds, as before, " I dare not attribute this to natural causes : it is the will of God." Thirty-two years before, he was in perpetual fever, and could hardly speak for coughing, and wrote his own epitaph, " not knowing how it might please God to dispose of me ; "

HERE LIETH THE BODY

OF

JOHN WESLEY

A BRAND PLUCKED OUT OF THE BURNING ;

WHO DIED OF A CONSUMPTION IN THE

FIFTY-FIRST YEAR

OF HIS AGE,

NOT LEAVING, AFTER HIS DEBTS ARE PAID,

TEN POUNDS BEHIND HIM :

PRAYING,

GOD BE MERCIFUL TO ME, AN UNPROFITABLE

SERVANT !

He ordered that this, if any, inscription should be placed on his tombstone.

The expressions and the " spacing " of this unique inscription are characteristic in the highest degree : and what did its author and subject, who had thus contemplated his

death at fifty, think of it if he read it again at eighty-seven ?
Few men indeed have lived a life at once so long and so
energetic.   S. Francis Xavier, who equalled him in missionary activity under far greater difficulties, in a short
time fulfilled a long time.   Most of those who worked as he
did, and Whitefield among them, have been snatched away
in their prime.   But Wesley's was a strength that was
never suffered to rest idle, and yet it endured to the end.

When he was in America, and aged thirty-four, these
were typical days of his.   After travelling all night he
arrived very early at Purrysburg, and, finding no guide to
Port Royal, set out without one an hour before sunrise.
After walking two or three hours he was told that he could
easily reach his destination in another five or six.   At
eleven he lost his way and wandered about in a swamp till
two, when he found a wood and traced and retraced his steps
there till towards sundown.   All he and his two companions
had to eat that day and next morning was one gingerbread
cake between them ;   for water they dug with their hands
three feet into the ground.   On the ground they slept,
though " the night was sharp."   Next morning, " neither
faint nor weary," they began the march again at six: between
one and two they came to a friend's house.   Next morning
a new start was made—" About sunset we asked our guide
if he knew where he was, who frankly answered ' No.'
However, we pushed on till about seven we came to a
plantation ;   and the next evening, after many difficulties
and delays, we landed on Port Royal island."   Such he
was in his thirty-fifth year : on his eighty-eighth Christmas
in London he began service " as usual at four o'clock," took
service at the West End in the morning, and preached
again at four o'clock : and that was a holiday.

Take another extract from the Diary, enough to show
the nature of his ordinary journeyings.   He is going to his
old home at Epworth :

" I was wondering the day before at the mildness of the
weather, such as seldom attends me in my journies.   But
my wonder now ceased : the wind was turned full north, and
blew so exceedingly hard and keen, that when we came to

Hatfield, neither my companions nor I had much use of our hands or feet. After resting an hour, we bore up again, through the wind and snow, which drove full in our faces. But this was only a squall. In Baldock Field the storm began in earnest. The large hail drove so vehemently in our faces that we could not see, nor hardly breathe. However, before two o'clock we reached Baldock, where one met and conducted us safe to Potten.

"Tuesday, 17, we set out as soon as it was well light. But it was really hard work to get forward. For the frost would not well bear or break. And the untracked snow covering all the roads, we had much ado to keep our horses on their feet. Meantime the wind rose higher and higher till it was ready to overturn both man and beast. However, after a short bait at Bugden we pushed on, and were met in the middle of an open field with so violent a storm of rain and hail as we had not had before. It drove through our coats, great and small, boots, and everything, and yet froze as it fell, even upon our eyebrows, so that we had scarce strength or motion left, when we came into our inn at Stilton.

"We now gave up our hopes of reaching Grantham, the snow falling faster and faster. However, we took the advantage of a fair blast to set out, and made the best of our way to Stamford Heath. But here a new difficulty arose, from the snow lying in large drifts. Sometimes horse and man were well nigh swallowed up. Yet in less than an hour we were brought safe to Stamford. Being willing to get as far as we could, we made but a short stop here ; and about sunset came, cold and weary, yet well, to a little town called Brig-casterton.

"Wednesday, 18, our servant came up and said, ' Sir, there is no travelling to-day. Such a quantity of snow has fallen in the night that the roads are quite filled up.' I told him, ' At least we can walk twenty miles a day, with our horses in our hands.' So in the name of God we set out. The north-east wind was piercing as a sword, and had driven the snow into such uneven heaps, that the main road was not passable. However, we kept on, a-foot or on horseback, till we came to the White Lion at Grantham. Some from Grimsby had appointed to meet us here, but not hearing anything of them (for they were at another house by mistake), after an hour's rest we set out straight for Epworth. On the road we overtook a clergyman and his servant ; but the toothache quite shut my mouth. We reached Newark about five.

" Thursday, 19, the frost was not so sharp ; so that we had little difficulty till we came to Haxey-Car. But here the ice which covered the dykes, and great part of the common, would not bear, nor readily break. Nor did we know, there being no track of man or beast, what part of the dykes were fordable. However, we committed ourselves to God, and went on. We hit all our fords exactly, and, without any fall or considerable hindrance came to Epworth, full as well as when we left London." Certainly, almost the first thing to remember about John Wesley is his amazing strength. Humanly, it is the cause of his amazing success.

" Something too much of this ! " but it is necessary to remember it, that we may understand why it was that no Englishman ever did greater work than John Wesley, or left results more tremendous.

Yes, the word is not too strong : for the results were all those which touch not only on this present life, and in it have profoundly affected the lives of English-speaking folk in growing force for more than a century ; but they belong also, and more than all else, to the power of the world to come. John Wesley before all else was a great converter of souls. Again and again there are descriptions in his Journal of scenes such as that at Gwennap when he spoke to over ten thousand people for nearly two hours amid the deepest attention and hoped that " surely here, in a temple not made with hands, was God worshipped in the beauty of holiness ; " or when on the following day, as he wrote :

" I was waked between three and four by a large company of tinners, who, fearing they should be too late, gathered round the house, and were singing and praising God. At five I preached once more on 'Believe on the Lord Jesus Christ, and thou shalt be saved.' They all devoured the word. O may it be health to their soul, and marrow to their bones!" Or when he carried the good news of Jesus into the prison and the madhouse, or when, on a Good Friday in bleak Northumberland, "the poor sinners were gathered together and gave earnest heed to the things that were spoken." But it is idle to multiply instances; every one who knows the name of John Wesley knows that he was not only a great orator but a preacher who brought sinners to the Saviour of the world.

It was but bare truth when he wrote, eight years before he died, "I have been reflecting on my past life; I have been wandering up and down between fifty and sixty years, endeavouring in my poor way to do a little good to my fellow-creatures." And thus it was that, in spite of the opposition to him, and in spite of his own extravagances, he changed the face of England.

To say this is not to forget his faults. He was self-willed and dictatorial and impatient of opposition; that his wife left him is almost the worst condemnation that can be passed on a minister of Christ; but it has been most truly said that "never was there a man more ready to forgive injuries, more ready to own his failings, more firm to his friends, and more patient with his foes."

What was such a man's opinion of literature, I cannot refrain from asking. He read Prior, and Home—the forgotten bombastic tragedy of *Douglas*—and Thomson, and was not at all afraid of novels, such as *The Fool of Quality*. Of travels he was an eager reader and a sceptical critic. Thus he writes of Captain Cook:

"Meeting with a celebrated book, a volume of *Captain Cook's Voyages*, I sat down to read it with great expectation; but how was I disappointed. I observed, 1, Things absolutely incredible: 'A nation without any curiosity: and, what is stranger still, without any sense of shame . . . men whose skin, cheeks, and lips are white as milk.' Hume or Voltaire might believe this; but I cannot. I observed, 2, Things absolutely impossible. To instance one, for a specimen. A native of Otaheite is said to understand the language of an island eleven hundred miles distant from it in latitude, besides I know not how many hundreds in longitude ; so that I cannot but rank this narrative with that of Robinson Crusoe, and account Tupia to be, in several respects, akin to his man Friday " (December 17, 1773).

It is strange that the man who could be taken in by the most preposterous impositions of sham " spiritualists " —if one may use the word—could, when he would, disbelieve so readily.

More interesting are his opinions of two famous books of his day. It is strange that his comment is entirely non-moral in the one case, wholly moral in the other. Thus he writes of the *Sentimental Journey* :

" Sentimental ! What is that ? It is not English : he might as well say continental.[1] It is not sense ; it con-veys no determinate idea ; yet one fool makes many. And this nonsensical word (who would believe it ?) is become a fashionable one ! However, the book agrees full well with the title ; for one is as queer as the other. For oddity, uncouthness, and unlikeness to all the world beside, I suppose the writer is without a rival."

And thus of Lord Chesterfield :

" I borrowed here [Oxford in 1775] a volume of Lord Chesterfield's *Letters*, which I had heard very highly com-mended. And what did I learn ? That he was a man of much wit, middling sense, and some learning ; but as absolutely devoid of virtue as any Jew, Turk, or heathen that ever lived. I say, not only void of all religion (for I doubt whether he believed there is a God ; though he tags most of his letters with the name, for better sound sake), but even of virtue, of justice, and mercy, which he never once recommended to his son. And truth he sets at open defiance ; he continually guards him against it ; half his letters inculcate deep dissimulation as the most necessary

[1] English usage has accepted both, and we hardly understand now why Wesley protested. We have suffered much worse things.

of all accomplishments. Add to this, his studiously instilling into the young man all the principles of debauchery, when himself was between seventy and eighty years old."

Whatever were the value of his literary judgments, they were like the rest of his Journal, profoundly genuine. He never disguised his feelings. His supreme characteristic was truthfulness. And next, with all his heroic enthusiasms and ecstasies, he felt very much as other people feel. It was this very human saint whom Churchmen must ever remember with affection. They may endorse the stern warning of the great Bishop Butler ; they must feel that, in laying hands on men to undertake the episcopal office, he was departing from all covenanted order. They cannot fail to see, what the acute lawyer Mansfield saw immediately, that " Ordination is separation ; " they will remember the lines which perhaps his own brother wrote :

> How easily are bishops made,
> By man or woman's whim !
> Wesley his hands on Coke hath laid,
> But who laid hands on him ?

But more gladly they will call to mind the many times when he asseverated his loyalty to the Church, and they will know that his errors, disastrous though they are bound to think them—and are not all Christians bound equally to think them disastrous, for who can regard disunion as anything but a grievous loss ?—were errors of the head and never of the heart. In his own mind he was never anything but a Churchman. He denied, in 1748, that his followers were dissenters : he sorrowed over Luther's " rough, intractable spirit, and bitter zeal for opinions so greatly obstructive of the word of God ; " he pitied those who can find no good at church ; he regarded Swedenborg as " one of the most ingenious, lively, entertaining madmen that ever put pen to paper ; " he warned his people of " the madness that was spreading among them, namely, leaving the Church." When he found the Manx people simple-hearted and loving, he said, " No wonder, for they have but six Papists and no dissenters in the island." He believed that the "glory " of his society was " to be not a separate body : " he asseverated " the more I reflect, the more I am convinced that the Methodists ought not to leave the Church. I judge that to lose a thousand—nay, ten thousand—of our people would be a less evil than this." He implored those who regarded his judgment, " Do not cast away the peculiar glory which God hath put upon you, and frustrate the design of Providence ; be Church of England men still." At the very end of his life he said, ' I declare once more that I live and die a member of the Church of England, and that none who regard my judgment or advice will ever separate from it ; " and the last sermon he ever preached was in a parish church.

This was no insincere or ignorant sentimentality ; it was a reasoned attachment, such as made him observe Lent, use the mixed chalice, pray for the faithful departed, keep all festivals and fasts, enjoy cathedral music at the Eucharist, and rejoice when he could " have the Lord's Supper daily, a little emblem of the primitive Church." But, as the years went on, the stability of his churchmanship yielded to the assaults of his strenuous individualism.

And in individualism lies the strength not only of the great sect which he founded but of the great party in the Church which he did so much to strengthen if not to make. But there was a greater service that he did than this service to a sect and a party.

" It is not only among Evangelicals that we must look for the good work of Evangelicalism. Just as Methodism had been indirectly a Gospel of blessing to many who were never Methodists, so also the Evangelical movement quickened the vital fire among multitudes who by no means adopted its characteristic modes of thought, and who certainly would not have called themselves by its name. Coleridge, for instance, and Wordsworth, and Southey, and those whose religious life they influenced, were in no sense of the word Evangelicals, but it may be greatly questioned whether they would have been what they were if Evangelicalism had never been." [1]   I like so to think of Wesley, and of that bright company of Evangelical good men.

Mr. Hugh Price Hughes in his Introduction to the recent edition of the Journal, almost the last thing he wrote, considered that George Fox and John Wesley stood together as the champions of Individualism, and that against them stood the spirit of John Henry Newman : the future of the British Empire depended, he thought, on which would prevail.   For " the true inwardness of the issue " he would send us to the Journal and the Apologia.   But, in truth, the future lies in something that is neither Individualism nor Papal Infallibility.   It lies in the energies of the individual worker, blessed by the grace of Jesus Christ, in the Society of the Catholic Church.   And that in his heart John Wesley realized : and it is for that most of all that England may thank him to-day.

[1] *The English Church and its Bishops*, 1700–1800 :   By Charles J. Abbey, Rector of Checkendon, late fellow of University College, Oxford, and joint-author of *The English Church in the* 18*th Century*, vol. ii. p. 148.

LAURENCE STERNE.

LAURENCE STERNE

Is it the most pathetic figure of the eighteenth century in England which is presented by Laurence Sterne, the priest and the wit ? Is it, with memories of crime and sorrow in our history which cannot be forgotten, only the influence of his own sentimental insincerity which makes us for a moment linger over his life ? A strange life indeed it was, and a sad one, not least when it was striving to be fancifully gay.

A Protestant country clergyman who suddenly became famous as a man of letters, not only in England but in France, among the most exclusive and critical societies of fashion and wit, was even in the eighteenth century a novel phenomenon. It was indeed an unusual distinction when " the protector of men of wit and genius," the wonderful Lord Bathurst, who at eighty-five had " all the wit and promptness of a man of thirty," who had been the friend, and " patron " of Pope and Addison, of Steele and Swift and Prior, sought the acquaintance of this country clerk, and said, " I want to know you, Mr. Sterne, but it is fit you should know, also, who it is that wishes this pleasure. You have heard of an old Lord Bathurst, of whom your Popes and Swifts have sung and spoken so much ; I have lived my life with geniuses of that caste, but have survived them ; and, despairing ever to find their equals, it is some years since I have closed my accounts, and shut up my books, with thoughts of never opening them again ; but you have kindled a desire in me of opening them once more before I die, which I now do ; so go home, and dine with me." A charming greeting, indeed, for a vain creature ; and the distinguished old man, as a man of learning, cour-

269

tesy, and feeling, had "a disposition to be pleased, and a power to please others beyond whatever" the happy clergyman had ever known; and they spent "a most sentimental afternoon, till nine o'clock."

The prodigious eagerness with which this unknown man was greeted in the fashionable world, as well as among that strange aristocracy, the aristocracy of letters, and the extreme severity with which he was also assailed by wise men as well as by jealous scribblers, was enough to turn any man's head. But Parson Yorick's head was not turned. In truth, it is more generally folk's hearts than heads that are turned; and perhaps Sterne had no heart to be turned.

Sterne's story is so strange that it is worth telling again; and then one may well ask, was it more tragic even than it was strange? The son of a poor subaltern and a sutler's daughter, an idle, mischievous boy who left school "without a shilling in the world," a sizar who lived in company that was as poor in morals as he was in purse, a life-long struggler against consumption who never took ordinary precautions of prudence in regard to health, a priest who owed his professional income, small enough, to the favour of an uncle with whom he vigorously quarrelled, a minister of religion who wrote books both coarse and indecent, if not deliberately immoral—the tale need not be prolonged. There shall be substituted for it the simple record of dates. Laurence Sterne was born in 1713. He went to school at Halifax when he was ten, to Jesus College, Cambridge, when he was twenty. He was ordained deacon in 1736, priest in 1738. He became vicar that year of Sutton in the Forest, and a prebendary of York in 1741. He married Miss Elizabeth Lumley in the same year, "overpowered" by her generosity. He added another living, Stillington, to Sutton in 1743. At Sutton he resided for more than twenty years, having an income of about £200 per annum, farming unsuccessfully, painting like an amateur, reading like a dilettante, jesting broadly among the country squires. The strange unpleasant story is all in Croft's reminiscences in the *Whitefoord Papers*, grossly exaggerated I hope. A prosy, not edifying, life it was: till the end of 1759 Sterne was a clergyman of some local distinction, against whom many hard things were said. At the beginning of the next year he had published a book which in a few months made him famous. *Tristram Shandy* had not long been out when its author was told that " there was not such a book to be had in London either for love or money ; " not long after, as one of his country neighbours tells us, a wager was laid in London that a letter addressed " to Tristram Shandy in Europe " would be delivered ; and " the postboy meeting Sterne on the road to Sutton pulled off his hat and gave it him."

Then there were barely seven years of life left him. In those he tasted the extremity of fame : he was received everywhere, flattered everywhere, happy so far as success could make him. He was constantly in London, in " the best society : " he visited France and Italy, to find himself as famous in Paris as at home. When he was in Yorkshire he had a new home in the living Lord Fauconberg gave him at Coxwold, where he improved an old house and called it Shandy Hall. But at the height of his fame, and when he might have been happy in possessing influence with the widest sphere wherein to exercise it, he was dogged by severe illness—which he bore with unfailing cheerfulness—and at last, when the world was at his feet, he died alone in a hired lodging. The story of his last moments, as the literary footman, John Macdonald, " a cadet of the house of Keppoch," tells it, is one of the most tragic in the history of men of genius. " I waited ten minutes ; but in five he said, ' Now it is come ! ' He put up his hand as if to stop a blow, and died in a minute." It was Friday, the 18th of March, 1768, and he was only fifty-five.

Sterne was a man of genius. It were idle for those who detest some parts of his books, or who (like the present writer, in spite of repeated efforts) have never succeeded in reading *Tristram Shandy* from end to end, to deny it. But what, after all deductions are made for a strangely lax society and for a singular temperament, are we to say as to the character of the man ? A bishop—but he was one who did not mince his words—is reported to have said that he was

" an irrecoverable scoundrel." Dr. Johnson spoke of him severely. One of the Crofts, a neighbour of his, says, on what is apparently good evidence, that " he was far from being a good man," and tells at least two stories which make him a man of licentious morals. One at least of his own letters is only by most improbable interpretation patient of any meaning but one disgraceful to a husband and a priest. But, on the other hand, it is only fair to remember, what is very often forgotten, that Sterne, when these scandals must have been as well known in the neighbourhood as they are now to students, was the guest of his own diocesan, Archbishop Drummond ; that at the same time he was an intimate companion of at least one other bishop, who offered him preferment in his own diocese ; that he was an indulgent husband, and certainly a very fond and devoted father ; and that within a year of his death he made a statement, when there was no reason whatever to volunteer it, which, if true, is absolutely incompatible with all the charges against his moral life. He certainly numbered good men and good women among his friends. A very acute judge of character, and a keen investigator, the late H. D. Traill, said, "As to the nature of Sterne's love-affairs, I have come, though not without hesitation, to the conclusion that they were most if not all of them what is called, somewhat absurdly, Platonic." Only six months before his death he wrote to a male friend of his freely enough. " The past is over, and I can justify myself unto myself— can you do as much ? . . . I take heaven to witness, after all their badinage, my heart is innocent." Yet, if he was innocent, the scandals which were constantly and lightly told of him make his story a pitiable one. If he was guilty, the pity is perhaps the greater because it is not unmingled with disgust.

It is not unnatural to turn for some help in deciding to Sterne's sermons, and to the memories of his life as a parish priest. The first characteristic that strikes the reader of the sermons is their sentiment without enthusiasm. It is unpleasant to find him deriding the work of the Methodists, acutely though he lays his finger on the weakness of the doctrine of instantaneous conversion and assurance. The tone of "rational" apologetic is a mere vestment of the age : "we have nothing to part with but what is not our interest to keep" is a typical eighteenth century argument for religion. On the other hand the author was far from thinking that he employed only intellectual arguments or sought only intellectual conviction. "As the sermons turn chiefly upon philanthropy, and those kindred virtues to it upon which hang all the law and the prophets," he wrote, "I hope they will be no less felt, or worse received, from the evidence they bear of proceeding more from the heart than the head." It is difficult to read the sermons, not excepting those which bear the affectation of the successful "Shandyism" stamped on them, without feeling that the preacher never said a word beyond what he really believed and meant. He believed the central truths of Christianity in full sincerity, and he saw the horror and shame of sin plainly enough. If he did not sympathize with Methodist ways of dealing with the evils of the time, he saw quite plainly what the evils were. Vice and folly did not escape his lash, and he knew how to rebuke the society of which he had become the favourite for its neglect of religious observance and its derision of religious belief. He says that it might naturally be expected that religion would be found among those whose education helped them to know its value, but, "if you examine the fact, you will almost find it a test of a polite education, and mark of more shining parts, to know nothing and indeed care nothing at all about it ; or, if the subject happens to engage the attention of a few of the more sprightly wits,—that it serves no other purpose but that of being made merry at, and of being reserved as a standing jest, to enliven discourse when conversation slackens upon their hands." It had come to this, he said, that church-going was as much neglected among the upper classes "as if religion was a business fit only to employ tradesmen and mechanics—and the salvation of our souls a concern utterly below the consideration of a person of figure and consequence." That the "lower ranks of mankind" would never become so far divorced from religion, was his strange prophecy, one of the most remarkable instances of the blindness of the eighteenth century that I can think of.

It might seem, from the tone of his published sermons as well as from such passages as these, as if Sterne addressed himself chiefly to educated people. And as a preacher, his bitter neighbour Croft tells us, " his delivery and voice were so very disagreeable " that half the congregation usually went out of church when it was his turn to preach in the Minster. There are " a many idle tales " of him which would show that he was no more popular with his country parishioners than was Crabbe. Once when he was skating and the ice broke not one of them would help to get him out. " Another time, a Flock of Geese assembled in the Church Yard at Sutton, when his Wife bawl'd out ' Laurie, powl 'em ' (*i.e.* pluck the quills), on which they were ready to riot and mob Laurie." They considered him, says the same reporter, to be crazy or crackbrained : it is the opinion generally held of a literary clergyman by his parishioners.

Truly a strange life, and a pitiable one ; and it is no happy memory that the places most often in his thoughts have to give. Nowhere indeed do we naturally think of him save at Coxwold. There is very little record or memory of him at Sutton or Stillington, except his signature in the register, and an account of orchard trees that he planted in the rectory garden. At Toulouse, which he thought so delightful, and where he found a house and garden so charming for so little money, certainly one does not think of him ; there are much greater memories in that most attractive city. It is safe to say that no one remembers that he died in Bond Street. His gravestone no longer covers—if ever it did—his remains. Only at Coxwold is his memory kept green.

There the splendid Early Perpendicular church looks down upon distant moors and forests, and, nestling among the woods, the Priory of Newburgh, where once, when it was a true priory, lived William, the most candid and wise of English medieval historians. A fine position, and a grand church, with remarkable features without and within.

STERNE'S PULPIT, COXWOLD.

Without, the great octagonal tower, a rare architectural work. Within, the old eighteenth century arrangement, practically as it was in Sterne's own time. There are the high pews, abodes of the privacy which does not always encourage devotion. The fine three-decker survives, and it is hung with red stuff and yellow fringes, just as we see in the churches " Phiz " would draw. The chancel was added to after Sterne's death, and it contains the fine Fauconberg tombs which go back before his time and the monuments which continue after it ; but it also has a feature entirely characteristic of the eighteenth century,—practically useful and really not at all ugly as it stands there,—the altar rails coming out like a peninsula into the chancel, They are good rails, and in that quaint church they look entirely in keeping, and it is sincerely to be hoped that no modern " ritualism " will be able to induce the strong Yorkshire conservatism to do away with them. There is a sad rumour that it was once tried—that a hasty archbishop said they must go, that he would not give confirmation in the church if they did not, that he would give ten pounds to help them away ; but the churchwardens were not obedient to archi-episcopal opinions, as the clergy are, and so the rails remain, and the church too, very much as Laurence Sterne saw it. Long may it so abide, with the parish church of Whitby, to testify to the ecclesiastical habits of our forefathers.

In the vestry are the registers, with Sterne's thin, clear signature ; and there is a pewter flagon, dated 1754, that he must have used. These and the pulpit are the most certain memorials of him in the church. In the village is the house he put together or added to, still called, as he named it, Shandy Hall. It has a pretty front looking on the road, and within you may see some panelling of his day, and the little room which is said to have been his study. But in truth he studied out of doors, in church, in the market, in the fields, or in the houses of other folk, not at all (though, like many famous writers, he was probably a plagiarist) among books. One fancies him for a time happy at Coxwold: so at least one of his letters shows him, delighted with neighbours' kindliness, with fish and fowl and cheerful company. That he was not a neglectful parish priest one would be glad to think. He had a kind heart and not at all a wise head. Probably no one would have thought so ill of him as many did if he had not spoken so ill of himself. At least his memory is worth a charitable record, if only for a warning of the great tragedy that lies waiting for great gifts not used for the highest ends.

SHANDY HALL, COXWOLD.

THE RELIGION OF DR. JOHNSON

By the side of these clerical studies it is natural to put the figure of one who in spite of the great position he occupied in the eyes of contemporaries was yet among laymen typical rather than dominating in religious interests.

Dr. Johnson's religion, even in his own day, was famous enough to be mocked at. The publication of his Devotions by his friend Strahan, Rector of Islington, provoked bitter comments in *A Poetical Review of the Literary and Moral Character of the late Samuel Johnson LL.D.* by John Courtenay, Esq., London, 1786. A line or two are enough to quote from it. Take these :—

> On Tetty's state his frighted fancy runs,
> And Heaven's appeas'd by cross unbutter'd buns :
> He sleeps and fasts, pens on himself a libel,
> And still believes, but never reads, the Bible.

Notes of quotation fortify the satire. It was true, but Johnson would not have minded at all, however he might have crushed the writer.

Any one who will take the trouble simply to look at the index to Dr. Birkbeck Hill's edition of the " Johnsonian Miscellanies," even if he does not go on to refresh his memory by a glance through Boswell, will need no convincing that Dr. Johnson was emphatically a man of prayer. To him all the chief incidents of life, the new work begun, the old accomplished, days of affliction or success, anniversaries, associations sacred and secular, were the occasion not merely for special and renewed devotion but for new and most seriously thought out meditations and prayers. And Johnson, when he wrote his prayers, was more natural, we feel, than in anything else that he wrote. He had, of course, an unconquerable sense of literary style and a deep feeling of the solemnity and awfulness of the sinner's approach to the Most High ; and he was trained in the language of the English authorized devotions ; but no less he was, in a very real sense, at home with God. In the midst of the utter self-abasement of penitence which marks almost all that he wrote in this regard there is a freedom from conventional language, from false or affected antithesis, and from ill-judged choice of allusion or quotation, which affords re-markable evidence of the sincerity of his pious mind. As a writer of prayers, indeed, he rivals the makers of the Book of Common Prayer, and he surpasses every one who has followed him. Take for example the prayer written not long before his death. In genuine feeling, in power, and depth, there is nothing of Wesley's to place beside it.

"O Lord, my Maker and Protector, who hast graciously sent me into this world to work out my salvation, enable me to drive from me all such unquiet and perplexing thoughts as may mislead or hinder me in the practice of those duties which Thou hast required. . . . And while it shall please Thee to continue me in this world where much is to be done and little to be known, teach me, by Thy Holy Spirit, to withdraw my mind from unprofitable and dangerous en-quiries, from difficulties vainly curious, and doubts impos-sible to be solved. Let me rejoice in the light which Thou hast imparted, let me serve Thee with active zeal and humble confidence, and wait with patient expectation for the time in which the soul which Thou receivest shall be satisfied with knowledge."

But he did not merely write prayers ; he lived them. Church-going, it cannot be said that he enjoyed : "I hope in time to take pleasure in public worship," is the best he can say ; and then deafness came and defeated his good intention. Nor was he ever able to bring himself to read the Bible constantly or for pleasure. But he had a con-tinual and vivid faith in God, and that faith was con-tinually and vividly expressed in his prayers.

It is difficult, indeed, to read the pages of that little book in which he wrote down his holy resolutions and tender offerings of supplication and love without a deep emotion. Here was a true man, we say, on his knees before God.

And his devotion belonged to a type peculiarly English and peculiarly the creation, as it seems to us, of the English Church. It was solemn, sincere, reticent, humble, ordered. When he prayed for the dead, as he did repeatedly, it was with " the usual preface of permission," that is, with the safeguard of " so far as is lawful "—in accord, that is, with primitive models and the will of the Almighty. When he made his Communion on Easter Day he fasted rigidly before, and sometimes even, it would appear, till the evening, in greater reverence for the commemoration—it is his own phrase—of the death of his Redeemer. And he observed the fasts of Holy Week with a strictness—recorded certainly with not the slightest suspicion of self-righteousness —which must have been rare in his day. His outward reverence was scrupulous ; we all remember stories of his rebukes to those who even pretended to be profane. He could understand, with shrewd common sense, the inner meaning of outward signs :—,

" Campbell is a good man," he said ; " a pious man. I am afraid he has not been in the inside of a church for many years ; but he never passes a church without pulling off his hat. This shows that he has good principles."

This, says the editor of a recent issue of the Prayers. " is sheer formalism." It is nothing of the kind—it is sheer common sense. Outward reverence is certainly not retained where the principle has been abandoned ; a man would not take off his hat at the sight of a church who did not believe in revealed religion and, to some extent at least, act up to his belief. Dr. Johnson's religion was systematic and ordered, but it was also a religion of robust common sense.

Terrors he had as to death. Is not the fear of death dreadful, asked Boswell. "So much so, sir," was his answer, " that the whole of life is but keeping away the thought of it." It may be that this terror was physical, but far more likely it was akin to that acute melancholia from which he continually suffered and which yet he never suffered to drive him to despair or to any real absence of faith in God, or to any abandonment of that continued renewal of resolution which as, Dr. Pusey said, is the life of perseverance.

"Whether I have lived resolving till all possibility of performance is gone by, I know not. God help me, I will yet try."

So he wrote ; and try he did, and triumphed in the end. When it came to dying, no Christian made a better death, for he died with the prayers and blessings about him of those whom his faith had strengthened and his charity had supported.

The editor whom I have referred to [1] says very truly :

"He had very regular and decided views on the great dogmas of the Christian Church. And it is equally clear from his habits of personal devotion that what the old divines used to call "the root of the matter" was in him. Day by day he tried to live, in the sight of the Eternal, a life of devout and Scriptural piety. That he enumerates and mourns his failures to do so with painful penitence and sorrow only emphasizes the sincerity and genuineness of his religion. As a matter of fact, no man of his time had larger, healthier, and saner views of the real nature of godliness and practical Christian duty."

It is strange that, when the editor should understand so much, he should yet speak of Johnson's " scrupulous observance of fast days " as " mere formalism." It was, as any one who knows the Book of Common Prayer, not to mention the practice of the eighteenth century pietists, would be aware, a part of the fixed, orderly devotion which the Church of England teaches and which Johnson, with his conservative spirit and his wide knowledge of the past, and his sound common sense, was far too wise to abandon. He knew that the ancient ways were the ways of experience, and his religion was one of inherited and corporate as well as personal devotion. And, indeed, there is a sense in which

[1] *Prayers and Meditations of Dr. Samuel Johnson.* With Notes and an Introduction by the Rev. Hinchcliffe Higgins, and a Preface by Augustine Birrell, K.C. London.

the sneer in which an eminent and very delightful writer indulges, when he introduces the edition I have been using by a lively preface, is surely contrary to fact.

" There is no taint of professionalism about his faith," says Mr. Birrell. " He is nothing of the cleric. He owns to hours of doubt and darkness." The strict adherence to rule, has, at least, no touch of the religious amateur about it, and when Johnson groaned and trembled before God he was of the company of the Wesleys and Whitfields of his age. But Mr. Birrell speaks very wisely when he says—

" Johnson has been blamed for the timidity of his piety by more confident spirits, but who can doubt its representative character ? "

It is, indeed, this " representative character " which makes the *Prayers and Meditations* of Samuel Johnson so welcome a possession. He thought and prayed as the member of a true and ancient Church, linked in piety to her rules, and with her to penitence and love. I write with a volume of Dr. Birkbeck Hill's edition, containing the Devotions, at my side, which bears the annotations of Dr. Bright, late Regius Professor of Ecclesiastical History at Oxford. How much I wish that true and loyal son of the English Church, that faithful Johnsonian, could have given us an edition of these beautiful prayers. Of him it was true indeed, as Strahan wrote of Johnson, that " his prayers and his alms, like those of the good Cornelius, went up for a continual memorial ; and always from a heart deeply impressed with piety, never insensible to the calls of friendship or compassion."

SOME MEMORIES OF GEORGE CRABBE. I

IT was strange in an age which affects to admire realism that Crabbe should have been forgotten. Here was a son of the people, who as apothecary and clergyman, was brought close to aspects the most sordid of common life, and who had the power to express them vividly and plainly. He saw life very clearly on many sides, and he wrote down, with an emphatic distinctness, exactly what he saw. Yet forgotten he certainly was. Since the collection of his works in 1834, two years after his death, they have only twice been reprinted except in selections ; and for separate biographies, since the memoir by his son prefixed to the seven volumes of *Works*, we were till 1903 content with Mr. Kebbel's bright and interesting sketch. It is strange indeed that a writer so characteristic, and in literary history so important, should have been long excluded from the *English Men of Letters*. No other proof is needed that one of the most popular writers of the beginning of the Nineteenth century was utterly forgotten at its close.

But Crabbe's memory will certainly not be suffered to perish. As a direct record, by an acutely observant man, of the social life of the early nineteenth century, his pictures can never lose their value ; and poets have always known the passages which compel them to rank him among themselves.

Perhaps it is too soon for a reaction in his favour. He died at Trowbridge only in 1832. Some at least who could remember him are still alive, and it is not hard to gather, in the places where he lived, some memories which go back to his days.

Aldborough, it is true, now calls itself Aldeburgh ; it has

lost houses, as it did while its most famous son still lived, and it has built more ; but a sojourner writes of it : " I will go so far as to say that its generally unprogressive character in the present does not point to any marked advance within the last hundred years or so." I should not dream of saying the same thing of Trowbridge, with its energetic clergy and its taste for lectures. Nor shall I attempt to describe Trowbridge, and for Aldeburgh I will be content to quote the almost forgotten description by Wilkie Collins in *No Name*, written in 1862. It gives the setting of Crabbe's early life very clearly.

" The most striking spectacle presented to a stranger by the shores of Suffolk, is the extraordinary defencelessness of the land against the encroachments of the sea.

"At Aldborough, as elsewhere on this coast, local traditions are, for the most part, traditions which have been literally drowned. The site of the old town, once a populous and thriving port, has almost entirely disappeared in the sea. The German Ocean has swallowed up streets, market-places, jetties, and public walks ; and the merciless waters, consummating their work of devastation, closed, no longer than eighty years since, over the salt-master's cottage at Aldborough, now famous in memory only, as the birthplace of the poet Crabbe.

"Thrust back year after year by the advancing waves, the inhabitants have receded, in the present century, to the last morsel of land which is firm enough to be built on—a strip of ground hemmed in between a marsh on one side and the sea on the other. Here—trusting for their future security to certain sandhills which the capricious waves have thrown up to encourage them—the people of Aldborough have boldly established their quaint little watering-place. The first fragment of their earthly possessions is a low natural dyke of shingle, surmounted by a public path which runs parallel with the sea. Bordering this path in a broken, uneven line are the villa residences of modern Aldborough —fanciful little houses, standing mostly in their own gardens, and possessing here and there, as horticultural ornaments, staring figure-heads of ships, doing duty for statues

among the flowers. Viewed from the low level on which
these villas stand, the sea, in certain conditions of the atmo-
sphere, appears to be higher than the land : coasting
vessels gliding by assume gigantic proportions, and look
alarmingly near the windows. Intermixed with the houses
of the better sort are buildings of other forms and periods.
In one direction, the tiny Gothic town hall of old Aldborough
—once the centre of the vanished port and borough—
now stands fronting the modern villas close on the margin
of the sea. At another point, a wooden tower of observation, crowned by the figure-head of a wrecked Russian
vessel, rises high above the neighbouring houses ; and
discloses through its scuttle window, grave men in dark
clothing, seated on the topmost storey, perpetually on the
watch—the pilots of Aldborough looking out from their
tower, for ships in want of help. Behind the row of buildings thus curiously intermingled, runs the one straggling
street of the town, with its sturdy pilots' cottages, its
mouldering marine storehouses, and its composite shops.
Towards the northern end, this street is bounded by the
one eminence visible over all the marshy flat—a low wooded
hill on which the church is built. At its opposite extremity
the street leads to a deserted martello tower, and to the
forlorn outlying suburb of Slaughden, between the river
Alde and the sea. Such are the main characteristics of
this curious little outpost on the shores of England as it
appears at the present time."

How stand the other places that Crabbe knew " at the
present time " ?

Of Muston and Allington I can speak more particularly.
The house in which Crabbe lived at Muston is now pulled
down. It is replaced by the one built higher up a slight
hill, in a position intended, says scandal, to prevent any
view of Belvoir. Crabbe, with all his ironies, had no such
resentful feelings, and, indeed, more modern successors of his
have opened what he would have called a " vista," and the
castle again crowns the distance as you look southward
from the pretty garden.

In the church and in the village Crabbe has left memories.

SOME MEMORIES OF GEORGE CRABBE

On the north wall of the chancel, close to the altar, is the plain marble slab :

NEAR THIS MEMORIAL
LIE THE REMAINS
OF SARAH, WIFE OF
THE REV. GEORGE CRABBE
LATE RECTOR OF THIS PARISH.
SHE WAS BORN 12TH DEC. 1751
AND DIED 21ST SEP. 1813.

In the Register, at the beginning of the new books which the law brought into use in 1813, after two burials entered in Crabbe's own hand, comes the record of his wife's interment on September 25, aged sixty-two. A neighbour read the service. Two more entries in Crabbe's writing follow, and then one in his son's. Within a year he had left the parish.

The last years there, as his son tells, had not been happy ones. The building of a dissenting chapel, and the teaching of a form of " enthusiasm " most distasteful to him, had embittered his relations with his parishioners. The " oldest inhabitant " used to say that he well remembered that the Rector, when he left, broke up all his furniture and crockery that he did not take away, and threw it into the pond just below the churchyard.

It is clear that at all times Crabbe was a stout " Church of England man " of the familiar eighteenth-century type. Of nothing was he more afraid than of " enthusiasm." He had heard, and he respected, John Wesley ; yet, as one of his notes shows, he regarded " a sober and rational conversion " as the very antithesis of " a methodistic call." The note reads strangely after the beautiful hymn which breaks upon the gloom of the madhouse.

> Pilgrim, burthen'd with thy sin,
>   Come the way to Zion's gate,
> There, till Mercy let thee in,
>   Knock and weep and watch and wait.
>   Knock !—He knows the sinner's cry :
>   Weep !—He loves the mourner's tears :
>   Watch !—for saving grace is nigh :
>   Wait,—till heavenly light appears.

Hark ! it is the Bridegroom's voice ;
Welcome, pilgrim, to thy rest ;
Now within the gate rejoice,
  Safe and seal'd and bought and blest !
    Safe—from all the lures of vice,
    Seal'd—by signs the chosen know,
    Bought—by love and life the price,
    Blest—the mighty debt to owe.

Holy Pilgrim ! what for thee
In a world like this remain ?
From thy guarded breast shall flee
  Fear and shame, and doubt and pain.
    Fear—the hope of heaven shall fly,
    Shame—from glory's view retire,
    Doubt—in certain rapture die,
    Pain—in endless bliss expire.

So careful was the author of these pathetic lines to dis-
claim any sympathy with Methodism that, while his charity
makes him insist that they are " not intended to make
any religious persuasion appear ridiculous," he thinks it
necessary to explain that " they are supposed as the effect
of memory in the disordered mind of the speaker, and,
though evidently enthusiastic in respect of language, are
not meant to convey any impropriety of sentiment."

The exaggerated safeguards in which Crabbe delights
might prove, if proof were needed, that it must have been a
rough society he had to deal with. Yet in one important
respect the morals of his parishioners, as evidenced by
the Register—and very likely because of his own strict
moral teaching—were much superior to what would be
inferred from his poems. The most interesting note that
he himself made in the Register is this baptism : " Brown,
Francis, son of Thomas Brown and Johanna his Wife,
was baptized this 2nd day of Jany 1806 beneath a Hedge
in ye Parish of Sedgbrook. He was born in a Hovel on
the 31st of Decr 1805, the Father a Chimney Sweeper
belonging to Market Harborough." But others appear to
have made sententious or facetious insertions, to his great
annoyance. In 1746 there had been the following entry :
" July 11th Died William Blundey, a servant man of Great

Panton. He was run over by a loaded wagon in Muston Lanes which broke his left Leg & Right Thigh and Run of a mortification. N.B. He was riding on the shafts and fell asleep—a caution to all carters. He was buried the day following." Fifty years later occurs the following curious imitation : " John Millthorp, Novr 7th 1796. John Millthorp belong to the 3 Rigemant of Dragoons was runed over with a bagig wagon with riding on it. [An illegible word] of wagon shaft had is left leg and Rite thy Both Broke wich kill im, let this caustion All drunken men." To this Crabbe had added : " It is requested that no more such impertinence may be entered in this book.—G.C."

The habit of irrelevant entry seems to have been an old one in Muston. At the beginning of the century the Rector had entered the following curious " Memorandum : John Manors first Duke of Rutland dyed at Belvoir Feb 3 170$\frac{10}{11}$ at eight in the morning in the 73 year of his age & was buried at Bottesford the 23 of Febr. *avec grand fracas.*"

Bottesford, where till recently the Rutland family were always buried, is only two miles from Muston. The famous tombs of the Mannerses are the great historical interest of the famous church. It is strange that Crabbe should have made so little of the social history they illustrate. There you read of Francis, sixth Earl of Rutland, whose two sons " both dyed in their infancy by wicked practise and sorcerye " ; of how Edward, third Earl, departed this life " 14th April being Good Friday 1587 nere Puddle Wharfe in London, from whence his Corps was hither brought and buried,"and of Lord Robert Manners, whose memory Crabbe commemorated in some of his earliest poetry, and who " died, covered with wounds, in the service of his country."

" In future times," wrote the poet of *The Village* in his most classical style :

> In future times, when smit with glory's charms,
> The untried youth first quits a father's arms ;—
> " Oh ! be like him ! " the weeping sire shall say ;
> " Like MANNERS walk, who walk'd in Honour's way ;
> " In danger foremost, yet in death sedate,
> " Oh ! be like him in all things, but his fate ! "

Crabbe seems, through his whole life—in spite of his attachment to the Rutland family, and the kindness that was
always shown him, even after the death of his own immediate patrons—to have never shaken off the unpleasant
feeling which his dependent situation had instilled. " The
situation he filled at Belvoir," says his son, " was attended
with many painful circumstances, and productive in his
mind of some of the acutest sensations of wounded pride
that have ever been traced by any pen." He was always
a man of the most independent spirit, and there could be
nothing more offensive to his whole temper than the state
of society which is very happily illustrated by a monument in a church not so many miles away from his Leicestershire cures :

SACRED TO THE MEMORY OF
Mr. JOHN STANGER
WHO BY A FAITHFUL AND DILIGENT,
DISCHARGE OF HIS DUTY
DESERVED THE CONFIDENCE
AND OBTAINED THE PROTECTION
OF LEWIS FIRST LORD SONDES
AND RAISED HIMSELF FROM AN HUMBLE STATION
TO ONE OF RESPECTABILITY AND COMPETENCE.
HE ACQUIRED CONSIDERABLE POSSESSIONS
IN THIS PARISH, IN WHICH HE EXPIRED,
JULY 28TH, 1820,
HIGHLY ESTEEMED FOR HIS HONESTY
AND INTEGRITY.

The days when such monuments seemed appropriate
memorials of the dead were days when life was not often
looked at from an ecclesiastical standing-point. It was
the age *par excellence* of the sporting parson. Crabbe's
son says of his father that " in accordance with the usual
habits of the clergy then resident in the vale of Belvoir,
he made some efforts to become a sportsman ; but he
wanted precision of eye and hand to use the gun with
success. As to coursing, the cry of the first hare he saw
killed, struck him as so like the wail of an infant, that he
turned heart-sick from the spot ; and, in a word, although

Mr. Crabbe did, for a season, make his appearance now and then in a garb which none that knew him in his latter days could ever have suspected him of assuming, the velveteen jacket and all its appurtenances were soon laid aside for ever." The son does not venture to suggest that his father ever went out hunting. He would certainly echo with approval Cowper's lines on " the rueful jest " of a " cassock'd huntsman."

> He takes the field. The master of the pack
> Cries, " Well done, saint ! " and claps him on the back.
> Is this the path of sanctity ? Is this
> To stand a way-mark in the road to bliss ?
> Himself a wand'rer from the narrow way,
> His silly sheep, what wonder if they stray ?

And his own terrible description of the suffering death-bed of the agricultural labourer ends with these couplets :

> But ere his death some pious doubts arise,
> Some simple fears, which " bold bad " men despise ;
> Fain would he ask the parish priest to prove
> His title certain to the joys above :
> For this he sends the murmuring nurse, who calls
> The holy stranger to these dismal walls :
> And doth not he, the pious man, appear,
> He, " passing rich with forty pounds a year " ?
> Ah ! no ; a shepherd of a different stock,
> And far unlike him, feeds this little flock :
> A jovial youth, who thinks his Sunday's task
> As much as God or man can fairly ask ;
> The rest he gives to loves and labours light,
> To fields the morning, and to feasts the night ;
> None better skill'd the noisy pack to guide,
> To urge their chase, to cheer them or to chide
> A sportsman keen, he shoots through half the day,
> And, skill'd at whist, devotes the night to play :
> Then, while such honours bloom around his head,
> Shall he sit sadly by the sick man's bed,
> To raise the hope he feels not, or with zeal
> To combat fears that e'en the pious feel ?

Lines such as these show what estimate Crabbe himself formed of a clergyman's duties, and there are many hints in his Life which indicate how thoroughly yet unostentatiously he carried them out. Indeed, the intimate knowledge of the life of the poor which his poems show proves how constantly he must have visited no less than how closely he must have observed. The bitterness of his resentment against the Huntingtonians, the sentiment with which he regarded the days before the Reformation, were other expressions of the sense he had of the needs of the country folk for a reasoned historic creed and some dignity of worship. Politically he was a Whig, influenced by Burke, yet more strongly sympathizing with Charles James Fox, and inclining in social matters towards what was coming to be called Radicalism. There is no wonder, then, that he often found himself out of harmony with his Leicestershire surroundings. He was of humble origin, and, in spite of the experience of Beaconsfield and Belvoir, he never became quite happy in the society of people much his superiors by birth. The county squires round Muston were eminently Conservative ; it is still remembered that they respected him and recognized his fame, but they cannot have been familiar with him. With one of the old families, however, he was closely associated. One brother was for some time his curate at Muston and West Allington, and another succeeded him in the latter cure, which he held for forty-three years till his death in 1867. Among their kindred no special memories of Crabbe seem to linger, and, with the death of the old labourer at Muston who remembered him, all direct links with his residence in Leicestershire have been broken.

The times have changed, indeed, as well as the men. No longer is it a diversion to drive over in the hot summer afternoons to the neighbouring town, summon the landlord of a well-known inn (a famous character whose son became a baronet), and order him to produce the best dinner that could be procured—salmon, a great joint of beef, and his old port ; then, after a walk round the ruined castle and a dish of tea, to return in the cool of an August evening. No longer do the clergy mingle their secular with their spiritual affairs so simply as did Crabbe, or perform their duties in a manner so unconventional without being irreverent.

SOME MEMORIES OF GEORGE CRABBE

" I must have some money, gentlemen," Crabbe used to say as he walked down from the fine Jacobean three-decker at Muston, meaning that the tithes were due. Sometimes he would stop his sermon when it grew dark, with " Upon my word I cannot see : I must give you the rest when we meet again," or walk into a pew near the window and finish his sermon standing on a seat. Outward conformity to rule and convention is more common in our day than it was in Crabbe's ; some parts of a clergyman's work which were then thought unusual acts of virtue are now regarded as ordinary obligations of the profession ; but it may be doubted if there are many better parish priests now than the author of *The Village*.

His position as an author can never be rightly estimated unless it be remembered that he was first and foremost a clergyman. He is one of those few clerical men of letters whose pastoral work has left its impression on the whole of their writings. He belongs to the class of George Herbert and John Keble, not to that of Herrick and Sterne and Swift. Yet good critics have considered him essentially a satirist. It is worth noticing that it is a designation which he expressly rejects.

> I love not the satiric Muse :
> No man of earth would I abuse ;
> Nor with empoison'd verses grieve
> The most offending son of Eve.

His poems, indeed, were simply pictures of life as he saw it, presented in the form of Pope as nearly as he could achieve it, but in the spirit of revolt against the whole school of Arcadian fancy, The style was conventional, the matter entirely fresh and directly truthful. Thus *The Borough* and *The Village* told exactly what he saw at Aldborough and Muston, but told it in such a way that persons could not be identified, and only the legitimate consequences of the principles upon which they acted could be understood. There was nothing in Crabbe of exact portraiture. He was a constant observer and an unsparing critic ; but when he had seen he went back to his study and thought out his visions till they came back to him in another form. He was like a great artist who, after long years' study of Titian, can paint a magnifico of to-day with an understanding that no one who has lived wholly among the moderns can show.

Thus, if you go through the Registers of Crabbe's parishes, you will find nothing to recall the incidents he tells in the poems he named after them. The patrons he writes of are not at all like the Duke of Rutland or Burke. No hall that he knew had such *Tales* as he told. And yet there are no poems in the English language that give a more complete picture of the times in which they were written. Crabbe's merits can only be adequately seen by copious quotation. It is a pity that FitzGerald's selection is not reprinted, but Mr. Deane's is as good.

A poet whom Scott and Tennyson, Newman and Fitz-Gerald, have ranked so high we cannot afford to despise. It is easy to parody the weak side of his work : perhaps the *Rejected Address* that copies him is the best of them all. In his earlier volumes the influence of Johnson is too apparent, and at the last he was content with the repeated use of too trivial subjects. But at his best he was a great poet. He had a deep knowledge of human nature, a passionate sympathy with the suffering, a distinct creative power. And in command of expression he was not deficient. Again and again lines strike you which for vivid effect it would be difficult to surpass. It would be hard to better the famous description of an autumn landscape :

> Early he rose, and look'd with many a sigh
> On the red light that fill'd the eastern sky ;
> Oft had he stood before, alert and gay,
> To hail the glories of the new-born day :
> But now dejected, languid, listless, low,
> He saw the wind upon the water blow,
> And the cold stream curl'd onward as the gale
> From the pine-hill blew harshly down the dale
> On the right side the youth a wood survey'd,
> With all its dark intensity of shade ;
> Where the rough wind alone was heard to move
> In this, the pause of nature and of love

SOME MEMORIES OF GEORGE CRABBE

When now the young are rear'd, and when the old,
Lost to the tie, grow negligent and cold—
Far to the left he saw the huts of men,
Half hid in mist, that hung upon the fen ;
Before him swallows, gathering for the sea,
Took their short flights, and twitter'd on the lea ;
And near the bean-sheaf stood, the harvest done,
And slowly blacken'd in the sickly sun ;
All these were sad in nature, or they took
Sadness from him, the likeness of his look,
And of his mind—he ponder'd for a while,
Then met his Fanny with a borrow'd smile.

Only in the last lines is Crabbe at all reminiscent of his worst side ; and that side belongs, almost of necessity, to his desire to sacrifice everything to the subject he has in mind. He admitted that his descriptive touches were generally additions ; they are often obviously such, and yet they are none the worse for it.

On the other hand, he knew his strength. Few poets have known better how to tell a story ; no one, perhaps, in English verse has ever told a tale of common life so well. It was a triumph, while using the conventional forms, to have so utterly departed from the artificial spirit. Crabbe's appeal is always forcible and direct. There are no disguises. Vice is painted as it is, and meanness, and folly. Where he describes nature, we feel that his knowledge is as complete as Wordsworth's. When he speaks of man, we know that he is living in the real world. He has often the minute touch of the dramatist : what he lacks is the sentiment of the romance writer. Thus it was on one side only that he appealed to Scott. *The Village, The Borough, The Tales of the Hall* were quite of the spirit of *S. Ronan's Well*. Certainly the gentle, kindly, acute mind of Crabbe had many points in common with the Wizard of the North, and there are few happier literary memories than those Lockhart recalls of the days the two spent together in Edinburgh. But, with all the sympathy between them, Crabbe was generations more modern than Scott. He was, one often feels, of the age of George Eliot : but he knew the poor as she never knew them. Perhaps, in that aspect, his true fame is yet to come.

SOME MEMORIES OF GEORGE CRABBE—II

THE revived interest in Crabbe is a delightful feature of
the modern popular interest in poetry. He had seemed
for nearly three quarters of a century to be buried and
forgotten ; now writer after writer has shown a knowledge and admiration of his genius, and, what is much more
important, cheap popular editions of selections from his
poems have given evidence of the appreciation he has
won among the people. Canon Ainger's charming, graceful
and simple biography comes as the fit climax of the revived
interest, and makes me take up my pen again to record
more memories of the poet and parish priest.

As a parish priest Crabbe has been sharply attacked.
He has on the one hand been judged by a nineteenth-century
standard, on the other he has been regarded as if he were a
parson of the last century but one. The time has come for
a more just estimate. Now the further we stand from
Crabbe's lifetime the more clearly we may see his position
in relation to his times. We are too apt to think of him
as a belated survival of the eighteenth century ; so at
least he has appeared in most literary estimates, when he
has been compared with Cowper and contrasted with
Pope. More really he belongs to the nineteenth, the century
of George III and Walter Scott and Wordsworth and
Lord Brougham, having a relation that is easily traceable
in regard to each of those very distinct influences. He
was a man of wide sympathies and liberal principles, in
some ways a more enlightened and a much less pedantic
Dr. Parr. He knew human nature both intuitively and by
study ; and these were some of his qualifications as a
parish priest.

SOME MEMORIES OF GEORGE CRABBE

It is impossible for any one who has read the meditations that his son printed, from his diary, in the Life, to doubt the sincerity and depth of his personal religion. He was a man—his poems too confirm the impression—with the fear of God ever before his eyes. On the love of God, it may be, he dwelt less constantly ; but this is perhaps only to say by nature his mind turned always to the terrible and the severe.

" It was, we are told, on a dull November morning, with a fresh breeze towards the land, and the big waves bursting in wild foam upon the shingle, that Crabbe looked his last upon the sea. This was as it should be. Crabbe's poetry is redolent of the ocean, but of the ocean under its gloomier and more lowering aspects ; not in its tempestuous grandeur, not in its blue and summer beauty, but swelling moodily under leaden skies, and rolling its turbid waters to the shore in accents of profound melancholy." So says Mr. Kebbel ; and there is at least a touch of this feeling in Crabbe's religion.

It might be expected that such a man would shrink at times from some parts of the work of a parish priest. The strain would be too great for a nature so charged with melancholy to endure with balanced mind. So it may have been ; and so perhaps something which harsher judges among his parishioners thought to be neglect might be explained. That his heart was in his high calling there can be no doubt ; and so such memories as survive would seem to say. The criticisms, though there are not a few of them, can be discounted ; the eulogies have the support of good books and the friendship of good men.

Crabbe was ordained at twenty-seven, when he was " a successful author patronised by some of the leading characters in the kingdom." From the first, he was content to take humble work in humble cures ; what Dean Church wrote of John Keble in his little Gloucestershire curacies might be said, with the change of a few words, of Crabbe in Suffolk and Leicestershire. It was not until 1814, when he was sixty, that he received the important living of Trowbridge. He was then a widower, depressed, failing ; but the new start in life revived his powers. Much of the literary interest of his life, for himself, belonged to the next eighteen years. They included visits to the literary world of London, from which he had long been separated, the acquaintance of Scott, and the knowledge of Rogers, Campbell, and Southey. As a parish priest he met opposition and he lived it down. As a Whig, and one who did not hesitate to express his opinions publicly, he found the manufacturers of his parish extremely hostile ; and they were not slow in discovering a social as well as a political divergence. He was too much, they said, with Lord Lansdowne at Bowood. And again " that, perhaps, impolitic frankness which made him at all times scorn the assumption of a scruple which he did not really feel, led him to violate occasionally, what were considered among many classes in that neighbourhood, the settled laws of clerical decorum. For example, though little delighting in such scenes, except as they were partaken by kind and partial friends, he might be seen occasionally at a concert, a ball, or even a play." The censorious busybodies of a provincial town were not slow to find fault. It was perhaps known that before he left Muston the bells were rung to welcome his successor. His personal kindliness did not condone the severity of his religious principles. The latter were the first to be observed ; only gradually the former won their way.

It is perhaps natural that very little memory survives, or is preserved, of Crabbe as an active parish priest. When stories that are recalled are analysed they are found to be little but a reflex of some familiar passage in *The Village* or *The Borough* or *Tales of the Hall.* When he is remembered chiefly for his love of natural history, or for long hunts he undertook for fossils, one may remember that the only tradition that could be recovered, after fifty years, of Bishop Butler at Stanhope, was that he rode about the parish on a black pony. But happily to the testimony of the acute and penetrating genius of the poems, so solemn, so real, so deeply inspired by the thoughts of " righteousness and temperance and the judgment to come," we can add the testimony of the sermons. They are characteristic of religious feeling as it was in England before the Oxford Movement gave it a new touch of life. Crabbe himself, his son tells us, grew as years went on, and especially in the last ten years of his life, in appreciation of the doctrines of Christianity. He added more and more to his faith, and to his good works, knowledge. He gradually approached " in substantial matters, though not exactly in certain peculiar ways of expression, to that respected body usually denominated Evangelical Christians of the Church of England, with whom, nevertheless, he was never classed by others, nor, indeed, by himself."

The description is borne out by the volume of Sermons which was printed in 1850, to procure money for Trowbridge Church and Schools. It was dedicated to Prince Albert. The subscription list contains many names of interest ; among the very few survivors is the Duke of Rutland, then Lord John Manners. The sermons it is especially noted, were neither intended by the author, nor ever prepared by an editor, for publication. They are printed as they were written. And probably few sermons preached to-day would bear such a test so well. The style is trenchant, clear, vigorous, and serious. They are sermons preached, as was said of a very different preacher, by a dying man to dying men. They have a directness which was, I take it, uncommon when they were delivered. They partake to some extent of the characteristics of an early age of homiletics ; they are rarely directly dogmatic or doctrinal. None the less, the whole scaffolding of dogma is implied in every page of them, the dogma, that is, of an ante-Tractarian teacher who was not acquainted in much detail with earlier English theology. They imply doctrines, however, which Evangelicalism at times neglected. " To you," Crabbe says to his people, " belong the real confession as to your heavenly Father, the real absolution, for ours can be but conditional." Of the power, apparently he had no doubt, but he knew its limits. He makes one of his characters thus protest against the parish priest :—

If sick, he comes ; You cannot die in peace,
Till he attends to witness your release ;
To vex your soul, and urge you to confess
The sins you feel, remember, or can guess.[1]

Fasting, too, he clearly recognized as an obligation. Again, he was no idolater of the Reformation, as indeed his poems show. "When the Reformation opened the Bible for all who were disposed for so interesting a study, many read and were profited, many read and were confused ; to some it was the savour of life unto life, to others of death unto death. Some pretended to have found doctrines which were but the fruit of their own fancies, and while there were those who were sober and judicious, others were led away from all the sobriety of truth and reason into strange and visionary opinions, taking the fanciful interpretation of men for the revelation and commandments of God. Hence arose various sects and extravagant doctrines, and many instead of seeking for the assistance of the Spirit of God . . . . became vain in their imagination and their foolish heart was darkened."

On the other hand the sacramental teaching is very meagre. A strangely inadequate sermon on 1 Corinthians x. 16 declares that "by the Body and Blood of Christ must be meant the benefits of His passion, and these only." Emblems and signs only are to him those holy mysteries. But theology indeed was not Crabbe's strong point. There is little trace in his life or writings of his having read much of the subject. But of his piety and his knowledge of human nature the sermons, no less than his poems and his life, afford convincing proof. Again and again an acute saying shows that the preacher knew the diseases of the soul. "False humility produces false security ; for it is very natural for those who think they are humble in heart, when they are only humble in manner and form, to think also they are secure when they are only confident." Or, "no one who looks within himself will stand or be willing to stand by his merits ; the deeper he looks the more he

[1] From " The Gentleman Farmer." The unbeliever who wishes to prove that " he alone is lord of him," says this.

will find of weakness and sin, and he will be more inclined (even if his life be more than commonly reputable or clean) to despair of mercy for his provocations than to hope for acceptance without it."

He seems to have held the Evangelical views of " the Sabbath ; " he certainly fell into the pitfall that so many Evangelical preachers delighted to fall into, and preached a moving sermon on " Almost thou persuadest me to be a Christian," from which a little Greek might have saved him. But criticisms of the sermons can be little more than illusory, for we have not even the satisfaction of knowing at what date they were written, whether they represented mature knowledge as well as mature judgment, or whether they would have been chosen by himself as typical of his customary teaching. They give material not for decision but for illustration : but at least they justify the words of the epitaph, which some have thought too eulogistic, that he entered " into the sorrows and deprivations of the poorest of his parishioners." Such at least was the opinion of those who knew him best, and who could speak of his association with the parish " in which he so long laboured and was so much beloved." It is recorded that in almost his last illness, when he heard of " the heartfelt interest which many of his parishoners had expressed for his welfare," he exclaimed with great emotion, " Here is something worth living for." " The meekest of mankind," one called him who knew him well ; and he added—

> To error lenient and to frailty mild,
> Repentance ever was thy welcome child ;
> In every state, as husband, parent, friend,
> Scholar, or bard, thou could'st the Christian blend

And this note he certainly had of the true Christian preacher, an undaunted courage. It is still remembered in Trowbridge, by those who heard him, how he preached a funeral sermon on George IV. from the text " The sting of death is sin."

This view was confirmed by Canon Ainger. He did not defend pluralities ; he insisted that Crabbe himself came to towards mercy. Canon Ainger tells a story of how Crabbe, when people were talking of the virtuous deeds of somebody or other, would sometimes whisper to himself a not altogether favourable explanation ; but it is equally true that he was no less on the look out, like Shakespeare himself, for the "soul of goodness in things evil, would men observingly distil it out."

SYDNEY SMITH : A CONTRAST

THE era of comfortable clergymen, a cynic might say, never ends ; but it might not be far from the truth to assert that the age of clergymen who were both comfortable and eminent came near its ending with Sydney Smith. The early eighteenth century when it made bishops drew the line to exclude Jonathan Swift ; but he made a very good Dean of S. Patrick's. The early nineteenth century, in spite of the polite and affectionate wishes of statesmen like Lord Melbourne and Lord John Russell, drew its line to exclude Sydney Smith ; but yet he was very comfortable as a Canon of S. Paul's, with his " three virgins "—as the lady said—with their silver pokers to precede him.

When one reads through the biographies of the witty clergy-man,—whether by his daughter, Lady Holland, which was perhaps the very first of the intimately personal and trivial kind that have become so popular, or that by Mr. George Russell, which (admirable though it be) is a paean of Whig eulogy with space for comparatively few of the jokes—one is struck most of all by the feeling that Sydney Smith, after all, though he was a wit and a clergyman, was much more a gentleman interested in politics.

His distinguished services to the cause of Roman Catholic Emancipation were political not religious : he was always most anxious to assert that he did not serve the interests of religion in the matter, but the interests of political justice. And at no other time did he show any consideration for the religious views of those with whom he disagreed, were they bishops, Quakers, or High Churchmen. No, he imbibed in early youth a concentrated series of political opinions, and these were agreeably confirmed by association—and dinners—with the Whig aristocracy ; and so he adhered to

"To call him a legislator, a reasoner, and the conductor of the affairs of a great nation," he says, " seems to me as absurd as if a butterfly were to teach the bees to make honey. That he is an extraordinary writer of small poetry, and a diner out of the highest lustre, I readily admit."

A man who thought thus of the great liberal statesman who did more for the good name of England in Europe and in America as a champion of freedom than any Whig that ever lived is not to be regarded as more than a blind partisan. But the last phrase really describes the writer himself with admirable exactness. He was a diner out of the highest lustre. Politically he was a mere respectable bravo. Personally he was most delightful to the great people of the Whig party. You met him everywhere, and he always made you laugh, even if he only asked for the mustard. But even this was not universally enjoyed. Creevey, who often met Sydney Smith at Whig dinner-parties and in his later years most frequently—sometimes with " Charley Gore "—at the Duke of Sussex's, certainly did not like him. It is astonishing how these Whigs abused each other : and, besides, two of the wit-trade do not agree. " I never meet Sydney Smith," wrote Creevey, " without thinking him too much of a buffoon."

And thus the memory that he has left is—unjustly no doubt—that of a maker of first-class, second-class, and third-class jokes. One could fill pages with them : Lady Holland does. But under them all is the supreme idea of comfort, which coloured his whole, and notably his clerical, view of life.

The contrast between Sydney Smith and others of his day is in fine one of ideal. Thus when he came to the Church side of the Emancipation question he was ready enough to say, " It is quite right that there should be one clergyman in every parish interpreting the Scriptures after a particular manner, ruled by a regular hierarchy, and paid with a rich proportion of haycocks and wheat-sheaves." His was the ideal of " establishment." Therein he differed from the Tories of his day, and most notably from such men as Canning and his true successor Disraeli. The

Tories did not regard the Church simply as an establishment. To them the Church was the representative of all that was pure and all that was romantic in national life, and they linked to its traditions the memories of a time—which Disraeli lived to see revived—when Monarchy was beloved and when men sacrificed themselves for a romantic ideal. Charles I., says Disraeli in *Sybil*, " laid down his heroic life not only for the cause of the Church but for the cause of the poor." It was an opinion which the Young England party put in the forefront when they fought the battle for a higher political liberty and a higher religious freedom than Sydney Smith ever dreamed of. " In this country," wrote Disraeli, " Oligarchy has been called Liberty ; an exclusive Priesthood has been christened a National Church ; Sovereignty has been the title of something that has had no dominion, while absolute power has been wielded by those who profess themselves to be the servants of the People."

Against such enthusiasm Sydney Smith had only to oppose the opinions of common sense in possession. The institutions that he would defend he defended on grounds unblushingly selfish. And this is so thoroughly English that we find English biographers naturally in sympathy with the amusing ecclesiastic.

But English writers are not the only or perhaps even the most interesting writers on the English clergy. M. Bremond, a Jesuit, in his book *L'Inquiétude religieuse*, contrasts Sydney Smith with Newman. And fitly he contrasts him. Sydney Smith died in February 1845 : in October Newman became a Roman Catholic. Two widely divergent influences ceased to affect Englishmen in the same year—for the influence that Newman exercised, long though it took to work itself out, belongs really to those days when he was still free from the foreign control that fettered his powers and dulled his appealing tones. And the contrast gives one to-day a strange shock. It is hard to believe that it was while Newman's voice was preaching righteousness, temperance and judgment to come and was drawing the hearts of young Oxford to the Cross of Christ, that Sydney Smith was still proclaiming the comfortable ideal of a Whig religion, in which there should be no political, but many a social, disability, enthusiasm should be banned, and the Gospel of the Son of God should be withheld from the nations of the East.

Not very much of this could be learnt from the book of M. Bremond. The chapter in it on Sydney Smith is a review of M. Chevrillon's book published so long ago as 1894. The sub-title, " Le Christianisme bourgeois," is a sufficient indication of the contention. Sydney Smith is regarded as having done the good work of " accelerating the renaissance of liberal ideas in England "—ideas which M. Bremond elsewhere condemns. He is painted as a thorough Anglican —that is to say, comfortable, rich, and heretical, but yet a man of sound sense, who did much to secure the emancipation of Roman Catholics. His Fifth of November sermon is described, with a witty survey of the banquet which preceded it :—

" La soupe à la tortue, le roast-beef d' Angleterre, le pudding et le porto échauffaient l'orgueil national. Puis on va en procession à la cathédrale remercier le Dieu d' Israël d'avoir exalté l' Angleterre au-dessus de toutes les nations."

All this prepares one to learn that the idea of the English clergyman of the day was not to save souls, but to make a fortune. They were all *bourgeois*, and Sydney Smith, with all his wit, was *bourgeois* of the deepest dye.

But M. Bremond does not quite understand Sydney Smith. What Frenchman could ?

" Voici en deux mots," he says, " le rôle de ce personnage. Par ses écrits, par ses discours, il a rendu possible et il a accéléré la renaissance des idées libérales en Angleterre et, par là, préparé l'admirable mouvement religieux des cinquante dernières années." Of true modern ideas, of real freedom, of the recognition of individual rights, of what is now called Christian Socialism, Sydney Smith had not an inkling. Just as little of connection had he with the religious movement which he ignored or despised. " Nothing so remarkable in England," he said of the Oxford Movement, "as the progress of these foolish people." No, serious theories

were not for Sydney Smith. He made an admirable advocate of political freedom for the Roman Catholics, a party
cry of the men to whose principles he was attached. But
he could not look deep into things. " Le *John Bull*, au
large ventre, aux joues colorées, au verbe haut, est tout
entier dans Sydney Smith, et c'est là encore une des raisons
de son succès." Material things were his standard of life :
cheaper food, shorter journeys, and—the French writer
would add—umbrellas and braces, were his test of progress.
He was a true representative of that " liberalism " against
which the Oxford Movement was, and will remain in history,
the enduring protest.

Take for example Sydney Smith's views on the motives
which urge parents to allow their sons to take holy orders,
and the wisdom of retaining these motives.

—" To get a stall . . . is the habit which the ambitious
squire is perpetually holding out to his second son. . . .
If such sort of preferment is extinguished . . . the service
becomes unpopular . . . capital is withdrawn from the
Church, and no one enters the profession but the sons of
farmers and little tradesmen, who would be footmen if
they were not vicars, or figure on the coach-box if they were
not lecturing from the pulpit."

Turn to the beginners of the Oxford Movement, and—
to see them almost at their worst—look at them with the
eyes of a French Jesuit.

With Pusey and Newman we come to a different atmo-
sphere. Pusey is *entêté*—that is how we sum him up. He
has so violent a prepossession in favour of the English
Church that nothing can shake him. His own learning and
his love for Newman go for nothing ; and all the Movement, which began at Oriel—" collège modeste et sans appar-
ence "—did not stir him an inch from his obstinate affection.
But how hard it is for a foreigner to understand the English
Church ; and the study of Sydney Smith does not make
the matter easier. M. Bremond seems to think that all
English priests were married. Newman, he says, when he
resolved to lead a single life, had never seen any other
than married priests. Has he forgotten that then all

Fellows of colleges were unmarried and nearly all were in Holy Orders ? Pusey is asserted never to have felt a doubt of the justice of his position, though, curiously enough, a few pages later a passage is quoted which shows the reverse to be true. Newman's interpretation of the Articles (which it is not stated agreed with that of a seventeenth century Jesuit) is said to have been naturally repudiated by "the heretical Church." *Und so weiter*. Pusey's invincible pre-possession gives M. Bremond a great deal of trouble, but he is confident in the end that he has found an explanation of it. Has it never occurred to him that the profound learning and the intimate acquaintance with Catholic antiquity which Dr. Pusey possessed made it impossible for him to surrender the convictions which every year of study served more strongly to confirm, and to show to be those of the Church of which it was his delight to be a minister ? The whole attitude of M. Bremond towards the Oxford Movement, is, in fact, vitiated by his ignorance of two essential features of the teaching and belief of its leaders. The first is that they studied Christian antiquity for themselves with absolute sincerity, and made, with the Church their mother, their appeal to the decision of " sound learning." This decision, they were certain, was pronounced in favour of the Catholic claims of the English Church. It is no invincible prepossession, still less is it ignorance, which keeps their successors, as it kept Dr. Pusey and Dean Church, from submitting to Rome ; it is the knowledge that Papal claims and modern Roman doctrine are irreconcilable with the teaching of the Church of the Bible and the Fathers. And, secondly, the leaders of the Oxford Movement found, as their successors find, the practical evidence for the truth of the English position, thus established on the foundation of the Catholic Fathers, in the marvellous gifts of God's grace through the Sacraments, visible in the saintly lives of loyal children of the English Church. The living epistles gave their witness, and those who had eyes could not fail to see.

The ideal of the Oxford Movement indeed was the religious complement of the political ideal of the leaders of

SYDNEY SMITH : A CONTRAST

Young Conservatism in the 'forties. Newman, and Keble, and Pusey, thinking of the comfortable religion of Whig clergymen, might have said what Disraeli did say, when he thought of the political dominance of the "Venetian oligarchy" of the Whigs.

—"Time that brings all things has brought also to the mind of England some suspicion that the idols they have so long worshipped and the idols that have so long deluded them are not the true ones. There is a whisper rising in this country that Loyalty is not a phrase, Faith not a delusion, and Popular Liberty something more definite and substantial than the profane exercise of the sacred rights of sovereignty by political classes."

Loyalty and Faith came back with those men who from Oxford strove to lead English religion by the old paths : and in the work of their disciples came back also the true Popular Liberty which would make the Church free from the bondage of political partisanship.

Index

Index

INDEX

INDEX

INDEX

INDEX

Crisp family—pedigree, 10, 90
Crisp, Martha, 10
Crisp, Mary (Mrs. Phesant), 10
Crisp, Mr., " the eminent lawyer of Chipping Norton," 10
Crisp, Samuel (Daddy Crisp, Lem)
  Burford Journal, request for, 78
  Burney's, Fanny, letters to *see* Burney, Fanny
  Chesington, residence at, 26
    Scheme for keeping on Chesington in case of Miss Hamilton's death, 64, *sqq.*
  Death—burial at Chesington, 85
  Dressing-up for a minuet story, 26
  Epitaph by Dr. Burney, 85
  Ill-judged economy on Mrs. Gast's part, protests against, 27, 45, 78
  Ill-health, 28, 30, 34, 36, 38, 39, 41, 62, 64, 73, 74, 79, 84—disregard of regimen, etc., 28, 30, 34, 64
  Letter to Mr. Shute—Exiled Stewart princes at the Marchesa Bolognetti's ball, Feb. 15, 1739, 106
  Letters to Mrs. Gast
    Burney's, Fanny, illness due to overwork on *Cecilia*, etc. (Mar. 1, 1781), 55
    Burney's, Fanny, journal continued—sending on to Mrs. Gast (Sept. 20, 1780), 47
    Burney's, Fanny, social triumphs—Mr. Crisp's ill-health, etc. (Mar. 28, 1779), 27
    Dechair's proposal (Jan. 25, 1779), 24, 28
    Electric treatment for rheumatism, price paid for *Cecilia*, Susan Burney's marriage (Jan. 25, 1782), 74
    Electric treatment for rheumatism, Captain Phillips, political situation, etc. (Feb. 26, 1782), 75
    Electric treatment for rheumatism, political situation, etc. (Dec. 29, 1781), 71

Crisp, Samuel (Daddy Crisp, Lem), *continued*—
    Gast's, Mrs., rheumatism, advice for, Fanny Burney not spoiled by success, etc., 35
    Gast's, Mrs., ill-health (Nov. 27, 1780), 54
    Hamilton's, Miss, illness, money affairs, etc. (July 13, 1781), 64
  Letters to Mrs. Gast
    Health, improvement in (Mar. 30, 1781), 60
    Leigh's, Nancy, marriage settlements, money affairs, Fanny Burney's triumph, etc. (Sept. 24, 1780), 43
    Lewis's, Doctor, account of the two sorts of nightshade (May 7, 1779), 33
    Little Sam's affairs, Fanny Burney's illness, etc., etc. (Oct. 16, 1781), 6, 81
    Mackail extract, etc. (Nov. 8, 1780), 51
    Money affairs, No Popery riots, danger in West Indies, etc. (July 27, 1780), 38
    Money affairs, disposal of Mr. Thrale's property, etc. (June 4, 1781), 61
    Money affairs of Mrs. Gast and Anne Crisp, Misses Mathias, etc. (Aug. 22, 1780), 41
    Political situation, Mr. Allen's miserable client, price paid for *Cecilia*, etc. (May 23, 1782), 79
    Ray, Miss, murder of, Hetty Burney's illness, etc. (April 9, 1779), 30
    " Splendid dinner " at Streatham, British losses in America, etc. (Oct. 2, 1780), 49
    Will, re-making, money affairs, Mr. Thrale's illness (Dec. 15, 1781), 54
  Trusteeship for Nanny Leigh, 41, 54, 55
Virginia, 10

Y

INDEX

322

INDEX

INDEX

Granville, Mary, *see* Delany, Mrs.

Graves, Lucilla Anna Maria—tablet in Claverton Church vestry, 216

Graves, Rev. Richard, 153
  Aldworth curacy, 215
  Bath, lines on, 184
  Batheaston Villa, connection with, 159, 217–222
    Answer to *Bath Chronicle* attack, 221
    Poetical Amusements, 221—lines on the Transmigration of Soul, 222
  Blackstone, friendship with—anecdotes in *The Triflers*, 214
  Claverton, residence at, 159, 162, 215, 216, 217
  Crabbe, likeness to, 222
  Education at Abingdon School and Pembroke College, Oxford, 211, 214
  Epitaph in Claverton Church, 216
  Fellowship at All Souls', Oxford, 214
  Fitz-Herberts in Derbyshire, connection with, 215
  Friends of, 158, 211, 212, 230
  Gainsborough's portrait, 231
  Humour, 223, 224, 228
  Kilvert's, Rev. Francis, account of, 194, 222, 223
  Landscape gardening at Mickleton, 179
  Marriage to Lucy Bartholomew, 215
  Ordination in 1740, 215
  Oxford friendships, 158, 211, 212
  Parish priest, Graves as, 222, 230
  Pupils of, 222
  Shenstone, references to, etc.
    Criticism on Shenstone's Philosophy, 187
    Character written at Oxford, 212
    Friendship begun at Oxford, 212
    Memorial'—Halesowen Church monuments, 183

Graves, Rev. Richard, *continued*—
  Recollections of some particulars in the life of the late William Shenstone, 158, 186
  Whistler, Shenstone's quarrel with, account of, 187
  Works
    Columella; or the Distressed Anchoret, 132, 189, 225
    Eugenius; or Anecdotes of the Golden Vale, 225—no copy in the Bodleian, 226
    Euphrosyne; or Amusements on the Road of Life, 159, 228
      Note omitted in second edition, 228
      Shenstone, lines on, 228
      Originality, lack of, 223, 228
    Plexippus; or the Aspiring Plebeian, 225
    Poetry, " A Chronical Disease "—Graves's own account, 228
    Reveries of Solitude, 226
    Rural Felicity — Day in the Country anecdote, 227
    Senilities; or Solitary Amusements, 227
    Sermons, 226
    Spiritual Quixote, 156, 185
      Caricature of Methodism, 224
      English country life, picture of, 224
    The Festoon—collection of epigrams, 159, 228
    The Invalid with the obvious means of enjoying health, etc., 229
    The Triflers, 214, 226
      Bath, source of information on, 194
    see also sub heading Shenstone

Graves, Richard, the Elder—antiquarian interests, described in *Spiritual Quixote* as Mr. Townsend, 210

Green, Mrs., 15, 42

Grenville's, George, classification of bishoprics, 251

Gurwood, Col.—collection of Wellington's despatches, 142

324

INDEX

325

INDEX

INDEX

INDEX

Newman, John Henry
Contrast with Sydney Smith—
M. Bremond's book *L'In-
quiétude réligieuse*, 307, 308,
309
Influence opposed to Fox and
Wesley—Mr. H. P. Hughes's
view, 268
Newton, Bishop (Bishop of Bristol
and Dean of S. Paul's, Lon-
don)—autobiography, etc.,
247 *sqq.*
Attendance at Bristol Cathedral,
distress at chapter's neglect,
251, 252
Education, 248
Literary criticisms, 252
Portrait by Sir Joshua Reynolds,
250, 257
" Sleepy, but not corrupt," 253
Source of preferment, 251
Statesmen, anecdotes of, 251 *sqq.*
Warburton, Bishop, remark on,
231
Nightshade, two sorts of—Dr.
Lewis's account, 33
Nixon, Mr., 153
No Popery riots, 39
Non-jurors at Burford—non-juring
chapel in the Great House,
22, 120
Northumberland, Duchess of—
Poetical Amusements at Bath-
easton Villa, 218
Verses by the Duchess, 220—Dr.
Johnson's remark, 221

O

Orton, Mr. Job—*Lettters to a young
Clergyman*, etc., 237
Blair's sermons, eulogy of, 241
Gentle criticism of non-residents,
etc., 238, 239, 240
Music in church services, advice
as to, 240
Sacramental Meditation, 237
Sincerity and genuine religion of,
241

Orton, Mr. Job, *continued*—
Stonhouse, Dr., prescription for,
239
Outing, Mr., 153, 166
Oxford
Jacobite riot in 1749, 116
for particular Colleges and Per-
sons, *see* their Names
Oxford Movement—M. Bremond's
book *L'Inquiétude réligieuse*,
etc., 309, 310
Essential features of teaching and
belief of leaders, 310
Ideal—religious complement of
the young Conservatives'
political ideal, 310
Popular liberty restored to the
Church by, 311
Smith, Sydney, on, 308
Oxfordshire Jacobitism, 111, 113,
114, 117, 120, 122

P

Palmerston, Lord—*Poetical Amuse-
ments* at Batheaston Villa,
218
Parr, Dr., 195
Ex-page boy's recollections of,
161
Hughes, Mrs., description, 135
Link between eighteenth century
Warwickshire coterie and
Walter Savage Landor, 160
Payne, Misses, 40 *note*
Chesington visit, 42
Sally—courtship by Jem Burney,
47, 70
Payne, Mr.—publisher of *Cecilia*, 81
Pedigree of Leigh and Crisp fami-
lies and relations, 15
Pembroke College, Oxford—sets
frequented by R. Graves, 211
Percy Lodge—seat of the widowed
Duchess of Somerset, 154
Phesant, Mrs., 10
Phillips, Captain, 73, 75, 76
Character, etc., 75, 76
Marriage to Susan Burney, 73, 74
Models presented to the Museum,
etc., 76

INDEX

330

INDEX

INDEX

INDEX

INDEX

INDEX

Wellington, Duke of, *continued*—
Chivalrous politeness—acknowledgment of crossing-sweeper's salute, etc., 148, 149
Consideration and charity, love of children, etc., 148
Contrast with Marquess of Wellesley, 141
Humorous aspects of correspondence, 144
Jenkins, Miss, correspondence with, 145–148
Portrait " In the other House," 102
Werther's Charlotte, mention in Graves's *Eugenius*, 226
Wesley, John
Bath, preaching at, 205
Burford visits, 7, 8
Church of England, loyalty to—repudiation of dissent, warning to followers, 258, 266, 267
Separation involved in ordination, 266
Epitaph composed by himself at the age of fifty, 260
Extraordinary strength and activity—travelling 8,000 miles and preaching 5,000 times in a year, 259, 260, 261
Faults, 264
Humour, 259
Individualism, champion of—Mr. Hugh Price Hughes's view, 268
Journal, 258
Birrell's, Mr. Augustine on, 258
Third instalment, reasons for publication of, 259
Literary tastes and judgments, 264, 265
Religious work, tremendous results of, 263—not confined to Evangelicalism, 267
West Indies, situation in (1780), 39
West, James—antiquary of Alscot Park, 154

Westmorland, Earl of—Jacobite agent, negotiations with Frederick the Great, 118
Westmorland, Lady, *see* Burghersh, Lady
Whistler, Mr., 153
Graves's description of, 158
Oxford friendships, 158
Shenstone's quarrel with, 187
Wilberforce, Bishop—" deadly leaven " of Hoadly's Latitudinarianism, 246
Williams, Sir Charles Hanbury—Mengs's portrait, 125
Winchester, Bishop North of, and his wife—attachment to the Burney family, 73
Winckelmann, Mengs on, 128
" Witlings, The "—Fanny Burney's comedy, 34, 37
Wolfe, Gen.—interview with Pitt at Bath, 204
Woods, Elder and Younger—architects of Bath, 201, 203
Woollen manufacture, Shenstone's lament on, 180
Wootton Wawen Church, architecture, monuments, etc., 159, 170
Wordsworth, influence of Evangelicanism on, 267
Wraxall, Sir Nathaniel, description of Charles Edward in 1779, 119
Wright, Mr.—hiding cash till the news came of victory at Culloden, 72
Wymondsold, Mrs., 166

Y

York's, Duke of, duel—Bishop Watson's letter to Lord Rawdon, 255
Young, Mrs., nursing Mrs. Burney at Chesington, 83

Z

Zinzendorf, Count — sermons preached in London, 243

Butler & Tanner, The Selwood Printing Works, Frome, and London.

THE CENTENARY EDITION

of

Emerson's Complete Works.

12 Vols.   6s. net per vol.

It has been the aim of the publishers to render this Centenary Edition not only perfect in every detail of bookmaking, but notable for

NEW AND SIGNIFICANT FEATURES

THE INTRODUCTION has been written by the editor, EDWARD WALDO EMERSON, who has given in brief compass a fresh and authoritative account of his father's life and work.

THE TEXT is that of the Riverside Edition, presenting, in the earlier volumes, the readings finally decided upon by Mr. Emerson himself, while the later volumes were collected and revised by his friend and biographer, Mr. J. Elliot Cabot.

MATERIAL HITHERTO UNPUBLISHED. In making a fresh examination of Mr. Emerson's Journals in preparation for the Centenary Edition, considerable material of marked interest, hitherto unpublished, has been brought to light. In the present opinion of Emerson's literary executors, there is sufficient unpublished manuscript to form three or more volumes. While the date of publication of this material cannot be definitely announced at present, the purchasers of the Centenary Edition will have the opportunity to secure it, on publication, in a style uniform with the preceding volumes. The twelve volumes published comprise :—

With Complete Index, and Five Photogravure Portraits—

Wild Wings: Adventures of a Camera-Hunter among the Larger Wild Birds of America on Land and Sea, by HERBERT K. JOB, Author of *Among the Water-Fowl.* Profusely illustrated from 160 Photographs. Square 8vo. 10s. 6d. net.

After reading the author's previous book President Roosevelt wrote to him :—

"I must thank you for your exceedingly interesting book. I have been delighted with it, and desire to express my sense of the good which comes from such books as yours, and from the substitution of the camera for the gun. The older I grow the less I care to shoot anything except ' varmints.' "

Two Bird-Lovers in Mexico, by C. WILLIAM BEEBE. With numerous Illustrations from Photographs. Large crown 8vo. 10s. 6d. net.

Mr. Beebe is Curator of Birds at the New York Zoological Park, and in his book he describes a journey, which he took in the company of his wife, across Mexico from Vera Cruz to the Pacific and back. His attention was chiefly devoted to the birds. But he also describes the mammals and insects with which he met.

A New Edition:

Canada in the Twentieth Century, by A. G. BRAD-LEY, Author of *The Fight with France for North America,* etc. With many Illustrations and a Map. Demy 8vo. 5s. net.

" A really practical volume of great utility, besides being exceedingly pleasant reading."—*Daily Telegraph.*

A New Edition:

An Essay on Comedy and the Uses of the Comic Spirit, by GEORGE MEREDITH. Pocket Edition. Cloth, 2s. 6d. net ; leather, 3s. 6d. net.

A New Edition:

The Private Papers of Henry Ryecroft, by GEORGE GISSING. A Pocket Edition on thin paper. With Portrait of the Author. Cloth, 2s. 6d. net ; leather, 3s. 6d. net.

" It is the revelation of a deeply interesting personality, and it is expressed in a prose of admirable strength and beauty."—*Daily Chronicle.*

The Romance of the Milky Way, and other Studies and Stories, by LAFCADIO HEARN, Author of *Gleanings in Buddha-Fields, Glimpses of Unfamiliar Japan*, etc. Crown 8vo. 5s. net.

The late Mr. Lafcadio Hearn is well known as the author of several delightful books on the customs and beliefs of Japan. The title essay in the present volume deals with the Japanese mythology of the heavens. Another essay is devoted to Herbert Spencer's Ultimate Questions, and a third to Japanese goblin poetry. There are seven papers in all. This is the last posthumous volume of the author's work.

The Risen Sun, by BARON K. SUYEMATSU. Demy 8vo. Cloth gilt. 12s. 6d. net.

This book on Japan, by a distinguished son of the land, is likely to attract a great deal of attention. Baron Suyematsu, being as well acquainted with Western civilization as with Oriental, is thus enabled to form an impartial, and therefore invaluable, estimate of his country.

CONTENTS : *Book I. Antecedent to the War.*—A Bird's-Eye View of the Far Eastern Question—Japan and Russia—How Russia brought on the War 1898–1903—First Hostilities ; Japan and the Commencement of the War.

Book II. A Nation in Training.—The Introduction of Western Civilization—Foreigners in Japan—Moral Teaching in Japan—The Japanese Character—The Making of a Soldier in Japan—Woman's Education—Harakiri—The Police System—The Ethics of Japan—Sense of Honour—Religions—Art and Literature—The Great Change—The Emperor : Ruler and Poet.

Book III. External Relations.—Chinese Expansion—Japan and France—War Indemnity—Treatment of Wounded and Prisoners by Japan—Unfair Charges against Japan—Epilogue.

Spiritual Adventures : a Series of Studies in Temperament, by ARTHUR SYMONS, Crown 8vo. 7s. 6d. net.

CONTENTS : A Prelude to Life—Esther Kahn—Christian Trevalga—The Childhood of Lucy Newcome—The Death of Peter Waydelin—An Autumn City—Seaward Lackland—Extracts from the Journal of Henry Luxulyan.

A Study of Aboriginal Life in Australia : The Euahlai Tribe, by MRS. LANGLOH PARKER. With an Introduction by ANDREW LANG. With Illustrations. Demy 8vo. 7s. 6d. net.

THE WORKS OF
GEORGE MEREDITH

THE ORDEAL OF RICHARD FEVEREL
BEAUCHAMP'S CAREER
SANDRA BELLONI
VITTORIA
EVAN HARRINGTON
THE EGOIST
ONE OF OUR CONQUERORS
LORD ORMONT AND HIS AMINTA
THE AMAZING MARRIAGE
DIANA OF THE CROSSWAYS
THE ADVENTURES OF HARRY RICHMOND
RHODA FLEMING
THE SHAVING OF SHAGPAT
THE TRAGIC COMEDIANS
SHORT STORIES
POEMS—2 Vols.
AN ESSAY ON COMEDY

POCKET EDITION

In 18 volumes, as above, on thin opaque paper, bound in red cloth, gilt lettered and gilt top, 2s. 6d. net per volume; in full leather, 3s. 6d. net per volume.

LIBRARY EDITION

In 18 volumes, as above, crown 8vo, each with a photogravure frontispiece, 6s. each.

"In the realm of creative literature Mr. George Meredith occupies by the common consent of educated men a position not only comparatively pre-eminent, but absolutely great, unique, and entirely worthy of the special kind of recognition which the Order of Merit alone represents."—*The Times*, Friday, June 30, 1905.